Pencils Down

RETHINKING *high-stakes testing and accountability in public schools*

EDITED BY WAYNE AU AND MELISSA BOLLOW TEMPEL

RANDALL ENOS

✎ A RETHINKING SCHOOLS PUBLICATION ✎

Pencils Down: *Rethinking high-stakes testing and accountability in public schools*
Edited by Wayne Au and Melissa Bollow Tempel

A Rethinking Schools Publication

Rethinking Schools Ltd. is a nonprofit educational publisher of books, booklets, and a quarterly magazine on school reform, with a focus on issues of equity and social justice. To request additional copies of this book and/or a catalog of other publications, or to subscribe to *Rethinking Schools* magazine, contact:

Rethinking Schools
1001 East Keefe Avenue
Milwaukee, WI 53212
800-669-4192
www.rethinkingschools.org

© 2012 Rethinking Schools Ltd.
First edition

Production Editor: Catherine Capellaro
Cover and book design: The Flynstitute
Cover and chapter head illustrations: Randall Enos
Proofreading: Amalia Oulahan
Indexing: Marilyn Flaig
Business Manager: Mike Trokan

Library of Congress Cataloging-in-Publication Data

Pencils down : rethinking high-stakes testing and accountability in public schools / edited by Wayne Au and Melissa Bollow Tempel.—First edition.

pages cm.— (A Rethinking Schools publication)

A collection of articles from Rethinking Schools magazine.

Includes bibliographical references and index.

ISBN 978-0-942961-51-5 (alk. paper)

1. Educational tests and measurements—United States. I. Au, Wayne, 1972- II. Tempel, Melissa Bollow, 1978- III. Rethinking schools.

LB3051.P46 2012

371.26—dc23

2012010474

We dedicate this book to Maya Lu and Masami
for bravely being the first in their school to opt out
of computerized testing;
and Makoto, Haden, Nehuen, and Ollie
in hopes that the testing will never reach them.

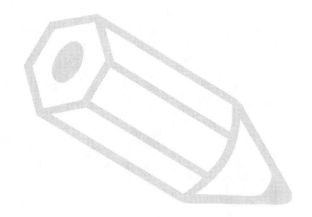

Acknowledgements

We thank *Rethinking Schools* editors Linda Christensen, Kelley Dawson Salas, Stan Karp, David Levine, Larry Miller, Bob Peterson, Stephanie Walters, Terry Burant, Helen Gym, Rita Tenorio, Dyan Watson, Kathy Williams, Kathy Xiong, Bill Bigelow, and Jody Sokolower for their ongoing work and support in shaping this book; Catherine Capellaro for helping shepherd this book through the process; Patrick J.B. Flynn for his artistic direction and patience; Randall Enos for his creative expression; Amalia Oulahan for her attention to detail; Kris Collett, Tegan Dowling, and Mike Trokan for doing so many things that make Rethinking Schools run; and, of course, the contributors to *Pencils Down* for everything they are doing to challenge high-stakes testing. We'd also like to thank our partners, Mira and Gene, for understanding the importance of getting this book published.

—*Wayne Au and Melissa Bollow Tempel*

TABLE OF CONTENTS

PART 1:

Testing, Testing, 1, 2, 3...

PART 2:

Testing Kids

PART 3:

Testing Teaching

PART 4:

Testing the Tests

PART 5:

Resisting and Responding to High-Stakes Testing

PART 6:

Beyond High-Stakes Standardized Testing

Introduction

It's time to put the pencils down

WAYNE AU AND MELISSA BOLLOW TEMPEL

In 2000, *Rethinking Schools* published *Failing Our Kids: Why the Testing Craze Won't Fix Our Schools*. In that volume, editors Kathy Williams (then Swope) and Barbara Miner pulled together a groundbreaking collection of essays, letters, articles, and analyses that challenged the juggernaut of high-stakes testing and accountability in public education policy.

And we thought things were bad then....

We now live in a world after the bipartisan passage of NCLB. The tsunami of high-stakes testing and accountability has crashed on our educational shores with full force—threatening the foundations of teaching and learning, as well as the democratic aspirations of public education.

Those of us who held even the slimmest hope that changes in presidential administrations might stem or perhaps turn back the tide have had those hopes dashed as waves of corporate-backed reforms pushed by Republicans, Democrats, and billionaire philanthropists continue to batter kids, teachers, parents, and schools.

Now, despite duplicitous official rhetoric that speaks of the importance of multiple measures to assess learning and teaching, high-stakes test scores are being used to quantify, rank, and judge everything in public schools. Schools are charged with overcoming every aspect of socioeconomic inequality to show test score gains. District administrators and their "clipboard police" enforce a strict, scripted curriculum focused on little beyond reading, writing, and math. Teachers and their unions are the new enemies of achievement because, despite decades of persistent inequality in education, they can't raise the test scores. Despite an economic crisis that has resulted in the massive defunding of public education, schools are expected to raise test scores.

Now, charter schools are being used to dismantle public schools, based on the false promise that charters can raise test scores. Teach for America is being used to attack unions and teacher preparation programs by placing undertrained and unqualified teachers in "high-need" schools, where need is determined by test scores. Following corporate hierarchies, district superintendents are rebranded as "Chief Exec-

> **Despite duplicitous official rhetoric that speaks of the importance of multiple measures to assess learning and teaching, high-stakes test scores are being used to quantify, rank, and judge everything in public schools.**

utive Officers" and use test scores to competitively rate and rank students, teachers, and schools within the new "free market" of education. Teachers and teaching are now reduced to being inaccurately described by measures of how much "value" they can add to their students' test scores.

Now, students = test scores.

Now, teachers = test scores.

Now, teaching = test scores.

Now, learning = test scores.

Now, education = test scores.

The entire package of corporate-like educational reforms hinges on the use of high-stakes standardized tests. These tests form the justification for charter schools, union busting, merit pay, value-added teacher evaluations, school closures, turnarounds, reconstitutions, and just about any other way free-market competition manifests in education policy today. Without the test scores, there is no basis for comparing students, teachers, principals, schools, districts, cities, states, and countries. And without an ability to make comparisons, the entire system of competition simply collapses on itself.

Democratic, Authentic Assessment

We want to be clear: We are not opposed to assessment or accountability. We take seriously the real concerns that parents—especially working-class parents and parents of color—have about the quality of their children's education. Opposition to testing does not mean opposition to accountability and documenting educational outcomes.

We firmly believe that assessment is critical to good, effective teaching, and that teachers and schools have a responsibility to their students and to the communities in which they teach. But the current systems of high-stakes testing and accountability are top-down models of reform that are fundamentally undemocratic: High-stakes tests and the policy makers who want to use them to hold educators accountable have no interest in the voices of students, teachers, parents, or administrators. Instead, they have to reduce us to numbers in order to fit all of us into their system.

But we know that students, learning, and teaching are more complicated than numbers. Education is a human endeavor, full of hope, struggle, and creativity; it involves failures and victories. We believe our systems of assessment and accountability need the flexibility and capability to capture all of that human messiness (in all of its beauty and power) if they are to provide fair and accurate measures of any aspect of education.

We need assessment that recognizes that learning and development happen unevenly, in spurts, with both backward and forward motion.

We need assessment that embraces the different learning styles of all children and also values the richness of cultural and community experience all children bring to the classroom.

We need teacher evaluation that acknowledges that teachers are both trained professionals and learners themselves. Such evaluation would, by extension, recognize that good teaching not only requires training and practice, but also opportunities for self-reflection, growth, and improvement (and yes, the chance to learn from mistakes).

> **We need assessment that embraces the different learning styles of all children and also values the richness of cultural and community experience they bring to the classroom.**

We need systems of accountability that honor our responsibilities to children and their communities. This accountability has to be based upon a shared commitment among teachers, students, parents, and administrators. It needs to be democratic and bottom-up, instead of the current crop of top-down, corporate-style reforms. This includes holding policy makers and administrators accountable for providing adequate and equitable resources to all children and schools.

Public education is not an island, but rather part of an interconnected and integrated network of social services and socioeconomic relations. We need systems of assessment and accountability that hold leaders accountable for providing resources such as health care, dental care, affordable housing, and other social supports.

We need systems of assessment and accountability that effectively and accurately identify sources of educational inequalities, particularly those related to race, economic class, gender, sexuality, home language, and immigration status.

Testing and Inequality

The impacts of systemic racism and other forms of injustice are real. They need to be exposed and fixed. Some have argued that test scores are one effective way to create such exposure. However, researchers have found that:

- Mandated high-stakes testing since the passing of the No Child Left Behind Act has not improved educational outcomes or closed any test-defined achievement gaps. So, high-stakes testing has not resulted in increased learning or equality.

- The ill effects of high-stakes testing—like narrowing learning environments to focus solely on reading, writing, and math, as well as the test-induced increase of high school dropouts—have had a disproportionately negative impact on low-income students and students of color.

- The construction and grading of standardized, high-stakes tests contain high levels of inaccuracy. The results, more often than not, are misinterpreted, misunderstood, and misused by policy makers and the general public.

- Racial, cultural, and economic class-based biases are embedded in many high-stakes, standardized tests. Although these biases have persisted for more than 100 years, test scores are still misperceived as accurate measures of intelligence.

Given these facts, we can only conclude that testing is the wrong way to expose educational inequality, and that the tests themselves are interfering with the accurate measurement of learning, teaching, and achievement.

This confirms what social scientist Donald T. Campbell identified in 1976 as Campbell's Law:

> The more any quantitative social indicator is used for social decision-making, the more subject it will be to corruption pressures and the more apt it will be to distort and corrupt the social processes it is intended to monitor. ... [W]hen test scores become the goal of the teaching process, they both lose their value as indicators of educational status and distort the educational process in undesirable ways.

Based on the evidence, high-stakes testing is exacerbating the inequality it is supposed to be measuring. Much of that evidence is highlighted in the pages of *Pencils Down*.

Time To Put the Pencils Down

Because high-stakes testing is so central to the entire apparatus of the corporate educational reforms that are being forced upon us—and because of the overwhelming evidence of the invalidity and injustice of using the tests as they are presently being used—we are publishing *Pencils Down: Rethinking high-stakes testing and accountability in public schools*. We are in the midst of a war on public education, and high-stakes standardized tests are the enemies' weapon of choice. *Pencils Down* is one attempt to expose the fallacy of high-stakes testing to the general public: We wanted to put together a collection of articles that provide thoughtful, emotional, and classroom- and research-based critiques of high-stakes tests—one we could put in the hands of students and teachers (future, present, and past), and also pass around to parents at PTA meetings, potlucks, and picnics.

In *Pencils Down*, we take the high-stakes tests to task, deconstruct the damage they cause to our education system, highlight their inaccuracy as tools of measurement, and offer visionary forms of assessment that are more authentic, democratic, fair, and accurate.

The first section, "Testing, Testing, 1, 2, 3..." covers the nuts and bolts of standardized testing and presents an overview of the enduring problems with the tests. Section two, "Testing Kids," offers views from the classroom of just what high-stakes testing is doing to the quality of education. The third section, "Testing Teaching," highlights the ways high-stakes testing stifles instruction and de-professionalizes teaching; and it examines efforts to bring standardized assessment to the process of teacher credentialing.

The fourth section of *Pencils Down*, "Testing the Tests," provides analyses of some lesser-known problems with the tests: their validity as a form of measurement, and the inconsistency found in their results and grading. This section is fundamental to any critique of high-stakes testing because the numbers produced by the tests carry an air of objectivity. (And pundits, policy makers, and philanthropists assert that such objectivity exists.) However, on closer examination, the numbers are far from objective.

One of the critical questions facing education activists today is, "What can we do?" From refusal and opting out to protests and organizing letter-writing campaigns, section five, "Resisting and Responding to High-Stakes Testing," takes a look at a wide range of efforts teachers, students, and communities have employed to oppose the testing regime.

Effective methods of assessing teaching and learning exist: They are just messier, more intensive, more democratic, and less punitive.

But critique, while important and necessary, can only take us so far. We need real, concrete visions of what alternative, non-high-stakes testing and accountability can look like. Many teachers, who have been hemmed in by the tests for years now, also need to learn (or relearn) how to provide quality assessment. That is why the sixth and final section of *Pencils Down*, "Beyond High-Stakes Standardized Testing," focuses on authentic forms of assessment, including portfolios and ongoing teacher and student self-reflection based on classroom evidence. Effective methods of assessing teaching and learning exist: They are just messier, more intensive, more democratic, and less punitive. And they require a bigger commitment to public education than the test-pushers are willing to make.

The powers that be continue to force high-stakes testing and accountability upon students, teachers, and parents. As a result, we are feeling...tested. Despite the infatuation with tests shared by policy makers, philanthropists, and corporate education reformers on both sides of the aisle, resistance continues to build. The struggle is far from over, however. As of this writing, the U.S. federal government has announced intentions not only to ratchet up the use of high-stakes tests to measure student learning and teacher effectiveness, but also to measure the effectiveness of teacher education programs by the test scores of the *students of the teachers* who graduate from the programs. This proposal sounds convoluted and ludicrous, but it is just another entry in a long list of examples of test abuse and misuse in education policy, and our kids are paying the price. It's time to stop the testing. It's time to put the pencils down.

PART I

Testing, Testing, 1, 2, 3…

RANDALL ENOS

Failing Our Kids

Why the testing craze won't fix our schools

KATHY WILLIAMS AND BARBARA MINER

"How is my child doing?" is the most frequent question a parent asks a teacher. "How are our schools doing?" is an equally common question asked by community members.

Both are important questions, but standardized tests can't adequately answer them.

Decades of experience and research show that misuse of standardized tests distorts student learning, exacerbates inequities for low-income students and students of color, and undermines true accountability between schools, parents, and the community.

The problem goes beyond the growing national obsession with test scores. The tests, often tied to state standards, can lead to a narrowing of the curriculum and the imposition of a restricted, official view of what constitutes knowledge. In addition, standardized tests are often "high-stakes" measurements. This high-stakes approach mandates that students who fail a particular test be retained, denied access to a preferred high school, or, in some cases, even refused a high school diploma. Some districts and states also use standardized test scores to evaluate principals, teachers, and entire schools.

Most important, standardized tests will never answer the question of what our children need to learn to be leaders and informed citizens in a multicultural, ever-changing world.

Many of the political and corporate backers of standardized tests skillfully use the language of high standards to promote an agenda that, contrary to the rhetoric, will increase divisions between the haves and have-nots.

Some advocates of standardized testing hope to use tests to improve teaching standards in low-achieving schools. Clearly, some schools do not adequately serve their low-income students, students of color, students with special needs, and students who do not speak English as their first language.

The irony is that an inappropriate reliance on standardized tests is likely to make problems worse for such students.

African American and Latino students, for example, are disproportionately failing "high-stakes" standardized tests. This has historical precedent. Dating back to the development of IQ tests at the turn of the century, standardized tests have been used to sort and rank children—most reprehensibly along racial and class lines—and to

> **Students often internalize the judgments of the tests, as if test scores were the final word on one's knowledge or potential.**

> **Teachers are increasingly pressured to drill students on the tests, even when they know the tests don't assess the most essential aspects of thinking and learning.**

rationalize giving more privileges to the already privileged. In fact, the first standardized tests were developed to support theories of the intellectual superiority of northern European whites.

Given the historical use of standardized tests, it comes as little surprise that the latest testing craze coincides with a conservative upsurge that looks down on programs designed to counter institutionalized discrimination, and with a growing division between the rich and poor.

Standardized tests do more than legitimize and preserve existing power relations. Standardized tests can shape teaching and learning in ways that can harm children. Teachers are increasingly pressured to drill students on the tests, even when they know the tests don't assess the most essential aspects of thinking and learning. Entire subject areas—such as music, art, social studies, and foreign languages—are de-emphasized in some schools because they aren't tested. Students often internalize the judgments of the tests, as if test scores were the final word on one's knowledge or potential.

In addition, when standardized tests become the engine of reform, they narrow the discussion of what is truly needed to transform schools: improvements involving funding equity, class sizes, teacher training, and reducing child poverty.

Standardized tests also come packaged with demands for more standardized curriculum. These calls are part of a broader effort to promote a narrow version of what children should learn.

As scholar and activist Harold Berlak notes, state-mandated standards and tests "are an effort to put an end to the most valuable asset of a multicultural society: its vibrant cacophony of views about what constitutes truth, knowledge, and learning, and about what young children ought and ought not to learn at school. Standardized curriculum and tests insist upon one set of answers, and only one."

Alternative Assessment

Acknowledging the origins and consequences of standardized tests is not the same as dismissing parent and community concerns about how well our children are learning.

In order to defeat calls for standardized curriculum and testing, it is essential that schools develop more equitable forms of assessment. Educators must acknowledge the need for schoolwide, districtwide, or statewide assessment. Historically, social justice activists have used such aggregate data to show how schools fail to provide a quality education to all children—to highlight what Jonathan Kozol refers to as "savage inequalities."

There clearly are potential benefits of "authentic assessments" or "performance assessments"—those assessments that simulate real-life tasks and knowledge.

We want to sound some notes of caution on alternative assessments, however.

New forms of assessment aren't inherently less biased than standardized tests; educators' unconscious racist attitudes can just as easily bias classroom observations or portfolio assessments. Moreover, new forms of assessment might simply be more effective ways of assessing a Eurocentric, low-level curriculum.

Entire subject areas—such as music, art, social studies, and foreign languages—are de-emphasized in some schools because they aren't tested.

The challenge is twofold. How can assessments help teachers to better know the strengths and weaknesses of their students' work so that the teachers can help students to engage in thoughtful and complex work? Second, how can educators use assessments to nurture critical inquiry, problem solving, and multiculturalism so students are better prepared to understand the world and change it?

The question, as is true with so many areas of school reform, is what will best foster more equitable schooling and promote skills and values that are necessary for a more just society. ✎

Common Questions About Standardized Tests

The following is based on an interview with Kathy Williams (formerly Swope), a former editor of Rethinking Schools *whose career in the Milwaukee Public Schools spanned 34 years. She taught for 20 years and has retired as director of the district's Division of Research and Assessment.*

Q. What is a standardized test?

A. Generally, people are referring to tests that are "standard"—they have the same questions, the same directions, the same time limits, the same answers—so that student scores can be compared. Standardized tests most often involve multiple-choice questions given to large numbers of students and scored by a computer, which recognizes only one "correct" answer.

Q. What's wrong with standardized tests?

A. One big problem is that the tests generally permit only one correct answer. Therefore the tests penalize multiple perspectives. The tests also avoid questions that require complicated, thoughtful answers. Because the tests are given under time constraints, they also privilege students who quickly come up with answers. In order to better sort students, the tests often have obscure or "trick" questions. Just two or three "wrong" answers can dramatically alter a score.

Many standardized tests are also norm-referenced. They are designed to compare, sort, and rank children. In a norm-referenced test, 50 percent of the children will always be "below average." They will fail, no matter what they do or know.

Standardized tests also have a long history of cultural bias. There have been attempts to eliminate bias, but the very structure, time limits, and types of thinking that are rewarded in standardized tests carry their own biases. There are many ways to process information and demonstrate one's intelligences. Standardized tests focus only on a limited range of standardized approaches and standardized answers.

Q. But some questions have only one right answer. The Declaration of Independence, for example, was signed in 1776, not in 1976.

A. Questions that only have one right answer tend to rely on rote memorization. They are fact-driven instead of being driven by critical thinking and analysis, which reflect higher levels of learning. We don't want to encourage students to merely regurgitate isolated facts. We want students to learn facts and procedures as part of thinking deeply about issues, events, and people—and to also make connections and integrate what they know.

Q. If we don't have standardized tests, how do we know how our schools and children are doing?

A. There are other methods of assessment. One alternative is performance-based assessments. These ask children to perform actual tasks or create things that are of value in the real world—essays, research projects, science experiments, and so forth. A second alternative involves portfolios, which take a look at student work over a period of time. Many teachers encourage student projects, such as building models to scale, or

Questions that only have one right answer tend to rely on rote memorization.

role playing and skits, or science fairs, or writing short stories or essays. Teachers can capture students' learning in any number of ways.

Q. But these assessments don't let parents know how their children's schools are doing compared to schools in other neighborhoods, districts, or states.

A. If we as a society establish high expectations for all students—including reading, writing, critical thinking, and deep analysis—and we assess how students are doing along a continuum to meet those goals, we would know how our schools are doing. Just as we give all students standardized tests, we could also give them more authentic types of assessments.

Q. The disparity in test scores can be used to argue for more resources for urban schools. Isn't that a good thing?

A. Can you give me one example where an urban school that had a large percentage of poor minority students received significant additional funding just because the school had low test scores? If so, then perhaps we can explore that as one reasonable use of standardized testing.

Q. People often refer to "high-stakes" testing. What do they mean?

A. Standardized tests are being used to make high-stakes judgments of students and, increasingly, schools. This is happening even though the test-makers themselves say the tests should never be the sole determinant of important educational decisions.

In essence, high-stakes means that, on the basis of standardized test scores, students are being flunked, denied access to a desired course or school, or even denied a high school diploma. In addition, some schools or principals are being judged primarily on the basis of standardized test scores. Important educational indicators—attendance, grade point averages, dropout rates, the rigor of the curriculum—are downplayed or ignored.

We should remember that the primary goal of assessment is to help students learn and to provide them with a quality education, not to constantly compare schools and students.

Finally, it is a myth that standardized tests are good indicators of student progress. Standardized tests merely show how well a student is able to perform on a particular test. They don't show how well a student demonstrates in-depth understanding of a given subject—or the way a student actually constructs and uses knowledge.

Q. Are all standardized tests bad?

We should remember that the primary goal of assessment is to help students learn and to provide them a quality education—not to constantly compare schools and students.

A. Some people would argue that, used in moderation, standardized tests are okay. However, the problem is not just with the standardized tests themselves, but also with how the tests are used. When the results are used to dictate what should be taught, when they are used to promote low-level thinking and memorization, when they are used to rank and track students, when they are used instead of more meaningful school reforms—these, in my mind, are educational disasters.

Q. Why do African American and Latino students generally score lower than whites on standardized tests?

A. This is a complicated question, and I will touch on a few points. First, students of color sometimes receive fewer opportunities and a less rigorous education. This can be manifested in less-experienced teachers, a more remedial-type curriculum, larger classes and less individualized attention, lower expectations, and fewer overall resources. Also, the parents' educational level is a strong indicator of how well a student will do on standardized tests. Due to the long history of discrimination and unequal opportunity, the families of many students of color have not had the economic and educational benefits of a higher education.

Second, standardized tests are culturally biased. The bias is not always overtly noticeable, and sometimes it is embedded in the very structure and design of the tests. For example, an overt bias might involve the subject matter—is the question about yachts or famous white writers? But bias can also be embedded in the way language is used.

Use of language is fundamentally tied to cultural experience. The language of a standardized test ordinarily follows European, Anglo-Saxon language patterns. Further, standardized tests tend to reflect a linear mode of thinking. Yet the linear mode of thinking is not consistent with an Afrocentric worldview and thinking style, which tends to be more eclectic and reflects what can be described as a spiral pattern.

Q. Testing is everywhere in society, and it's an important survival skill. What's wrong with teaching kids how to take standardized tests?

A. We have an opportunity—and a responsibility—to create a more just and more equitable world. We cannot do that if we continue to rely on the status quo in education and testing. Just as we have evolved technologically in the last quarter century, we need to evolve with our assessment practices.

Q. Whether we like it or not, students need to pass standardized tests to get into college. They can't wait for a more just and equitable world.

A. Students perform better on standardized tests when they have richer classroom experiences. Assessments and practices that actually improve teaching and learning in kindergarten through high school will help students perform better on standardized measures.

Some people advocate a dual strategy: We need to get rid of the reliance on standardized tests, while still ensuring that low-income students and students of color do well on these tests. Because of prejudice, discrimination, and bias over time, many people of color and other disenfranchised people feel the need to demonstrate, without a doubt,

> **We have an opportunity— and a responsibility—to create a more just and more equitable world. We cannot do that if we continue to rely on the status quo in education and testing.**

that they are achieving at levels equal to their white and middle-class counterparts. And they are using standardized tests to demonstrate that achievement.

But ultimately, the problem is with the prejudice, discrimination, and bias in society at large. When students of color perform well on standardized tests, that doesn't guarantee equal access to quality education. Other forms of institutional prejudice and discrimination remain in place.

Q. A standardized test doesn't take up that much time in a classroom. So why all the fuss?

A. Every minute of classroom time is valuable. Nothing should be taking place in a classroom that does not enhance teaching and learning. In some cases, teachers spend an inordinate amount of time preparing for a standardized test—by practicing test-taking skills, teaching specifically to the test, and so forth.

In addition, the breadth of a curricular area cannot be captured on a standardized test. If teachers limit themselves to emphasizing what is on the standardized test, then students are being cheated out of the richness of a rigorous, comprehensive curriculum.

Q. That sounds great if students are in a school with a rich curriculum. But what about schools where very little real learning goes on?

A. Some districts and administrators use standardized tests to ensure that students get a minimal level of education. But the level of education we should be demanding for all students requires that we go way beyond what is inspired by standardized tests. My concern is that standardized tests are becoming the top bar of expectations, not the minimal bar.

Furthermore, if you rely on standardized tests to close the achievement gap, that's terribly misleading in terms of who will get a quality education. Students in more privileged groups will get not only the material on the standardized tests, but may also receive drama, art, music, and important elective courses. It's essential to understand that relying on standardized tests has been shown to dumb down the curriculum. ✎

Standards: Decoy or Quality Control?

ASA HILLIARD

The following is condensed from a speech by the late Asa Hilliard, professor of urban education at Georgia State University in Atlanta. Hilliard was the author of numerous books and articles on education, particularly the education of African American children. Hilliard gave the speech at a conference in the fall of 1999 at Howard University on "Moving Beyond Standards To Provide Excellence and Equity in the African American Community."

Is the standards movement a quality control movement, as it is advertised, or is it a decoy for something else?

We have been here before, with the standards movement. In fact, we reach a standards movement almost every three or four years. Some governor wants to manipulate the test score requirements or get a new test. Some president wants to manipulate test score requirements or get a new test. Somebody wants to change the standards of education, presumably as a way of raising the quality of schools and schooling and the achievement of children. I say presumably, because I don't think I can remember a time when that was really the reason for having a standards movement. If you want to raise quality, standards manipulation is probably the last place you would start.

Let me say at the outset that no one fears high standards, at least no African Americans I know. We do not fear clear standards. We do not fear uniform standards. We do not fear public standards. In fact, we have been at the forefront of standards of the highest order.1

But what we need is honest school improvement that acknowledges high standards as well as high-quality school input. To establish the standards of output without having standards of input is a travesty. To hold children responsible for outcomes without giving the same level of sophisticated attention to guaranteeing the standards of exposure is an abandonment of the responsibility of adults for the education and socialization of children.

That's why I used the title that I did: "Standards as Quality Control or Decoy?" I believe the standards movement is generally a decoy. I don't care whether it's a Democrat or a Republican who calls for it. Usually, when people put so much emphasis on standards as a school reform tool, it means that they want to look like they're performing a reform effort, but they're actually moonwalking. They look like they're going forward, but they're going backward.

What most of us fear is that we will be held responsible for achievement without being given the same quality of treatment on the front end. We're not afraid of standards. We're afraid of hurdles, of obstacles.

Standards, Assessment, and Instruction

There are several things to deconstruct here, because they're all tied together. When we say standards, you can talk about setting standards. You can also talk about the instruments to measure

I believe the standards movement is generally a decoy. I don't care whether it's a Democrat or a Republican who calls for it.

the standards—whether they're valid, invalid, biased, or unbiased. And you can talk about the quality of instruction to enable people to meet the standards. All of that is tied together. But we generally break these apart. As a result, we usually make mistakes in our analysis. If you're talking about using standards to get the achievement level of U.S. students up to snuff, then you're going to have to talk more broadly and deeply than we've been talking so far.

I'm a little bit tired of people getting credit for improving education by doing the cheapest thing they can do, which is to call for the manipulation of test scores or to create new standards. These new standards are not going to be any better than the ones the College Board developed in the "green book": *What Students Need to Know and Do in Order to Graduate from College.*[2] They're not going to be any higher or better than the standards of the National Alliance of Black School Educators.[3] In fact, I'll take any standards that you come up with, as long as they're high enough. If you get a consensus of a group of thinking people, I don't think you can write a set of standards that *won't* make sense.

Are you going to say "no" to calculus as a standard for the high school level? I think calculus is a reasonable standard. All children are brilliant enough to learn calculus, if you want to offer it to them. But if you want to teach calculus, you have to know calculus. And most teachers don't. So why blame the child for the inability to achieve when the deficiency is in the other place? Obviously, if you want the child to achieve in calculus, and teachers don't know calculus, then now you've got to prepare the teachers. Now you're talking about staff development. See how it's all connected?

If you really want to raise the achievement of children, you've got to recognize reality in the classroom. Once you do so, you'll know that we'll have to do what we did in the 1960s. When this country thought that the Russians were ahead in the space race, when they put up Sputnik, the next thing that happened was that the United States massively mobilized for science education. It was science, science everywhere. We had a National Defense Education Act. Look at the language: Education became a matter of national defense. When the rubber met the road,

If you want elephants to grow, you don't weigh the elephants. You feed the elephants.

they knew they had to do something, and they funded the process of doing it.

What's happening now? The budget is bankrupt on social welfare issues, and nobody wants to do anything about it. So you manipulate the standards to make it look as if you're doing something. But you cannot fix the problems in the public sector without providing resources.

If you want to reform schools, don't do it with testing. We used to say, "If you want elephants to grow, you don't weigh the elephants. You feed the elephants." Children will not grow unless they get quality instruction.

In some ways, I see the standards movement as *Trivial Pursuit*. We know it's not a reform tool, and yet we move ahead as if it's a reform tool. I know why we ended up with national standards. After the Republicans gutted the social services budget, the politicians still wanted to look good to the people, so they could say they were making the best effort they could under the circumstances. In other words, they had to address the question, "What can I do with no money?" Basically, nothing but showboat.

IQ Is a Scam

I also want to say something about irrationality and mental measurement, because part of this job is to find tests that tell us the truth. The mental measurement movement is typified by irrationality.

IQ is the biggest scam in the history of education. Nobody needs IQ testing. Nobody benefits when you do it. I'm in a very different position than most of you; I don't want an IQ test for black kids, and one for green kids, and one for yellow kids, and one for red kids. I don't want any for anybody, because it offers no benefit to anyone. The issue is not bias. Sometimes, people get up here to discuss bias, when we should be asking, "Why is this foolish question about IQ being asked? Who said that teachers have to know a child's ultimate capability before they start to teach?"

We have got to learn to ask new questions and not simply give a black version of the white question. So intelligence testing should go out the window, as far as I'm concerned. Now, if you want to know how we know it's irrational, get the book edited by Helga Rowe, *Intelligence: Reconceptualization and Measurement*, which includes papers from a summit meeting of psychologists in mental measurement in Melbourne, Australia, in 1988. They were trying to figure out what was the state of the art in measurement, especially intelligence measurement, and they came away with three conclusions. Actually, there were probably more conclusions, but these are the three that interested me:

They couldn't agree on what intelligence was. That's what you might call a construct validity problem. It's a little hard to measure precisely when you don't have agreement on the construct.

There's no predictive validity to IQ tests unless you use low-level thinking as your achievement criteria. If you use high-level, conceptually oriented problem

solving, then there's no correlation between IQ scores and achievement outcomes. This is serious, because that's
where the IQ test is supposed to be
making its contribution, in predictive
validity. But it's not there unless you

**IQ is the biggest scam in
the history of education.
Nobody needs IQ testing.**

measure something that somebody has already had time to process.

If they can ever agree on what intelligence is—and if they can ever measure
it—they will have to take context into account. That's what the black psychologists have been arguing for before I was born: that the context is what gives meaning to a response. You can't universalize a dialogue, linguistically or culturally. It's
scientific idiocy to do so. So you have to understand whose IQ is being tested—
those who make the irrational IQ tests. IQ testing doesn't do any good for any-
body other than people who need work. It's a professional welfare program.

IQ tests, universally, are invalid. You cannot measure in absence of understanding of the context of the person. That means their culture; that means the
political situation; that means their exposure to curriculum—all of that adds up
to context.

Standards and Curriculum

I'm often called on to testify in court cases. In one case in Florida, the judge asked
me, very impatiently, "Well, just give me an example of a biased item!" I said,
"Well, Judge, all of them are biased." And he said, "No, no, no. I don't want to
hear that; I want to hear a specific example!" I said, "Well, OK."

The transgressions are so gross in these tests, it's so easy. That's a softball
question for me. So I said, "You know, let's take this section of this test. This is
about geography, the section on geography." He said, "Well, what's wrong with
it?" I said, "Florida doesn't teach geography."

Wouldn't you think that would be a content validity problem? He reluctantly
had to rule in favor of the plaintiffs. Afterward, officials actually had to go back
and institute a statewide curriculum in Florida. So now Florida has a curriculum,
supposedly. They went through a process, and now they say, "We have a curriculum, so we can have a test, and we can make measurement." But all they really
have is a standard measure with no match between the standard and what is actually taught in school.

I could go on. But the issue is, when we finally get down to the end of this standard dialogue, where will we stand on national assessment? Will the assessment
be rational? Will it have true content validity? Will there be an empirical way to
test it or will we still fool ourselves on mental measurement?

There's also the question of a common national curriculum. If you're not
ready for a national curriculum, you're not going to have national standards. And
you certainly won't have national, standardized assessment, because there will be
a mismatch between the assessment and the sets of standards that go with each
state, and maybe even substandards within each state.

If you're not ready for a national curriculum, you're not going to have national standards.

Opportunity to Learn

What I want to talk about is the common treatment opportunity—that is, opportunity to learn. You can't hold children to the standards unless you give them a chance to master those standards. You have to check to see if the opportunities are there. We are a country typified by savage inequalities—I love the title of Jonathan Kozol's work, *Savage Inequalities*—and it's not the children who are savages; it's the people who savagely distribute the resources inequitably. Here's what Kozol finds out: $10,000 per year per child at New Trier Township High School, $5,000 per year per child at DuSable High School. Where you live determines what level of resources you get. That's a policy issue that is not being addressed by the standards movement. They're not even looking at the inequality. They're looking only at the output, not the input.

Content validity of achievement tests, the standards, and the curriculum—all three must be aligned with each other. But I see no hope that that's going to happen in this country any time soon. Too many vested interests have reason not to see that happen.

So where do we go from here? As I said, we need to connect standards with instruction so that the standards themselves are content-valid, and then we need to connect the assessment instrument to the standards. If that happens, then maybe we can make some moves forward.

I have no expectation that that's going to happen, however. Therefore, I think the standards movement is going to be abandoned, and we'll be doing this again in another five years when somebody else has the problem of how to raise achievement with no money. But if we can turn the discussion around so it focuses on the quality of service rather than on the analysis of children and their families, then maybe, just maybe, we might be one step ahead when the topic comes up again. ✎

Endnotes

1. Asa Hilliard, Barbara Sizemore, et al., *Saving the African American Child*, Washington, DC: National Alliance of Black School Educators, 1984.

2. The College Board, *Academic Preparation for College: What Students Need to Know and Be Able to Do*, New York, NY: The College Board, 1983.

3. Hilliard and Sizemore, *Saving the African American Child*.

A Child Is Not a Test Score

Assessment is a civil rights issue

MONTY NEILL

"The function of education is to teach one to think intensively and to think critically. Intelligence plus character—that is the goal of true education."

—MARTIN LUTHER KING JR.

On the 2008 campaign trail, President Obama declared, "We should not be forced to spend the academic year preparing students to fill in bubbles on standardized tests." Obama also called for "a broader range of assessments that can evaluate higher-order skills."

If the nation's goal is a high-quality education for all, why not use assessments that can at least tell us if that goal is being met? Why not rely on multiple sources of evidence to inhibit narrowing curriculum and teaching-to-one-test format? Why not make decisions about students and schools based on information gathered over time? Why not transform assessment and accountability to serve the educational needs of all students? A truly healthy educational system will prioritize high-quality classroom instruction and use school-based assessment information to monitor classroom, school, and district progress. Sadly, the nation's public education system does not function that way.

Standardized tests have been prevalent for much of the latter half of 20th century. The emphasis on standardized testing has intensified in recent decades as elected officials, business leaders, and others have fostered the idea that the U.S. economy will decline unless student achievement and school progress are increasingly monitored through testing.

In 2002, President George W. Bush won passage of the No Child Left Behind Act (NCLB), which pushed the emphasis on multiple-choice, paper-and-pencil tests to new heights. Under NCLB, an ever-escalating number of students in every public school and district was expected to score at a proficient level on statewide standardized tests each year. Under the original configuration of NCLB, students as a whole and also specific ethnic and racial groups were required to meet this "Adequate Yearly Progress" (AYP) requirement.

The pressure to pass standardized tests intensified dramatically under NCLB. Schools that repeatedly failed to make AYP faced escalating sanctions, culminating in "restructuring," which can include replacing a school's staff or turning it over to private management. Schools that have struggled the most to make AYP are those with the highest percentages of poor students, schools that typically have fewer resources. In these schools, teachers are frequently expected to rigidly "deliver" a preprogrammed, often tightly scripted curriculum, each day covering a set of skills to prepare students for the tests. Teachers often lack the authority to deviate from the mandated curriculum regardless of student needs, emerging issues, or the teachers' recognition that these curricula fail to prepare students for future success. School staff members fear that if they do not narrow the curriculum and tailor the instruction to fit the tests, then their students will fare poorly, putting the students themselves and their schools at risk of severe sanctions.

One risk students face in a majority of states is the graduation test. These tests began in Florida in the late 1970s. A lawsuit delayed the use of the graduation test on the grounds that many black students had not had a fair opportunity to learn the material on which they were tested because they had attended schools that were segregated by law. The courts ruled that the tests could be used once students who had begun school after the end of de jure segregation had graduated. This ruling ignored the extensive de facto segregation and the vastly disparate resources available to blacks and whites.

Graduation tests quickly spread across the South and then to northern states with large populations of students of color in their cities, such as New York, Ohio, and New Jersey. In 1995-96, 11 of 16 states in the Southern Regional Education Board had exit exams, compared with only six of the remaining 35 states (including Washington, D.C.). Those states also tested an average of 7.5 grades, substantially higher than the national average of 5.28 grades. In effect, the worst-performing systems and those with the highest proportions of African Americans were most likely to implement high-stakes testing.

The next wave of states that enacted graduation tests—after a halt in the mid-1990s—included states with disproportionately high Latino populations. New Mexico and Texas, which imposed exit exams in the first wave, were joined by Arizona and California, for example. States with tests comprise about 70 percent of the nation's student population, but more than 80 percent of its African American and Latino students. The states without graduation tests form a belt from Illinois to Idaho, and north of Oklahoma—and in most cases have predominantly white student populations. Thus, youth of color, those who speak English as a second language, students who have disabilities, and students from low-income families are disproportionately denied diplomas because of test scores.

The same is just as true for tests students must pass to move to the next grade, which are found in Florida, Louisiana, Texas, and many large cities like Chicago and New York. As with diploma denial, the damage of grade retention falls disproportionately on youth of color. Extensive research has demonstrated that students who are held back progress more slowly than comparable students who are promoted: They suffer significant losses of self-esteem, and they are far less likely to graduate.

The Educational Consequences of High-Stakes Testing

Across the country, students have exposed the damaging educational consequences of high-stakes standardized tests. They have decried being denied diplomas because of test scores, and they have exposed the way incessant test preparation deforms curriculum, instruction, and learning.

Macario Guajardo, a 16-year-old from South Texas who for years boycotted the state's standardized test, the Texas Assessment of Knowledge and Skills (TAKS), explained to a state legislative committee on education reform the consequences for learning: "When I was in elementary, schools were basically like a TAKS factory, and students were almost like little robots. I don't remember there being any room for serious, creative, and critical thinkers."

> **So long as such a system remains in place, the pipeline to college and good jobs for low-income and minority-group youths will remain narrow, but the pipelines to prison and unemployment will remain wide.**

Carolyn, also 16, wrote in the *California Bee*, a daily newspaper, "District tests, including the high school exit exam, should be eliminated since there is no educational point to them...Too much classroom time is wasted on test preparation and taking tests. That time should be spent on actual learning of subjects, not on the steps of how to eliminate answers." She added, "The focus of our education system should not be based on tests, but on the individual needs of students."

The sharp disparities in educational opportunity are also visible to at least some students. Afrisha Lavine from Akron, Ohio, compared her school to a wealthier school that was nearby: "If they . . . put the same programs in the failing schools, then they would be good schools. The failing schools are not bad, it's just that they have a great disadvantage."

Jackie, a Boston high school student, similarly explained, "In going to other schools and finding what opportunities other students are getting made me realize what opportunities I am not getting at my school."

Districts in poorer communities—especially communities of color that have fewer qualified teachers and inadequate books, laboratories, and libraries—are expected to perform at the same levels as districts that have far more financial and educational resources. The inequity is compounded when districts gut art, music classes, and sports for the rote memorization, constant quizzing, and testing that limit time for creative and analytical thinking. Wealthier districts, whose students are better prepared for these tests, devote far less time to test preparation and don't suffer the impact of narrowed curricula.

A Californians for Justice report explained, "Any conversation with high school students from around the state reveals that students are extremely demoralized by the exit exam. It is clear that large numbers of students of color, low-income students, and immigrant students feel that their futures are being destroyed by a test for which they have not been prepared."

As Boston student Gregory pointed out, "They are just training us for the workforce . . . trying to train you to sit in one place and do simple operations for eight hours." Caroline added, "You always have a lot of people saying that you kids are the future. But how can we be the future if we are not getting what we need?"

The stories of educational damage occur and recur because high-stakes standardized testing has come to dominate learning and class time. Tests are widely used as a sole hurdle for student grade promotion, graduation, or program placement, and they control opportunities, curriculum, and instruction in the name of accountability.

The interaction of under-resourced schools and testing most powerfully hits students of color. They are disproportionately denied diplomas or grade promotion, and the schools they attend are the ones most likely to fare poorly on the tests and face sanctions such as restructuring.

Professor Gloria Ladson-Billings uses the term "education debt" to explain the lack of adequate educational opportunity for African American students that has been accumulating since slavery and segregation. She thinks that focusing on this inequality is far more meaningful than the commonly used term "achievement gap," which only refers to unequal test results. The debt includes the school-based debt in resources. It also includes the housing debt that forced people of color to suffer inferior living conditions, exemplified by the racial covenants that ensured African Americans could not move to many suburbs after World War II. Billings speaks also of pervasive historical and current unequal access to medical and the employment debt; African American families earn three-fifths of what white families earn in the United States, and income inequality is growing rapidly.

Test-based "school reform" like NCLB, which passed with support from both Democrats and Republicans, is an effort to improve results while ignoring the existence of the education debt.

The tools used to improve results—tests and sanctions—actually make things worse. Low-income students, who are disproportionately children of color, attend under-resourced schools that serve up a thin gruel of test preparation. So long as such a system remains in place, the pipeline to college and good jobs for low-income and minority-group youths will remain narrow, but the pipelines to prison and unemployment will remain wide.

What is it about the use of standardized tests as the primary arbiter of school quality that is problematic? The trouble arises partly because, in the face of escalating sanctions, some schools and districts have taken harmful actions such as increasing suspensions and expulsions of low scorers—removing perceived problem kids from the classrooms instead of dealing with their problems. And partly the trouble is the damage done to teaching.

Testing's control over teaching is unevenly applied. The drill-and-kill school practices that guarantee students will not be ready for college, skilled employment, lifelong learning, or effective citizenship are most prevalent in schools serving low-income children of color. No one has documented this more powerfully than Jonathan Kozol in *Shame of the Nation*. Building on his earlier exposé of the vastly unequal opportunities provided in different communities across the nation, *Savage Inequalities*, Kozol describes in painful detail the brain-deadening, emotionally stultifying consequences of scripted curricula and test preparation in what he terms "apartheid education."

Suburban middle- and upper-class schools succumb to a degree to teaching to state exams, but teaching to the test is nowhere near as prevalent or powerful in those communities. And the suburban schools certainly do not employ the tightly scripted curricula widely used in urban schools.

The learning gaps revealed by standardized tests mask worse gaps in more advanced learning areas. For example, students in well-to-do schools typically learn to write research papers, which colleges expect students to do. There are no research papers on standardized tests. If the primary goal is to boost test scores, teachers will not take the time to teach needed research and writing skills.

> **Using a variety of assessments is the best means to obtain evidence about school quality and student learning. This shift is necessary to get out of the dangerous, educationally destructive trap of high-stakes testing.**

As noted psychologist Robert Sternberg wrote, "The increasingly massive and far-reaching use of conventional standardized tests is one of the most effective, if unintentional, vehicles this country has created for suppressing creativity." That suppression, too, most powerfully affects students who are most subject to the tests.

The Impact of Low Graduation Rates

With tests as one key factor, African American and Latino graduation rates barely reach 60 percent. The consequences are severe. Non-graduates have significantly lower lifetime earnings and less stable families; they are more likely to be unemployed or imprisoned.

Graduation rates for low-achieving minority students and girls have fallen nearly 20 percentage points since California implemented high school exit exams, according to "Effects of the California High School Exit Exam on Student Persistence, Achievement, and Graduation," a research paper published by Stanford University's Institute for Research on Education Policy and Practice. In 2007-08, 40,000 more students failed to graduate than did so in pre-test years.

Similarly, more than 40,000 Texas students were denied diplomas in 2007 because they did not pass all four parts of the state's graduation exam. These casualties are a direct result of high-stakes accountability systems designed to maximize test scores.

Current research by John Robert Warren and his colleagues demonstrates that graduation tests increase the number of dropouts, do not lead to better test scores, and do not produce improved results in college or employment. They are, in effect, wholly negative.

The "Standards for Educational and Psychological Testing," produced by the American Educational Research Association, American Psychological Association, and National Council on Measurement in Education, warn against these practices: "[A] decision . . . that will have major impact on a student should not be made on the basis of a single test score." Similarly, the American Evaluation Association concludes, "High stakes testing leads to underserving or mis-serving all students, especially the most needy and vulnerable, thereby violating the principle of 'do no harm.'" Policy makers have ignored the wisdom of the very people who make, use, and research tests.

Civil rights organizations have long battled these make-or-break tests. They point out how systems that deny diplomas or promotions based on test scores typically fail to provide adequate or equitable opportunities for all students to learn the material on the tests. This places the burden of accountability on the backs of children, hitting hardest those children within the worst education systems with the fewest resources.

African American and Latino children are more frequently retained in grades than are whites. In Chicago in 2008, 98.6 percent of white students passed the grade promotion test, compared with 85.5 percent of African Americans. These disparities have not changed much over the years. Since 2002, 12.9 percent of Chicago's black students have been held back, whereas only 2.3 percent of white students have faced the same fate. In 2008, 5.4 percent of Latino students were retained.

Chicago-based researchers evaluated the consequences and concluded that retention is harmful. Retained students did not do as well academically as comparable students who were promoted, and retention increased the likelihood of dropping out.

The Chicago studies confirmed decades of previous research showing that flunking students diminishes their self-esteem, reduces their likelihood of graduation, and fails to increase achievement. Because grade retention is harmful and test-based policies lead to more retention overall with disproportionate increases for African Americans and Latinos, test-based retention intensifies race-based inequalities in school systems like Chicago's public schools.

There is a ready solution to the "social promotion" versus "retention" dispute: Promote students, but provide intensive extra support to those who are not doing well as soon as academic problems are identified. Providing such support would help schools avoid inflicting the damage of retention while offering the help many students need. Helpful support would focus not on boosting test scores, but rather on strengthening real academic knowledge and skills.

Better Assessments in an Improved System

A good assessment—one that helps us understand what students have learned—is essential for teaching and learning. It is also is a core component of holding students, teachers, schools, and districts accountable for their work, class time, and resources. Although the processes of assessment and accountability often overlap, they do not go hand in hand. Many assessments used in education have nothing to do with accountability. And demonstrating a student's, teacher's, or school's success—in short, accountability—should involve far more than academic assessments.

In *Grading Education: Getting Accountability Right*, authors Richard Rothstein, Rebecca Jacobsen, and Tamara Wilder write that the general public, legislators, and school board members view the aims of education broadly and think education should serve many purposes. It should include the teaching of academics, critical thinking, arts and literature. And it should prepare students for skilled work while promoting social skills, work ethics, citizenship, physical health, and emotional health.

In *Empowering Schools and Improving Learning*, the Forum on Educational Accountability (FEA) proposes accountability structures that would look at inputs: what students are getting on the front end, including the quality of health care and housing, teacher quality, and school resources. The FEA proposes that schools and districts collaborate with families and communities to meet the needs of the whole child—cognitive/intellectual, social, civic, emotional, psychological, ethical, and physical—while preparing students for successful citizenship in a multicultural world.

> We might agree to prioritize reading, writing, and math, but all of those skills can and should be integrated into richer opportunities—and assessments and accountability need to take those broader needs into account.

Assessments should include multiple kinds of evidence: multiple-choice questions, essays, projects, teacher observations, and student self-evaluations. Good teachers know how to use a broad range of assessments, and they know it is possible to use many different tools to assess knowledge. Unfortunately, pressure to boost scores on standardized tests has reduced the range of assessments teachers use. For example, one teacher, in a FairTest report on NCLB, described how she had to reduce the number of book reports she assigned because of the time required for test prep. These kinds of stories have been told thousands of times across the nation.

Teachers use high-quality assessment results to adjust their teaching ("formative" assessing) and to evaluate student success ("summative" assessing). This means that good teachers use a variety of measures to gather a great deal of evidence about student learning. Most of the time, this evidence stops with the teacher. It may show up as a grade, or in a discussion with parents or next year's teacher, but it rarely informs efforts to improve schools or shape policy or provide public accountability. In short, a much richer sampling of learning is ignored in favor of a narrow set of data called test scores.

Good and meaningful learning often involves more extended work. Assignments and projects produce a great deal of information about the learning process and student achievement. But it is not easy to create meaningful tasks, and teachers cannot be expected to create all the tasks they might need. Therefore, districts, states, consortia of districts—and even test companies—should assemble banks of high-quality tasks. The tasks would be available for teachers to use during their courses, as they deem appropriate. The completed tasks would become part of the record of student achievement. Some tasks might be administered statewide, but research suggests great caution in trying to make sound inferences based on the results of one or two tasks. One study found it would take between nine and 10 one-hour tasks to be able to make a fair judgment about what a student learned in a high school biology class. No state can or should administer 10 tasks, but a good teacher can do so during the course of the year. However, when regarded as one part of the overall evidence, centrally required tasks can be a useful component of assessing learning.

It is not easy to gather evidence over time from the many kinds of work students complete and assemble the pieces in a useful format. It requires a strong evaluation structure. An example of such an evaluation structure is the Learning Record (LR), first developed in London, England, for use with multilingual, multicultural immigrants. Without dictating the specific content, the LR provides a structure for gathering samples that can illuminate the teacher's evaluation of a student. It provides a means for scoring: in the case of the reading record, by placing students on progress (developmental) scales. If anyone else looks at the LR, its structure enables rapid verification of the teacher's evaluation. If teachers had low expectations or did not have students read much material of consequence, then that would be revealed. If the students read challenging novels and plays and wrote thoughtful papers, then that would be revealed.

"Sampling" procedures, such as those employed by the National Assessment of Educational Progress (NAEP), also can be used. NAEP is the only nationally representative and continuing assessment of what students in the United States know and can do in various subject areas. NAEP assessments are conducted periodically in mathematics, reading, science, writing, the arts, civics, economics, geography, and U.S. history. It reports at state and national levels, as well as in a few large cities. A state sampling procedure will not produce individual student scores, but rather school-level scores. These standardized tools, which can include performance tasks, can serve primarily as a check on the system.

New assessment approaches require teachers, administrators, and other professionals to learn more. Unfortunately, teachers are poorly prepared in college and in their early years of teaching to do assessments in beneficial ways, even though assessments are a primary component of teaching. Collaborative professional development, primarily at the school level, can include a focus on developing and using better, broader, richer assessments. Educators can then use the resulting assessment data for further staff learning.

Standardized tests can be part of the assessment and accountability mix. However, there is no reason for the federal government to mandate that states test all children with a standardized instrument every year. (No other country comes close to mandating as much testing as the United States, and many are doing better on international comparisons of student learning.) If states continue to choose to test annually, those tests should be used in accountability the same way sampling would be: Where there are significant shortfalls in a school district, the state would investigate to determine the cause. If warranted, the state could use the results to direct any needed changes to help teachers, students, and school administrators.

Using a variety of assessments is the best means to obtain evidence about school quality and student learning. This shift is necessary to get out of the dangerous, educationally destructive trap of high-stakes testing. Escaping that trap does not mean no one will be watching or that schools and districts won't be held accountable. The assessment alternatives outlined here provide a richer set of accountability tools, and they provide far richer information than standardized tests. The information provided in a Learning Record or a set of complex tasks can be used to guide improvement efforts with much greater accuracy and effectiveness than the sparse data from 40-to-50-item standardized tests.

Is it okay to offer little or no consideration for the whole child and students' relationships to actual communities?

The Big Picture

High-quality performance assessments with strong local components functioning within a supportive accountability and improvement system are vital components of educational opportunity and equity. Such assessments can contribute to improving education where an overemphasis on standardized tests coupled with misguided accountability procedures cannot.

Schools alone cannot overcome poverty, but they can make a powerful difference. A focus on improvement must also address the reality that the nation cannot wish away inequity and inadequacy with the magic wand of testing. Rational efforts must use input, process, and outcome information to guide improvement and each develop each school's capacity to serve all children well, as the FEA proposes. This means holding government accountable for providing adequate and equitable resources for all children. Schools like those in the New York Performance Standards Consortium demonstrate that students in under-resourced schools might not catch up on standardized tests, but they can be prepared for the more important goal of succeeding in college because they can learn to think and use knowledge well.

What do we, as a nation, want to prioritize? Spurious and illusory steps toward equity through standardization, or real improvement efforts in which high-quality assessment is one essential part?

More significantly, how much less should low-income communities, communities of color, and their advocates settle for? It might be pie in the sky to think that all kids will attend schools that spend $25,000 per pupil each year—as many elite private schools do—or spend upwards of $15,000 per pupil as many wealthy suburban schools do. But is it acceptable to completely eliminate art classes or science labs? Is it okay to offer little or no consideration for the whole child and students' relationships to actual communities? We might agree to prioritize reading, writing, and math, but all of those skills can and should be integrated into richer opportunities—and assessments and accountability need to take those broader needs into account.

To settle for less is accepting obvious inequality, and it consigns the children of the poor to perpetually less. It does not give those children the educational opportunities they need to succeed in higher education, at work, and as effective citizens. Settling for less means leaving them behind while pretending to enable them to catch up. Martin Luther King Jr., who spoke so eloquently about the "goal of true education," might wonder at our society's current emphasis on rote learning of "basics" and drills for filling in the bubbles on multiple-choice tests.

Changing this system depends on activism by parents, students, educators, communities, and organizations. Without a concerted push for change, our nation is likely to continue undermining education for our most vulnerable youth. ✎

A version of this article appeared in the Fall 2009 issue of Root & Branch, *2(2), 28-35.*
www.rootandbranchmagazine.org

The Straitjacket of Standardized Tests

Where is the standardized test that can measure passion for learning, respect for others, and human empathy?

TOM MCKENNA

When I first met Sol Shapiro, he was in his 80s and living alone in a retirement home. He was the first person my Portland, Oregon, high school history class interviewed for an oral history project about our city's immigrant community, Old South Portland. My students were primarily African American. Sol was Jewish. They were young. He was old. Neither party was really excited about the encounter.

We met in Sol's apartment. He was helpful as the students set up their equipment. After about 20 minutes of uncomfortable introductions, the interview began.

"My name is Sol Shapiro. I am very familiar with old South Portland." Silence. One that seemed much longer than it actually was. Quietly, almost imperceptibly, Sol began to weep. My students were stunned. They turned off the video camera and tape recorder. Soon Felicia ventured forth and placed her hand on Sol's shoulder, "It's OK, Mr. Shapiro. We understand."

Sol cleared his throat, removed his glasses, and dabbed his tears. "Thank you," he said as he looked down.

"Excuse me, please, I'm very sorry." He rose from his couch and headed for a back room. My students looked at me with puzzled expressions.

"What do we do now?"

We waited. After a few minutes, Sol returned. He reclaimed his seat on the couch and shared artifacts from his life with us, accompanying each with a tale from his past. Students feasted on a steady stream of photographs, letters, religious pieces, and historical documents. Much of what he shared over the next hour never got recorded on tape. Students came to class the next day with a new outlook on interviewing old people and oral history. They wanted more.

Unfortunately, given the demands of current educational reform in Oregon, teachers are finding it difficult to give students the "more" they desire.

Teachers Under Pressure

Increasingly, teachers feel pressured to prepare students to do well on state-administered standardized tests. We feel we have to teach to those tests; we have to "cover the content" because these tests will be the measure of our teaching and our students' learning.

A well-respected classroom veteran recently told me, "All this standardized

A well-respected classroom veteran recently told me, "All this standardized test stuff has changed the way I teach."

test stuff has changed the way I teach." He wasn't comfortable with his realization. There seems to be little room left for the use of oral history, much less time to pursue the kind of in-depth project described above. What happens if my students don't do well on the tests? What happens to my school in a district that has already "reconstituted" two other schools for low scores? What happens to my job in a state that recently took away teacher tenure? Those pressures are real, and I do not want to downplay them. I also want to emphasize that those pressures and the reality they reflect are the reasons why using teaching methods like oral history are so important.

Clearly, high-stakes standardized testing—where a single multiple-choice test administered out of the context of the classroom is used to ascertain both student learning and teacher effectiveness—affects much more than the way student academic performance is assessed. It also threatens to define the way teachers teach. In a world enriched with difference, the hidden curriculum of much current educational reform is singularity, sameness, and compliance.

What score would I give students on the South Portland project? What would a multiple-choice test tell state legislators about what we all learned? Lives changed. People overcame significant historical barriers that threatened to keep them apart forever. Students were moved to social action. They came to class religiously. They sat in an orthodox synagogue with yarmulkes on their heads and learned about Judaism. They became passionate experts about urban renewal. They uncovered obscure historical documents on Saturday mornings in an Oregon History Center where they did not feel welcome.

Oral history can be a powerful classroom tool. I'm reminded of this each time I think of the South Portland video project and when I use oral history techniques with students. Out of necessity, students acquire and apply valuable skills in pursuit of learning that matters. They formulate questions for interviews. They work collectively to solve problems that threaten to derail hours of work. They need to write text and then critique, revise, and polish it. Discovery leads to questions, and research is needed to find answers to those questions. Research leads to surprise, surprise breeds excitement, excitement spills over into passion, and students find a connection in the classroom they aren't likely to find in a more traditional setting. I know. I used to teach in a more traditional way.

Students Transformed

James never missed history class. Often, he had to sneak in and out of my room to hide from the dean, because he rarely attended his other classes. He was our No. 1 cameraman and interviewer. Jennifer uncovered a quote from a neighborhood meeting, on document long lost in dusty boxes, and it moved her to angry tears. History came alive for her. She wove it into our collective narrative text. The words of a state official resonated when she read his comment about the people who would be moved by urban renewal: "Frankly, we don't give a damn about the renters."

The end result of our work was a 30-minute documentary about South Portland and about the urban renewal that destroyed it. We were invited to show the piece at the Portland Art Museum auditorium. I got there early and stood outside on the street trying to help direct my students and their families to a facility where none of them had ever been, in a part of town where few of them had ever ventured.

> **What would a multiple-choice test tell state legislators about what we all learned? Lives changed. People overcame significant historical barriers that threatened to keep them apart forever.**

About 250 people attended our premiere that night. The students deftly answered questions from the audience and talked extensively about their experience.

Sol Shapiro was in the crowd. Shortly before the show was scheduled to begin, I saw him walking toward me. He had on a plaid sports jacket with contrasting dark blue tie and trousers. I waved. He waved back with noticeable hesitation. We greeted. "Tom, I didn't know if you would remember me," he said.

"Sol, how could I forget?" I replied, and grabbed his hand. I tried to hug him, but he pulled away.

"I need to tell you something," he said. "Before meeting your students, I was doing very little. What did I have to live for? My wife is gone, the community. But those young people reminded me I still had something to offer." I tried to interject.

"No, listen, I used to be a tailor, as you know, for years," Sol continued. "I said to myself, why not share what I know with others? So, I'm now helping out at the local community college in their fashion design program. I came here tonight to see the show and to thank your students."

We smiled. Sol gestured as if to tip his hat, and then he made his way into the auditorium.

Students, their families, and former residents of South Portland gathered at my home for a reception after the show. Students commandeered my stereo, and their music boomed throughout my home. I went to turn it down. I stopped when I saw what was going on in my living room. Dancing hand in hand around my house were two groups of people who were about as different from each other as I could imagine and who, when I first approached them about getting together, had resisted the idea of cooperating. Young and old, African American and Jewish were joined together in a celebration of each other. They celebrated a new understanding that our project helped them achieve. They embraced the differences that one time kept them apart.

Find me the standardized test that can measure the meaning of that embrace. ✎

This article is adapted from a story that originally appeared in The Oregonian. *The names have been changed.*

Racism in the History of Standardized Testing: Legacies for Today

ALAN STOSKOPF

At the beginning of the century, one of the most damaging experiments in public education began. Under the banner of educational reform, the American eugenics movement captured the hearts and minds of some of the nation's most influential educational researchers and policy makers. Although the history of the eugenics movement has been virtually written out of U.S. history textbooks, this history nonetheless has had an insidious effect on the lives of students and the organization of public schools. It also has become part of an unexamined legacy that shadows today's standards and testing movement.

A Legacy of Bias

The English mathematician Sir Francis Galton first coined the term "eugenics" in 1883. He wrote, "Eugenics is the study of the agencies under social control that seek to improve or impair the racial qualities of future generations either physically or mentally."[1] What Galton saw as a new branch of scientific inquiry became a dogmatic prescription in the ranking and ordering of human worth. His ideas found their most receptive audience at the turn of the century in the United States.

Eugenics fed off of the fears of white middle- and upper-class Americans. In the early 20th century, the United States was experiencing rapid social and economic change. As the nation became more industrial and urban, millions of poor immigrants from Southern and Eastern Europe flocked to the United States seeking a better life. Simultaneously, thousands of African Americans were beginning a great migration to Northern cities from the Jim Crow South. Competition for jobs intensified existing frictions along class and racial lines.

Periodic economic recessions created further social unrest. Labor unions, civil rights groups, and the women's suffrage movement pressed for greater equity. At the same time, nativist and racist groups like the Ku Klux Klan pulled in the opposite direction. It was out of this cauldron of social upheaval that the American eugenics movement emerged. It promised prosperity and progress, not through strikes or ugly race riots, but rather through a new science that would combine advances in the field of genetics with the efficiency of the assembly line.

Eugenicists used a flawed and crude interpretation of Gregor Mendel's laws on heredity to argue that criminality, intelligence, and pauperism were passed down in families as simple dominant or recessive hereditary traits. Mainline eugenicists (who were explicitly preoccupied with issues of race) believed that some individuals and entire groups of people (such as southern Europeans, Jews, Africans, and Latinos) were more predisposed to the "defective genes." Charles Davenport, a leader in American eugenics, argued for laws to control the spread of "inferior blood" into the general population. He told an international gathering of scholars "that the biological basis for such laws is doubtless an appreciation of the fact that negroes and other races carry traits that do not go well with our social organization."[2]

Davenport's wishes were partly realized. Eugenic advocates convinced 30 state legislatures to pass involuntary sterilization laws that targeted "defective strains" within the general population, such as the blind, deaf, epileptic, feeble-minded, and paupers. On the national level, eugenic supporters played a decisive role in the congressional passage of the draconian Immigration and Restriction Act of 1924, which established blatantly racist quotas. President Calvin Coolidge embraced the eugenic assumptions behind the law when he declared, "America must be kept American. Biological laws show that Nordics deteriorate when mixed with other races."[3]

> **Although the history of the eugenics movement has been virtually written out of U.S. history textbooks, it nonetheless has had an insidious effect on the lives of students and the organization of public schools.**

Lasting Effects

Although those laws have been repealed, the impact of eugenics on public education was more enduring. Eugenic ideology worked its way into the educational reform movements of the 1910s and '20s, playing a key role in teacher training, curriculum development, and school organization. It also provided the guiding ideology behind the first IQ tests. Those tests were used to track students into separate and unequal education courses, establish the first gifted and talented programs, and promote the idea that educational standards could be measured through single-numbered scores. Eugenic ideas about the intellectual worth of students penetrated deeply into the fabric of American education.

Eugenics was a common feature in college curricula. Universities offering courses in eugenics proliferated from 44 in 1914 to 376 in 1928.[4] A recent analysis of 41 high school biology textbooks used through the 1940s revealed that nearly 90 percent of them had sections on eugenics.[5] Major figures in education were attracted to eugenics and wrote books for teachers and the general public. Eugenics became a top-down model of education reform for these educators. A cadre of university experts was trained in the latest testing methods; these experts embraced eugenic principles, believing they could make schooling a more efficient enterprise. Schools would be places where students learned basic eugenic principles and where they were tracked into their future roles as dictated by their biological worth.

A sampling of influential textbooks used in colleges of education gives us a better sense of some of the eugenic visions of educational reform. Lewis Terman, professor of education at Stanford University and originator of the Stanford-Binet intelligence test, is remembered today as an early proponent of tracking. But his views on tracking and school organization—which were rooted in a eugenic conception of humanity—are less known. Terman expressed these views in his textbook, *The Measurement of Intelligence* (1916). The book would be used for decades in teacher training. He wrote:

> Among laboring men and servant girls there are thousands like them [feeble-minded individuals]. They are the world's "hewers of wood and drawers of water." And yet, as far as intelligence is concerned, the tests have told the truth. . . . No amount of school instruction will ever make them intelligent voters or capable voters in the true sense of the word . . .
>
> The fact that one meets this type with such frequency among Indians, Mexicans, and negroes suggests quite forcibly that the whole question of racial differences in mental traits will have to be taken up anew and by experimental methods.
>
> Children of this group should be segregated in special classes and be given instruction which is concrete and practical. They cannot master, but they can often be made efficient workers, able to look out for themselves. There is no possibility at present of convincing society that they should not be allowed to reproduce, although from a eugenic point of view they constitute a grave problem because of their unusually prolific breeding.

Terman and other educational psychologists successively convinced many school districts to use high-stakes and culturally biased tests to place "slow" students into special classes, rigid academic tracks, or entirely separate schools. The racist and class-based assumptions behind these recommendations were justified as scientifically sound because the "tests told the truth." IQ tests soon became the favorite eugenic tool for identifying "superior" and "inferior" students and then charting their educational destiny.

The tests were also seen as an instrument to identify students deserving special treatment. Today's gifted and talented programs had their origins in the eugenic use of IQ tests in the 1920s. Leta Hollingworth, a professor at Teachers College at Columbia University, was a founder and persuasive advocate of gifted and talented programs in schools. She and other educational leaders thought only the students from the right biological stock were capable of achieving high academic standards.

In *Gifted Children: Their Nature and Nurture*, a book frequently cited by researchers of "gifted" programs today,[6] Hollingworth wrote:

One result recurs persistently wherever American children are tested by nationality of ancestors. American children of Italian parentage show a low average of intelligence. The selection of Italians received into this country has yielded very few gifted children.

[Eugenics would] ultimately reduce misery if the stupid, the criminal, and other mentally, physically, and morally deficient would refrain from reproduction.[7]

President Calvin Coolidge embraced the eugenic assumptions behind the law when he declared, "America must be kept American. Biological laws show that Nordics deteriorate when mixed with other races."

As with Terman, Hollingworth's ideas were not on the margins of educational thought. Eugenic themes proliferated in educational journals and textbooks from the 1910s through the 1930s. In particular, the popular belief took hold that IQ tests could label and accurately place students into academic tracks according to their inherited abilities. For example, an educational consultant for the San Jose, California, school system recommended that the district use test scores to guide "children for their proper economic life activities in accordance with their abilities." The great majority of Mexican-American school children in the district were to assume lower academic tracks because the tests supposedly revealed their inferior intellectual quality.[8]

Reflecting on the Consequences

We do not know all the ways eugenic notions affected public education. We do know that by the early 1920s, more than 2 million American school children were being tested primarily for academic tracking purposes.[9] Eugenic notions of student worth influenced at least some of the decisions about where to allocate resources and how to select students for academic or vocational courses.

It is important to recognize that an active minority of educators, journalists, labor groups, and parents resisted these ideas. In particular, African American scholars such as W. E. B. Du Bois, Horace Mann Bond, and Howard Long offered informed critiques. They decried the use of tests to rank racial groups. In "Intelligence Tests and Propaganda," Horace Mann Bond issued a warning about the misuse of IQ tests:

But so long as any group of men attempts to use these tests as funds of information for the approximation of crude and inaccurate generalizations, so long must we continue to cry "Hold!" To compare the crowded millions of New York's East Side with the children of Morningside Heights [an upper-class neighborhood at the time] indeed involves a great contradiction; and to claim that the results of the tests given to such diverse groups, drawn from such varying strata of the social complex, are in any way accurate, is to expose a fatuous sense of unfairness and lack of appreciation of the great environmental factors of modern urban life.[10]

IQ tests soon became the favorite eugenic tool for identifying "superior" and "inferior" students and then charting their educational destiny.

Too few white Americans read these words. It was not until the 1960s that these early rebuttals were widely recognized as important contributions to the body of academic literature that refuted racist and biologically determinist interpretations of IQ tests.

Bond's cautions also were not heeded by Richard Herrnstein and Charles Murray when they wrote the bestseller *The Bell Curve* in 1994. Many reviewers within the academic and lay communities have criticized the thinly veiled racism and the voluminous but misleading data found in the book. These authors' tendencies were reminiscent of the eugenic advocates' interpretation of tests in the 1920s. Furthermore, Murray and Herrnstein rewrote history when they claimed that the eugenic elements of tests were not used to draw negative conclusions about immigrant groups in the country and played no role in the immigration hearings of 1924.[11] This kind of denial of history makes it all the more important to re-examine how standardized tests are being used in educational reform today.

Standardized tests can provide important diagnostic information for educators. Achieving standards of academic excellence through ongoing assessment of student work is a vital component of a young person's learning. However, too often, standards and assessment have become synonymous with top-down, externally mandated tests. Learning becomes reduced to test preparation and test taking. Test scores are often seen as proxies for intelligence or as the most important indicators of what students are learning. Quick judgments and quick fixes are the products of this kind of reform. And this phenomenon is not just a relic of the past.

Even if many supporters of high-stakes tests might recoil at the assumptions that underpinned the use of standardized tests earlier in the century, the consequences of this version of education reform might not be so different from the 1920s. This connection becomes even more apparent when comparing performances between poorer and more affluent school districts. Doing well on high-stakes tests is strongly correlated with income levels and only confirms the educational inequities that have characterized U.S. education throughout the century. The academic tracking begun by yesterday's eugenicists is an institutional legacy we live with today. Education reform that is driven by high-stakes tests stands a good chance of entrenching that legacy.

The history of eugenics in American education needs to be examined in more depth and brought to bear in discussions on the use of high-stakes tests to raise academic standards in public schools. This history raises some challenging and disturbing questions for all of us today. What is the economic and political context in which the contemporary version of educational reform is being touted? What are the assumptions about student learning that fuel the current wave of testing? What are the effects of this testing on the lives of students and the educational climate of schools? How do these tests affect the equitable distribution of educational resources and opportunities between different school districts?

Test scores are often seen as proxies for intelligence or as the most important indicators of what students are learning. Quick judgments and quick fixes are the products of this kind of reform.

These questions need to be discussed with educational policy makers and representatives from diverse communities in open forums. Parents, students, and teachers have to be brought into these conversations. The eugenics movement is a reminder of what can happen when the assumptions and consequences of educational reform are not put to the test of real-life experience. ✎

Endnotes

1. Francis Galton, *Inquiries into Human Faculty and its Development*, New York, NY:Macmillan, 1883.

2. Steven Selden, "Conservative Ideology and Curriculum," *Educational Theory* 3, 1977.

3. Calvin Coolidge, "Whose Country is This?" *Good Housekeeping* 72,1921.

4. Hamilton Cravens, *The Triumph of Evolution: American Scientists and the Heredity-Environment Controversy*, 1900-1941 , Philadelphia, PA: University of Pennsylvania Press, 1978.

5. Steven Selden, *Inheriting Shame: The Story of Eugenics in America*, New York, NY: Teachers College Press, 1999.

6. Ibid, p. 102.

7. Ibid, p. 103.

8. David Tyack, *The One Best System: A History of American Urban Education*, Cambridge, MA: Harvard University Press, 1974)

9. Sarah Glazer, "Intelligence Testing," *CQ Researcher*, 1993.

10. Horace Mann Bond, "Intelligence Tests and Propaganda," *The Crisis*, 28, 1924.

11. Richard Herrnstein and Charles Murray *The Bell Curve: Intelligence and Class Structure in American Life*, Free Press, 1994.

For Further Reading

The Bell Curve Debate: History, Documents, Opinions edited by Russell Jacoby and Naomi Glauberman (Times Books, Random House, 1995), chapters 6-8.

Inheriting Shame: The Story of Eugenics in America by Stephen Selden (Teachers College Press, 1999).

Confronting the Forgotten History of the American Eugenics Movement by Alan Stoskopf, et al. (Harvard/Facing History Project, 1999).

PART 2

Testing Kids

RANDALL ENOS

Testing Kindergarten

Young children produce lots of data

KELLY MCMAHON

I remember my kindergarten experience from 25 years ago. Way back then, kindergarten focused on letters, sounds, counting, coloring inside the lines, cutting straight along the solid black line, and learning how to get along with others. I remember looking forward to rest time, recess, snack, and show and tell. That was kindergarten before the days of No Child Left Behind. Kindergarten post-No Child Left Behind is being turned into a school experience that results in many children disliking school and feeling like failures.

I have spent the last six years teaching 5-year-old kindergarten for Milwaukee Public Schools (MPS). During this time, I have seen a decrease in district initiatives that are developmentally appropriate and an increase in the amount of testing and data collection for 5-year-olds. Just when I thought the district couldn't ask for any more test scores or drills or practice, a new initiative and data system popped up for my school to complete. My school had not met our Adequate Yearly Progress (AYP) for the past three years. Due to our failure to meet AYP, we became a School Identified for Improvement (SIFI), with Level Two status.

The students in my classroom during the 2008-09 school year completed more assessments than during any of my prior years of teaching kindergarten:

- Milwaukee Public Schools' 5-Year-Old Kindergarten Assessment (completed three times a year)
- On the Mark Reading Verification Assessment (completed three times a year)
- A monthly writing prompt focused on different strands of the Six Traits of Writing
- 28 assessments measuring key early reading and spelling skills
- Chapter pre- and post-tests for all nine math chapters completed
- Three additional assessments for each math chapter completed
- A monthly math prompt
- Four Classroom Assessments Based on Standards (CABS) per social studies chapter (20 total)
- Four CABS assessments per science chapter (20 total)
- Four CABS assessments per health chapter (20 total)

I recently learned my students will also be expected to complete four benchmark assessments beginning in the 2010-11 school year. This list does not include the pre- and post-Marzano vocabulary tests (which I refuse to have my students complete because the assessment design is entirely developmentally inappropriate) or the writing and math portfolios we are required to keep.

In the spring, the literacy coach at my school handed us a copy of the new

MPS Student Reading Portfolio, which includes a list of 10 academic vocabulary words per semester that kindergartners are expected to know. My students will once more have to complete pre- and post-tests each semester. When I brought the MPS Student Reading Portfolio to the Milwaukee Teachers' Education Association's (MTEA) Early Childhood Committee, the members were surprised and disgusted. This new reading portfolio asks kindergarten students to define terms like Venn diagram, sound out, understand, poetry, tracking, sight word, expression, and describe; it also expects kindergartners to produce 20 different sounds, including the blending and digraph sounds *ch, qu, sh, th*, and *ing* at a proficient level. This developmentally inappropriate assessment tool was designed without the input of early childhood educators. The early childhood committee submitted our comments and recommendations for proposed changes to both the MPS Reading and Early Childhood Departments. We have yet to hear a response.

Kindergartners Need to Play

One negative impact of continued assessment-crazy data collection on my school has been the total disregard for the importance of children's social and emotional development. As more and more of my students spend less time interacting with their peers outside of school, I am forced to severely limit the amount of time dedicated to play centers in my classroom. Without the opportunity to interact with their peers in structured and unstructured play, my students are losing out on situations that allow them to learn to problem-solve, share, explore, and deepen their learning.

As Edward Miller and Joan Almon point out in their book *Crisis in the Kindergarten: Why Children Need to Play in School*, "Research shows that children who engage in complex forms of socio-dramatic play have greater language skills than nonplayers, better social skills, more empathy, more imagination, and more of the subtle capacity to know what others mean. They are less aggressive and show more self-control and higher levels of thinking."[1]

Apparently young children stopped learning through play the moment the bipartisan No Child Left Behind bill passed Congress and was signed into law by President George W. Bush.

Sleepless in Milwaukee

The issue of allowing young children in kindergarten to rest has now become a battle all across MPS. MPS issued a guideline for rest time for early childhood programs. The district guidelines proposed a maximum 45-minute rest time in the fall for all-day 4-year-old kindergarten, followed by a maximum of 30 minutes of rest in the spring. The guidelines suggested a maximum of 30 minutes to be used for rest in the fall in 5-year-old kindergarten classrooms, and for rest to be *entirely phased out* in the spring.

These policies fly in the face of brain research, which suggests that sleep allows the brain to cement the learning that has taken place. As Merilee Sprenger writes in her book *Learning and Memory: The Brain in Action*:

Through prior knowledge or interest, the new information may be added to the old and form more long-term memory. The process may have to be repeated several times before long-term memory is formed. The brain will process some of this information during sleep. Studies have shown that while rats are in the sleep stage called REM (rapid eye movement) sleep, their brains reproduce the same patterns used for learning while awake.[2]

I'm left wondering how much more testing and data collection I might be expected to do, and how many more developmentally inappropriate initiatives I will be asked to implement.

But MPS insists that I wake a sleeping child who might have only gotten five or six hours of sleep each night.

My administrators allotted my students 20 minutes of rest time each day for the 2009-10 school year. However, by the time my students finish using the restroom and get a drink of water after their one and only recess for the day, they will have roughly 10 minutes to rest. Every year I have at least one child in my classroom who is not getting adequate sleep every night.

There was a young boy in my classroom last year who went to day care directly from school and stayed there until 11 p.m. By the time his mother picked him up, drove home, and gave him a snack, it would be 1 a.m. before he finally got to bed. This child would then be up roughly five hours later to start his day all over again. He entered my classroom exhausted and in need of additional sleep. When he allowed himself to fall asleep at rest time, it was nearly impossible to wake him.

When district officials came into my classroom, I had to defend my professional judgment in allowing this child to continue to sleep after I began afternoon instruction. I have multiple students in my classroom this year with similar sleeping schedules at home, yet they are allowed only 10 minutes for rest. I am experiencing far more behavioral problems in the afternoon this school year due to the decrease in time my students are allowed to rest.

As I enter my eighth year of teaching in Milwaukee, I'm left wondering how much more testing and data collection I might be expected to do, and how many more developmentally inappropriate initiatives I will be asked to implement. I also wonder exactly how much longer I can continue to "teach" under these circumstances.

Endnotes

1. Edward Miller and Joan Almon, *Crisis in the Kindergarten: Why Children Need to Play in School*, College Park, MD: Alliance for Childhood, 2009.

2. Merilee Sprenger, *Learning and Memory: The Brain in Action*, Alexandria, VA: Association for Supervision and Curriculum Development, 1999.

Testing Lang

AMY GUTOWSKI

Lang was a student of mine, an 8-year-old with big brown eyes and a shy, quiet nature. He hated writing; putting pencil to paper was a brutal task for him. Yet he wrote, with his sharpened lead pressing hard onto the paper, and with his forehead wrinkled in concentration and pain.

Lang taught our class how to say "hello" and "goodbye" in his first language, Hmong. He loved math and could spot an equivalent fraction from a mile away. He would add numbers into the hundreds of thousands and stun the class.

During morning work, I would often have the kids try to find as many words as they could using the letters from a larger word—like finding the word "leap" within the word "apple." Lang would discover the word "nectar" in "concentration" and wow his fellow 3rd graders. He spelled the word "hypothesis" in our heated classroom game of spelling hoops, which allowed him the chance to make the final, winning shot. I said a small prayer before the orange-sized Nerf basketball left Lang's hands—he so deserved to experience the glory. When the ball swished through the net on the mini-basket, the other students went wild and sprung to their feet, cheering. Lang went back to his seat, with his hands warm from high-fives and cheeks red from excitement, smiling.

Lang also devoured *Captain Underpants* books, checking them out weekly from the classroom library. His excitement for reading increased with each new adventure. In March, we had to give the 3rd-grade standardized reading test, a thick booklet brimming with multiple-choice questions and treacherous reading passages. The kids knew it was coming; we had prepared, worked in practice booklets, and perfected the art of filling in the bubbles.

But as the other kids finished their tests, my heart grew heavy. Lang still sat there, with his forehead wrinkled in pain. His pencil filled in perfect, lead-heavy circles. He was almost finished when I noticed his bloody lip, bitten from anxiety. I told him that he did his best, and that was definitely enough.

He smiled, wiped his lip with a wet tissue, and asked if he could go to music. Months later, I sat at my desk after school reading the test scores that had just been shipped back to us. I sat in silence, lights off, while sun streamed through the window. According to the test, Lang wasn't "advanced" and he wasn't "proficient." He was "basic," which couldn't have been further from the truth.

How many other students and teachers have this same experience when the test scores come back? Lang and I will survive this, of course, but as the tests approach this year I wonder which of my students will find themselves explaining test scores to parents who thought no child was going to be left behind. ✎

All Work and No Play

How educational reforms are hurting our preschoolers

SHARNA OLFMAN

Education in America is undergoing a sweeping reform. Its guiding mantra "standards, accountability, testing, and technology," and its effects reverberate from ivory towers to Head Start programs.

At the preschool and kindergarten level, it translates into early academics, "scripted teaching," desk work, computer-based learning, and a paucity of play. As a result, a rich multidisciplinary literature demonstrating the critical role of play for cognitive, social, emotional, and ethical development—a literature that was decades in the making—is being ignored.

Remarkably, current educational reforms are not driven by the findings and recommendations of educators and child-development experts, but rather by politicians and policymakers at the federal, state, and local levels, with the express intention of ensuring America's competitive edge in the new information-based economy. This agenda was first articulated in the 1983 report *A Nation at Risk*, issued by President Ronald Reagan's National Commission on Excellence:

> If only to keep and improve on the slim competitive edge we still retain
> in world markets, we must dedicate ourselves to the reform of our educational
> system.... Learning is the indispensable investment required for success in the
> "information age" we are entering.

The "high-stakes" testing movement and race to "wire the classroom" were launched by Reagan in 1983, given renewed vigor by Presidents H. W. Bush and Bill Clinton, and gained further momentum with George W. Bush's 2001 No Child Left Behind Act, which received overwhelming bipartisan support. In 2003, the federal government announced that it was implementing a standardized assessment of all 4-year-olds in Head Start programs nationwide to assess reading readiness, thus officially delivering high-stakes testing to preschoolers.

A Failing Grade for Testing and Technology

Given that education reform is now spearheaded by politicians and the corporate elite rather than by experts in childhood, it comes as no surprise that the "accountability" movement and its handmaiden, the "wired classroom," have not only failed to improve education, but indeed, have undermined it. Results of the congressionally mandated National Assessment of Educational Progress (NAEP)—commonly referred to as the Nation's Report Card, which has been assessing school performance for more than 30 years—reveal that states with the highest stakes attached to standardized testing are more likely to perform below average on the NAEP, whereas states that give minimal import to standardized tests are more likely to perform above the average. Furthermore, in 1998, the highly acclaimed Third International Math and Science Study (TIMSS), which compared a half-million students from 41 countries, revealed that U.S. high school seniors were tied for last place in math among developed nations.

"Teaching to the Test": Narrower and Shallower

The impact of tying teachers' and administrators' bonuses, salaries, and job security; state and federal and funding of schools; and students' graduation to standardized tests is that teachers are compelled to "teach to the tests." The tests, which are usually multiple-choice, merely sample the curriculum and do not assess depth of understanding, meaningful application of knowledge, or original thinking. Consequently, the curriculum becomes narrower and shallower, and drills, rote learning, and practice tests increasingly dominate the teaching methods.

In the race for high test scores, kindergarten students and even preschoolers are now subjected to a similar barrage of academic drill work at an age when they are meant to learn through play and hands-on experience. If the NAEP and TIMSS results are any indication, these teaching methods are unsuccessful; yet, these methods are being introduced to students of increasingly younger ages in the vain hope that they'll somehow "take" if we start young enough.

The Key to Testing and Technology's Popularity

And yet, despite these dismal prognoses, the titans of testing and technology remain popular among policy makers and the general public. Given the appalling results of these reforms so far, their appeal is remarkably robust. Why? Perhaps the rhetoric surrounding them contains a piece of the puzzle. Standardized testing and access to the internet are nowadays touted as the great levelers in society that will ensure quality education for all. Parents are told that all children and schools will be held to a uniform standard of excellence and given access to the same vast store of information through the internet. And so, whether particular children become presidents or street people depends exclusively on those students' own effort and resolve.

These rhetorical strategies are irresistible on two counts. First, any thoughtful and ethical individual supports, indeed *demands*, high standards and accountability from the public school system. With the cooptation of the language of "standards," it becomes difficult to stand in opposition. Unfortunately, the critical debate about what these standards should be and how they should be measured is not taking place. Second, the rhetoric of "standards" embodies the quintessential American Dream: "Hard work and fair play will liberate us from the bondage of blood lines, social class, and racism."

The reality, however, is that the "accountability" movement is profoundly deepening divisions along lines of class and race. As Peter Sacks noted in *Standardized Minds*:

[I]f social engineers had set out to invent a virtually perfect inequality machine, designed to perpetuate class and race divisions, and that appeared to abide by all requisite state and federal laws and regulations, those engineers could do no better than the present-day accountability systems already put to use in American schools.

We are captivated by the deterministic notion that all of our traits, including personality, intelligence, creativity, and mental health, are chiefly determined by our genes.

Egalitarianism vs. Genetic Determinism

This sad state of affairs reflects a curious paradox at the heart of U.S. culture. On the one hand, we embrace ideals of egalitarianism and self-determination. On the other, we are captivated by the deterministic notion that all of our traits, including personality, intelligence, creativity, and mental health, are chiefly determined by our genes.

Genes do contribute significantly to our physical and psychological makeup, but their effects are exquisitely sensitive to environmental input. Nevertheless, the media feeds our insatiable appetite for stories about the genome project, cloning, or the latest claim that gene A is the "depression" gene and gene B dictates our preference for Pepsi over Coca-Cola. And in this climate of striking cultural contradictions, we allow intelligence and achievement scores, which allegedly disclose children's true abilities, to determine children's futures regardless of abilities in the real world.

Similarly, we seek to enhance our genetically programmed brains, which we liken to organic computers. If children are struggling in the classroom, we are more likely to tinker with their "hardware" by using drugs that increase attention or lessen anxiety than we are likely to address the underlying psychological or socioeconomic issues that give rise to their symptoms.

Environment has little role in our gene-driven discourse on learning nowadays, so we have no qualms about holding different children or different school districts to the same standard, despite dramatically diverse circumstances. As a result, the following scenarios become increasingly common:

Mary attends a school that is rich in resources, with small classes, state-of-the-art science labs, yearly textbook upgrades, a beautiful library, weekly field trips, well-paid and well-educated teachers, and an abundance of parent volunteers. She lives in a safe neighborhood with lawns that beckon her to play, and has access to the finest medical care.

In contrast, Susan dodges bullets and drug dealers on her walk home from school. Her school is drafty, overcrowded, and has a high turnover rate of underpaid teachers struggling with dated textbooks. She had to enter the hospital as an emergency case before receiving treatment for a recent infection, and her devoted mother, a single parent, works two full-time, minimum-wage jobs to make ends meet. At 10 p.m., Susan still waits anxiously for her mother to return home from work, with the noise of the television to bolster her courage and keep her "company." Before her mother returns, she warms a can of soup for herself and her little brother. She struggles to make sense of her homework, but fear and loneliness overwhelm her.

Mary and her school district performed well above average on the state's mandatory end-of-year assessment. Her parents are proud of her test scores, and district teachers received handsome bonuses. But Susan missed the cutoff score by a few points and has to repeat her year. Her school district is in desperate need of resources and teachers, but was denied both state and federal aid and placed on notice. Susan feels demoralized; her self-esteem is shaken. Her mother tries to enroll her in a neighboring school district with better resources, but she is told that the school has a waiting list.

Meanwhile, Susan's 4-year-old brother Joseph is enrolled in a Head Start program. His class is large, and the support staff has been downsized because a portion of the budget went to the purchase of new computers and reading software. Play has been eliminated from the curriculum to give children like Joseph a "leg up" in the academic race.

Joseph is small for his age, slightly malnourished, chronically asthmatic, and longs for affection and the opportunity to run freely and play, unfettered by concerns for safety. He struggles to sit still in front of the computer terminal. On the recommendation of his teacher, Joseph is sent to a local clinic where he receives a diagnosis of attention-deficit hyperactivity disorder (ADHD) and a prescription for Ritalin. He no longer disrupts the class. However, by the time Joseph is in middle school, he will have been held back twice and taken Ritalin for a decade. Lacking hope and incentive to do better, he will now hoard Ritalin and sell it on the street to buy clothes, CDs, or drugs that are more to his liking.

By the logic of "accountability," Mary and Susan were measured by the same yardstick. So either Susan didn't try hard enough, or she is simply less capable than Mary. Clearly, though, the root cause of Susan and Joseph's classroom struggles is not genetics or the absence of standards, but rather poverty, a two-tiered school system, and the absence of essential family services such as subsidized and regulated day care and after-school programs, a living wage, and humane medical coverage. Thus, under the guise of equality, the system privileges wealthy families and the corporations who manufacture the testing and computer technologies.

Admittedly, the story of Susan and Joseph might have turned out differently. They might have beaten the odds, succeeded academically, and gone on to successful careers; many such children do just that. However, the issue is not whether it is *possible* to do so, but rather whether it is morally defensible to require some children to leap over so many additional hurdles along the way. ✎

Reprinted from: All Work and No Play: How Educational Reforms Are Harming Our Preschoolers. *Edited by Sharna Olfman. Copyright 2003 by Sharna Olfman. Reproduced with permission of Greenwood Publishing Group, Inc., Westport, Conn.*

A Dark Cloud on the U.S. Horizon

A teacher's experience in England is a cautionary tale

MELISSA SCHIEBLE

I lasted two long, bitter years. Sadly, those years were the first two of my teaching career. After months of job searching and phone interviews, armed with a teaching certificate and two crammed suitcases, I moved to England in 2001 to teach abroad, to work side by side with British colleagues in a public secondary school.

I knew little about the English educational system, but one thing was certain: High-stakes testing was extremely important. With the determination of a novice, I assumed the system change would be rough, but manageable. I had done a little test preparation during student teaching, so how shocking could it be?

Schooling in England is under tight government control, regulated by a rigid system of standards and testing—known as the National Curriculum—first introduced by the Education Reform Act (ERA) in 1988. Given the heavy testing agenda under U.S. federal education policy and the increasing number of U.S. educational reformers who talk about a standardized "core" curriculum and look to England as a model system, my experiences offer a warning about where this may lead.

Extreme High Stakes

As a secondary English teacher at Oliver Park School, part of my heavy workload required me to teach two classes of year 11 (grade 10). Year 11 is considered an "exam year"—the final year of secondary school—and teachers spend nearly all of this year on explicit test preparation and practice. If students fail to achieve at least a passing grade of "C" on a minimum of five tests, their hopes of one day "going to university" die. Students who do not pass at least five of their exams may then be steered toward technical schools or labor jobs such as construction, cosmetology, and other trades.

The grades leading up to year 11 are spent teaching to the standards in order to prep students with the skills needed for the exam at the end of each "key stage": the ages of 7, 11, and 14. Oliver Park is recognized nationally for graduating students with high exam results. In fact, parents are so desperate to enroll their kids at Oliver Park (the English system is one of open enrollment) that while I taught there, the school had a six-year waiting list for students outside its boundaries. Because of the constant pressure to keep scores high, a rigid system of tracking was in place at the school.

Years of poor test scores and lack of engagement—in part a result of the testing craze—dumped the year 11 students who struggled to achieve into the bottom

These students were at the bottom of 12 sections, ranging in descending order from the "high flyers" to the hopeless, neatly sorted by test scores.

English class of a 12-track system. Yes, these students were at the bottom of 12 sections, ranging in descending order from the "high flyers" to the hopeless, neatly sorted by test scores. I taught this class, referred to at the school as the "bottom set," and my job was just to get them through the exam year.

My bottom-set students, not surprisingly, represented the few students of color at the school and the kids from low-income families in the area. Many of the students talked about living in the subsidized housing estate across from the school, and the shabby and often tattered appearance of their uniforms separated them from the general population at Oliver Park. Some aspired to get labor or technical jobs the following year, and others remained silent about what lay ahead. Teachers and administrators openly discussed how these kids would never pass the high-stakes exam at the end of the year, which was known as the General Certificate for Secondary Education (GCSE).

Unfortunately, the students in the lowest track received very little care or attention from the school, as their projected examination scores did not fall on the critical "C"/"D" borderline: a group of students whose test results are crucial to the school's improved annual success on the high-stakes exam. Teachers' projections, mock exams, and exams from years past helped to make these predictions. In fact, because exam results were so important, more experienced teachers were strategically arranged to teach the classes that contained the "borderline" students. New teachers (like me) or less-qualified teachers taught the bottom set.

My struggling students suffered tremendously, bound by a system that failed to recognize their gradual and delicate progress as significant. The National Curriculum is precisely what bound them. Throughout year 11, we painstakingly trudged through the depths of what we were required to do under the National Curriculum. Forty percent of a student's final grade came from coursework—a series of essays and speaking activities. Each essay had to focus on a topic or reading under categories such as Shakespeare, pre-1914 prose, and 20th-century drama, to name a few. This system is stacked to reward middle- and upper-class students, and it disadvantaged my bottom set.

Given that the majority of students at Oliver Park come from middle-class, white households, the school's high examination results do not reflect better teaching (though its teachers are talented and dedicated), but rather the results reflect that most of the school's students are set up by the system for success. Exam questions—such as tracing the successful elements of an article's argument in standard, sophisticated English—come much more easily to students who have had similar conversations at the dinner table their entire lives.

The remaining 60 percent of a student's final grade for English was determined by the high-stakes exam. The exam for English and English literature consisted of a series of essay questions and writing prompts, all designed for students to display their mastery of form, genre, and literary analysis within standard English. Exams were sent away and graded by "external markers," largely teachers working for extra pay at the end of the year. Although there was some room for discussing personal and social issues in books or articles we read—or for exploring issues with a critical eye in writing assignments—often these experiences were sidelined or glossed over to focus on mastering the art of "taking the exam." Because the exam was so important, a substantial number of my lessons were spent frantically teaching to the test: "Don't forget to read the question, take notes on the piece of nonfiction text, remember to follow the bullet points, use connectives and rich vocabulary—don't forget time!—analyze the presentation of the article and any graphics or pictures that accompany it, write with fluency and originality."

> **My struggling students suffered tremendously, bound by a system that failed to recognize their gradual and delicate progress as significant.**

I rushed through all of this (because the exam was always looming, and we had mounds of skills and questions to prepare for) with a class of bored and frustrated students. My students would frequently ask, "Why do we have to do this, Miss?" And, under pressure to achieve good test results, I would craft an answer that supported the National Curriculum and the exam. But in the back of my mind, I asked myself the same question.

Disconnected Curriculum

My students possessed immense abilities to articulate certain injustices or personal thoughts about literature, but they needed time to hone these skills in writing; they needed more time than the National Curriculum deemed necessary. In my opinion, we could have helped my students develop their reading and writing skills by discussing young adult novels and poetry that connected to their lives. I wanted to provide opportunities for them to understand society as it exists, rather than teaching a series of lessons on test taking with no application to the world beyond the boundaries of schooling. But I had no choice: I had to follow the National Curriculum.

Student behavior is a significant problem in England and rarely discussed in international test-score comparisons. Because my students were bored with test preparation and frustrated with the tasks at hand, we battled our way through the year. Many of the students in these bottom-set classes were frequently suspended or placed on reduced timetables for offenses ranging from swearing to refusing to do work, disrupting and harassing other students and staff, fighting, breaking windows, and a number of other nightmarish situations. I hate to admit it, but my colleagues and I dreaded teaching these classes due to sheer exhaustion from constantly dealing with difficult behavior. The behavior issues stemmed from students' boredom with the drill-and-kill curriculum and from their reaction to their status in the school. Even teachers with many years of experience struggled. Inspiring students through meaningful work was nearly impossible.

My students weren't the only ones who were frustrated. I desperately wanted to respond to their boredom with creative lessons and projects that built on their interests, rather than forcing them to write a standard, five-paragraph character essay on Mrs. Havisham from *Great Expectations*. What these students needed was to feel their lives connected to our materials in class; they needed to be thrilled and excited by their readings, because many had not experienced the pleasure that reading a good book brings. These are the reasons I went into this profession—and it did not take long for me to want out.

During exam time at the end of the year, I helped other teachers in school supervise the English and English literature test. My eyes darted from one long face to another with every passing minute, hoping that at least one part of the exam would be recognizable to my students. I watched in dread as their body language conveyed defeat: fidgets and restlessness, irritating pencil-tapping on the desk, doodles marked all over what should have been pages of fluent prose.

The students in my bottom set were incredibly sensitive to their place, determined by exams and tracking in this school. Earlier in the year, when I tried to teach a combined lesson with a teacher whose class was at a more advanced level, my students pleaded with me not to make them go into the other classroom. They said the other students were the "boffins," English slang for students who are too attentive to schoolwork. Their put-downs indicated to me that my students felt they did not measure up. Hours upon hours of wrestling with mock tests seemed in vain—a clear waste of what could have been useful class time. This exam served as nothing more than a final slap in the face after a year of struggle writing essays and sitting through hours of mindless test preparation under the National Curriculum.

The Price

The National Curriculum in England comes with a heavy price paid mostly by England's struggling students, many of whom are low income or of color. Few teachers in the United Kingdom would deny that the National Curriculum has significantly narrowed what can be taught and that it has reinforced, if not introduced, a skill-and-drill approach to schooling. This type of teaching is virtually impossible to avoid when the system places such an emphasis on examination results and classroom teachers are held accountable for students' test scores.

Back home in the United States, I've heard praise for the British system—how "accountable" teachers are there, and how equitable it is to have a "rigorous" and uniform curriculum. Well, I've seen this future, and it's not so great. Teachers will spend even more time on test prep. Inequality will become more pronounced. Students' behavior will deteriorate as they rebel against an empty curriculum. Fewer and fewer students will be exposed to material that encourages them to reflect critically about social issues. As the United States moves more and more toward a standards- and test-driven curriculum, I hope my experience offers a warning about what lies ahead. ❧

Testing Our Sanity

A 4th-grade bilingual teacher shares her story
of preparing students for mandated tests

KELLEY DAWSON SALAS

President George W. Bush claimed no child would be left behind under the Elementary and Secondary Education Act (ESEA). But testing required by the ESEA results in educational practices that are developmentally inappropriate and discriminatory for English language learners. In addition, pressure to raise test scores is causing significant negative changes in bilingual programs. Our Wisconsin school district and state government have a commitment to bilingual education. But our ability to follow through on that commitment has been seriously compromised by the ESEA.

Prior to 2002, our district tested most of our Limited English Proficient (LEP) students in their native language, Spanish. Then, in September 2002, the state informed teachers that all students with an English proficiency level of three or above must take the state standardized tests in English. Previously these students had been tested in Spanish, but the state Department of Public Instruction had negotiated the level-three cutoff with the federal Department of Education. This cutoff was of great concern to bilingual educators, because level-three and -four students, by definition, do not read and write at grade level in English. In fact, most level-three and -four students I know have good verbal English but are just beginning to read and write in English.

I was teaching 4th grade at La Escuela Fratney, a bilingual elementary school in Milwaukee, when these changes took place. When we learned our level-three and -four LEP students would be tested in English, the rush began. We were supposed to prepare about 25 LEP students to take a 4th-grade battery of standardized tests in English. We had about a month to get them ready.

We created small, intensive English transitional reading groups, unrealistically hoping we could raise students' reading levels from roughly a 1st- or 2nd-grade level to a 4th-grade level in a month. We began teaching math bilingually, explaining concepts in Spanish but pushing students to write explanations of their mathematical thinking in English, because that's how they'd have to do it on the test. We enlisted several non-classroom teachers in this test-preparation effort so that students could learn in small groups.

The teaching strategies mentioned here—transitional reading groups, a

> **We created small, intensive English transitional reading groups, unrealistically hoping we could raise students' reading levels from roughly a 1st- or 2nd-grade level to a 4th-grade level in a month.**

Most 4th graders make great gains in all of these areas over the course of a year as they academically transition to their second language—but it cannot be done in one month.

focus on math problem-solving, and helping students write in English—are normal, positive aspects of our 4th-grade program. Most 4th graders make great gains in all of these areas over the course of a year as they academically transition to their second language—but it cannot be done in one month. What was inappropriate about this test-preparation scheme was not necessarily the teaching methods we used, but rather the fact that we tried to force our students to make nearly a year's worth of progress in one month so they would be ready for the test in November.

Another problem the test-prep routine presented for our school was that several specialists including our special education teacher and mentor teachers, were pulled from their other duties in order to work intensively with our 4th-grade students on test prep and to administer the tests. This helped our 4th graders, but it had a negative impact on students at other grade levels.

In addition, our normal curriculum was interrupted for two months while we carried out this emergency test-preparation plan. We put our math statistics and data unit on hold so we could focus on general problem-solving skills and helping students learn to explain mathematical thinking in English. We shortened Spanish reading instruction to 40 minutes a day. We shortchanged our social studies unit on conflict resolution and our science unit on the Milwaukee River ecosystem. We focused instead on packing in English reading and math before November.

In the two months leading up to the test, I attended planning meetings and work sessions with my partner teacher and several other staff members. We planned test-prep curriculum, organized the testing groups, and tried to figure out how to make the necessary accommodations for our LEP students. Each of us spent between two and six hours a week outside of the school day doing the work. This not only diverted our time away from other planning and teaching duties, but it also cost our school a considerable amount of money, since we were paid for our work.

Finally the tests began.

"Teacher, This Is Crazy!"

Department of Public Instruction officials had informed teachers that they expected us to make every allowable accommodation so that LEP students could do their best on the tests. Allowable accommodations for LEP students included extra time on all five tests (English Reading, English Language Arts, Science, Social Studies, and Math); reading aloud the science, social studies, and math tests; and providing a verbal translation in Spanish of the science, social studies, and math tests.

These accommodations nearly tripled the time that LEP students needed to complete their tests. Our English proficient students spent about six and a half hours altogether to complete their five timed tests. It took us seven days at two and one-half hours a day to finish the tests with our LEP students—17 and a half hours of tests.

A bright girl, who had high expectations for herself and was making great progress in English before the tests, appeared increasingly downtrodden as the days went on.

One day, I asked students to write about their experiences with the tests. The LEP students and English proficient students had different kinds of responses. English proficient students said things like: "It was fun because we took the test for an hour and we got to play math games and read for the rest of the morning," (while they waited for their LEP counterparts to finish). LEP students wrote things like: "It was hard because it took so much time, and I got tired."

The math, science, and social studies tests took the most time and were the most grueling. We administered the tests in groups of six LEP students. We read each test item aloud twice in English, stated the translation twice in Spanish, and then gave the students time to think, work, and mark their answers. We moved on to the next question when everyone was ready. Imagine being 10 years old and paying attention in this type of a learning situation for almost three hours every morning—not to mention trying to "do your best" on the test.

Students coped with the testing in their own ways. Some shrugged it off and did their best even though they got tired. One boy shut down each day after about half of the time, putting his head down and refusing to answer any more questions. A bright girl, who had high expectations for herself and was making great progress in English before the tests, appeared increasingly downtrodden as the days went on. An extremely quiet girl suddenly burst out with, "Teacher, this is crazy!" as I read the umpteenth question on the science portion of the test.

We teachers did not have the easiest time of it, either. During testing weeks, we blew off steam by taking the kids out for kickball every day at noon when the tests were done and by counting the days of testing left. But the months of time and energy we spent preparing our students for a test we did not think was educationally useful took its toll on many of us. One colleague said she felt she was going crazy trying to reconcile what we were doing with her own vision of what education should be. I also experienced an enormous amount of stress and desperation about the whole situation.

The process of trying to prepare the LEP students for the tests and administering the tests to them was unreasonable and educationally inappropriate. But my school and other schools engage in these kinds of practices because the law requires us to, and because the stakes are high. Many of our bilingual schools are on the "schools in need of improvement" list. If we do not improve our scores, we face sanctions.

The ESEA and its testing requirements are implemented somewhat differently in each state; the federal Department of Education negotiates the details

The process of trying to prepare the LEP students for the tests and administering the tests to them was unreasonable and educationally inappropriate.

with each state's education department. Some states, like California and Texas, offer Spanish standardized tests to students who have been in the United States for less than three years; other states, like Wisconsin, did away with Spanish testing and give alternative assessments to the small percentage of students who are not required to take the tests in English. But all states are under pressure to test more English language learners in English, and to begin testing these students after fewer years of English instruction.

National research shows that English language learners learn English best when they learn to read and write in their native language first. Then they can make a successful transition to reading and writing in English. This process is not quick; research shows that it takes five to seven years for students to function at grade level in academic English. Unfortunately, there are too many teachers, principals, and schools feeling pressured to ignore that research. They are short-changing literacy in students' native languages and pushing English early because of pressure from the ESEA and English standardized tests.

Schools, districts, and states that want to provide quality bilingual education are finding that harder and harder to do given the pressure from the federal government. The ESEA seems designed to force English upon English language learners before they are academically prepared—a practice that is both pedagogically harmful and developmentally inappropriate. ✎

Edwina Left Behind

SÖREN WUERTH

The woman from the state education department had come to show us "the data." She stood in an auditorium, in front of Ketchikan school district's some 300 teachers and staff members and began a choppy PowerPoint presentation that described the standards on which students would soon be judged.

The official, dressed in a black blouse and black sport jacket, called herself a "recovering" math and middle school teacher.

During her presentation, which I'd seen before, we were quizzed on the meaning of acronyms and asked multiple-choice questions about federal education policy. Judging from the comments and muffled heckling I could hear coming from behind me, I was not the only teacher who considered the education department's presentation demeaning.

As I listened, I reflected on Edwina, a student in the 12th-grade language arts class I taught in the remote Cu'pik Eskimo village of Chevak. Chevak School is the dominant feature in the rural Western Alaska village. Just over 300 students shuffle from small, modular homes to the K-12 school, leaning into the wind most of the year to get there, crossing swells of snow drifts in the winter.

Edwina was tough. She had a round face, always wore the same sweatshirt and oval glasses, and maneuvered through two communities rife with drugs and alcohol like a running back moving past hapless opponents.

Edwina's family lived in the coastal village of Hooper Bay, but she attended Chevak's school 20 miles inland, hoping her education would be superior to that of the neighboring village. On weekends, she'd leave her grandmother's place and drive a snowmobile 40 miles across frozen tundra, in weather that dipped to 60 below, to visit her home village. Edwina beat up boys who picked on her brothers, swore, and chewed tobacco. She turned to her schoolwork with the same rugged self-assurance.

A senior, Edwina needed to pass the state's High School Graduation Qualifying Exam to receive a diploma. Early in the year, I downloaded practice tests the state education department offered on its site. The sample test was three years old, and students were so familiar with it they had memorized many of the answers.

Edwina didn't complain. She took the test seriously, as she did most of her school assignments. She remained after class to finish projects, always smiling, easily falling into laughter. She was a good writer. One of her stories, detailing the time she got lost riding through a blizzard behind her father on

Students shuffle from small, modular homes to the K-12 school, leaning into the wind most of the year to get there, crossing swells of snowdrifts in the winter.

his snowmobile, eventually appeared in a journal of high school writing. A disciplined student, Edwina maintained a straight-A average throughout her school career. When a storm gripped the village and other students decided not to go to school, Edwina would invariably trudge through wind-packed snow to ensure an immaculate attendance record.

As the woman from the state droned on about formulaic assessment, I thought of how, as far as the state was concerned, Edwina's entire education—all that she'd learned and all that she had endured to obtain it—would come down to one test.

Kids in the village struggle to memorize vocabulary and concepts with which they have no connection. A counselor in my village told me the story of an elementary student who began crying during a test. When the counselor asked her what was wrong, the girl pointed to the word "curb" and said she didn't know what it meant. In her community, on a dusty knoll above thousands of acres of barren tundra, residents travel on dirt paths with four-wheelers and snowmobiles.

Cultural Ignorance

It seems every teacher who has worked in Alaska's rural school system has a story of the cultural ignorance of standardized tests. A question that stumped a student in my wife's 2nd-grade class asked for the best choice on how to get to a hospital: boat, ambulance, or airplane. Since the nearest hospital is 300 miles away, the student circled the logical, yet "incorrect," answer: airplane.

In Alaska, only about 40 percent of Native students graduate from high school, compared to almost 70 percent for all other ethnicities combined. There were 13 dropouts in Chevak the year I taught there. Generally, white students pass high-stakes tests at double the rate of their Native counterparts. In the region encompassing Chevak, an area the size of Iowa and dotted with more than 50 villages, only about a quarter of the students pass reading tests.

Edwina had lived her entire life in the remote villages of Hooper Bay and Chevak. It's a desolate region where the wind blows almost constantly across a vast delta of winding rivers, sloughs, and subarctic tundra. Edwina had to work hard to support her family. Her anna (grandma) and atta (grandpa), as well as other family members, relied on her to help prepare food, cook, wash laundry, run to the village store, and perform hundreds of other tasks.

She tried to stay awake in class and, when I joked with her once about her sleepiness, she erupted in uncharacteristic anger: "I've been up all night working, babysitting, helping my anna and atta!"

Yet, the state graduation-qualifying exam would not ask about her snowmobiling experience, subsistence hunting on the frozen ocean, collecting driftwood, or preparing a traditional sauna called a "steam."

Worried about previous years' lackluster test results, Edwina took a supplementary class, from another teacher, designed specifically to "teach to the test." In my classroom I deviated from language arts units geared toward critical thinking, inquiry-based learning, and cultural literacy, and devoted several weeks of classroom instruction to reviewing test strategies, test content, and preparation.

We analyzed sample tests, practiced using the process of elimination to discard distracting choices, and even discussed cultural biases in test questions.

But in a village where kids are raised with a linguistically distinct form of English—called village English—and where young people struggle daily with the effects of economic hardship, domestic violence, and cultural disintegration, tests that ask students to compare personal digital assistants are irrelevant. Alaska Natives in rural villages have far greater concerns. With Alaska's Native communities suffering from the highest rates of Fetal Alcohol Syndrome, teen suicide, and child abuse in the nation, staying healthy—and even alive—is the paramount motive.

> A counselor in my village told me the story of an elementary student who began crying during a test. When the counselor asked her what was wrong, the girl pointed to the word "curb" and said she didn't know what it meant.

I tried to take these real concerns into consideration in my classroom by making learning relevant to conditions my students faced in their communities while maintaining high expectations in an academically rigorous curriculum. We read books by Native American authors such as Sherman Alexie, reconstructed traditional narratives into plays, and analyzed comparisons between "home" language and Standard English.

I conducted a grant-writing unit so students could realize an authentic outcome for composition. Edwina wrote an introduction to a grant that was ultimately awarded to her senior class.

Little did I know, however, how severely high-stakes tests would undercut my efforts to motivate my Alaska Native students to excel at reading and writing. Near the end of the year, the counselor came into my classroom. She stood solemnly by the door, as someone would who is about to deliver the news of a death in the family. She held the test results and waited until students were sitting down. When the seniors looked at their test scores, some seemed unfazed by the results. Edwina, however, said she felt sick.

Because she didn't pass the test, Edwina didn't get a diploma when she graduated later that spring. None of her female classmates did.

Edwina wrote a letter about her shattered hopes and her view of schools—how she'd "been working hard in school all this time" since kindergarten, how she wanted to earn the diploma her older sister never received, how she's afraid she'll end up living with her mother the rest of her life. When she read her letter aloud, other students in class fell silent. I suggested she send her letter to the editor of the Bethel paper, but drawing attention to oneself and one's problems is not customary among the Cu'pik Eskimo.

In Ketchikan, the representative from the education department closed her presentation, saying, "Everyone's goal is to increase student achievement."

Edwina accomplished that goal. The state and the school district failed her. ✎

The Scripted Prescription

A cure for childhood

PETER CAMPBELL

Afew days before my daughter Vivian started prekindergarten at a public school in Portland, Oregon, she was asked to come in and be tested. As part of the test, the teacher asked Vivian to write her name on a piece of paper. My 4-year-old daughter looked up at me with huge, puzzled eyes. I looked at the teacher with equally huge, puzzled eyes. Write her name? On the first day of pre-kindergarten? Vivian didn't know how to hold a pencil, much less write her name.

Traditionally, or so I've been told, the first meeting has been a time for the new student and the teacher to get to know each other. But there was no conversation about what Vivian liked to read, what she liked to do, or anything else that might have given the teacher some insight into Vivian's personality. Her teacher appeared to believe all that she needed to know about Vivian could be discovered from this test. It saddened me to think that my daughter's first impression of school was based on taking a test and failing it.

Now, Vivian regularly brings home worksheets that she did in school—photocopies of activities like sorting, graphing, letter tracing, and letter recognition. She's very busy at school. The first 45 minutes or so of class is open, but it's surprisingly structured and fettered. The kids often work alone. There's not much in the way of spontaneous expression or originality, and there is no time for them to engage in non-adult-supervised open-ended play situations or unstructured, whole-body activities. They have several areas set up for them—a puzzle here, a set of crayons and coloring books there.

And there is hardly any noise.

After the initial 45 minutes, the teacher has the students work in "centers." Each center is focused on a specific task, usually associated with a literacy skill. According to the teachers I've spoken to, these skills were the sorts of things 6- and 7-year-olds used to do in 1st grade. Now 4- and 5-year-olds are being asked to do them in prekindergarten.

Next year, if Vivian stays at this school and attends kindergarten, she will be in school all day, and she will be even busier. As a kindergartner, she will have exactly 20 minutes of recess, and then she'll get back to work.

I met with the principal and with Vivian's teacher. I expressed my concern that this practice might not be developmentally appropriate; some kids are just not ready for a heavy dose of academics and skills. The principal looked at me, rolled her eyes, and said calmly and confidently, "Well, it's not going to do them any harm."

I'm not so sure. Should we place such a heavy emphasis on academic skill development at such an early age? Is this a developmentally appropriate practice?

The truth is, we don't know. That's because this heavily skills-based, academic approach has never been taken before in prekindergarten and kindergarten classrooms in this country; there simply are no long-term data. Yet the lack of data on long-term effects

It saddened me to think that my daughter's first impression of school was based on taking a test and failing it.

has not stopped us from forging full steam ahead. Proponents of this approach think this emphasis on academic achievement is good for very young children. But we don't actually know what effect it's having, nor do we know what effect it will have five, 10, or 15 years from now.

Where I'm from, we call this "driving with your eyes closed." Others call it hoping. Call it what you will, but the fact of the matter is that our children in public schools—my daughter included—are participating in a giant experiment that none of us agreed to. Our children are guinea pigs, to put it nicely. Others might call them lab rats.

My daughter came home the other day in an incredibly grumpy mood.

"How was school today?" I asked.

"Terrible," she answered.

e said.
your friends?"

ddition of academics that worries me, as it
e seem to have lost the balance here. What
e for all of this skill building? Art, music,
e being cut to make more time for skills,
rting in prekindergarten.
ator at the Office of Teaching and Learn-
 can be about play, socialization, and fun.
teracy and numeracy in kindergarten, but
al instruction."
e too late."
hat?"
d neither is my daughter. But kids are be-
ier and earlier ages. The rush to raise test
mandates has only exacerbated this trend

Should we place such a heavy emphasis on academic skill development at such an early age? Is this a developmentally appropriate practice? The truth is, we don't know.

that David Elkind chronicled in his 1981 book, *The Hurried Child.*

Elkind argues that in blurring the boundaries of what is age appropriate by expecting—or imposing—too much too soon, we force our kids to grow up far too quickly. He referred to it as nothing less than an assault on childhood.

I'm worried that we're setting kids up to fail. We may succeed in getting some of them to read, write, and complete math equations precociously. But we may also be creating a cohort of 4- and 5-year-old children who look at school as a place where they simply don't belong, as a place that is devoid of fun. I'm concerned that children like my daughter are forming a negative self-image when asked to perform cognitive tasks they are clearly not able to complete or not comfortable doing. Children may not only develop negative self-esteem, but they may also form negative impressions about school, learning to feel it's too competitive or too stressful.

Competition and stress may or may not be something we want kids to learn to handle. And I'm not one of those parents who want to shield my little shnoogums from nasty people who don't think she's as marvelous as I do. But do we really want 4-year-olds to deal with these things in prekindergarten, the grade *before* the beginning grade of elementary school? When are children ever allowed to be beginners? Surely *pre*kindergarten is a good place for kids to be beginners. Or so we used to think.

The notion of children being "kindergarten ready" is a bizarre oxymoron. It's like saying you have to know how to play the piano before you can learn how to play the piano. But if you are not "kindergarten ready," then you are considered *behind*.

Children learn to play together by playing together. They learn how take turns by taking turns, how to share by sharing, how to resolve conflicts by resolving conflicts. In order to learn to do these things, children need to experience them firsthand. They need to *do* these things. But if they are not being given the time to have these experiences, then how are they supposed to learn from them?

In the context of the educational assessments that children like Vivian are subject to, we see a diagnostic model that specializes in both quantifying educational deficiencies in very young children and providing an antidote that meets the needs of the diagnosis. We see the emergence of large publishing companies that control the definition of the symptoms as well as prescribe and furnish the cure—for a hefty price. We see the emergence of the scripted curriculum, where "scripted" means an explicit formula to cure what ails them, as in "prescription." The prescription goes by various names, but they all have this in common: invent, identify, and remediate deficiencies—all in one slick package.

So what do I want? I want what Vivian wants: for her to be able to spend time with her friends, being a little kid. She doesn't have any children on her block, so school is the only place where she can socialize and interact with her peers. I want her to have the chance to make friends. I want her to have the opportunity to play. I want her to learn how to share and solve problems with

There will be time for such academic pursuits when she's a bit older. But there's only so much time she's allowed to be a little girl.

her peers. I want this more than I want her to be phonemically aware. She will have time for such academic pursuits when she's a bit older. But there's only so much time she's allowed to be a little girl.

Lest this sound a bit touchy-feely and out of synch with today's calls for accountability, consider this: A 2004 study by the Paris-based Organisation for Economic Co-operation and Development looked at literacy and reading skills for 15-year-olds. Finland was the top-ranked producer of readers. The United States was 15th out of 30 countries surveyed.

So what does Finland do? Children in Finland start learning to read in 1st grade. The Finns believe that play is the most effective learning tool in the early years and that it sets the stage for a lifelong love of learning.

I want this for all young children, not just my daughter. I want all children to have the opportunity to develop intellectually, socially, and emotionally. But most importantly, I want children to be allowed to have childhoods. ≈

Testing Our Limits

MELISSA BOLLOW TEMPEL

I walked away from the rest of my class and over to the three computers in the corner of my classroom. Two of my 1st graders, Jasmine and Jayden, sat at their computers with their headphones off, waiting for me to reset their computers to Measure of Academic Progress (MAP) test No. 2.

"I got 162," said Jasmine. "You got 142."

"You did better than me," replied Jayden with a frown. Shelly sat at the third computer. "I don't wanna do the computer test," she pleaded. "Do I have to?"

In the past three years I have experienced unimaginable computer frustration. Don't get me wrong: I treat my MacBook Pro like a third child, and I definitely use technology in the classroom to enhance teaching and learning. I've been accused of being in love with my iPhone, which serves as a timekeeper, meteorologist, and DJ in my classroom. And the opaque projector is an excellent, plastic transparency-free alternative to the overhead projector. Computers and technology have come a long way in the past 20 years, and they hold a big place in the lives of this generation of students. Unfortunately, one use of technology is failing in my classroom: the rapidly increasing use of computers for testing.

Computerized testing, like the widely used MAP test, has infiltrated the public schools in Milwaukee and across the nation like an uncontrollable outbreak of lice, bringing with it a frightening future for public education. High-stakes standardized tests can be scored almost immediately via the internet, which makes it possible to see scores within 24 hours, resulting in more frequent testing. Testing companies can now easily link districts to their online data warehouses; this allows districts to quickly access test scores (which would be good if the tests were generating usable data). This system provides momentum to those who believe more tests should be given to "track progress" throughout the year. In my district this means that every classroom teacher tests students at the beginning, middle, and end of the year—administering four tests in math and reading each time.

Limited funding and less staff in our district, like most urban public schools, creates even more of a problem because there are fewer adults to serve as proctors. Setting up these tests is a tedious, time-consuming job involving a web of long, nonsensical passwords and codes. Teachers are being mandated to use many hours of valuable instructional time and limited teacher planning time to complete these tasks. In schools like mine that don't have a computer lab, teachers have only a few computers in their classroom. We are asked to simultaneously teach while setting up and administering a few tests at a time, seriously compromising the quality of instruction we are able to deliver.

To illustrate the scenario, picture this: I have three computers on one side of the classroom, set apart from our learning area, so three children can take the test at one time. First I go to each computer and log into the network using an assigned proctor name and pass-word. Through this network, scores are uploaded to the testing website at the end of the day. Then I log into the test application using a different random alphanumeric name and nine-digit password. Once in, I select the

The new age of computerized high-stakes standardized testing is a frightening use of our advancing technology, but we can resist.

test the child needs to take, select the student's name, then sit the child down at the computer to begin, making sure he or she has the headphones on properly. (Yes, one of my students took the test wearing the headphones attached to her neighbor's computer. If I'm not watching carefully, others have taken the whole test without headphones on at all!) Then I hurry back to the rest of the class and continue teaching. When the child has a question, I have to go help. When the child is done taking the test, I have to go over and enter yet another proctor pass-word to finish the test and start the process over for the next child. Part of the score accounts for how long it takes a child to complete each question, so if the child has to use the bathroom I need to enter a code to pause the test. Each test takes about 20 minutes to complete; however, students do not finish at the same time, so I am going back and forth three different times to enter the passwords for the children and to set up the next student. I'm doing all this while I attempt to teach a lesson, lead an activity, or help the rest of the class do their work. The alternative is to stop instruction altogether for a few days and give my students "busy work" while three students at a time take the tests. And have I mentioned that we have no art, music, or physical education teachers at our school, so I have no prep time?

Unfortunately, the issue of time wasting and misuse does not even scratch the surface of the computerized testing chaos. Computerized testing now starts with students as young as 4 years old. MAP test data are reviewed and used in the screening process for children for special education. Those already receiving special education services with IEPs are required to take the grade-level test re-gardless of their instructional level. In Milwaukee, all students attending 4-year-old kindergarten are required to take the district's computerized test beginning their second week of school—ever. One of the literacy tests is 53 multiple-choice questions long, and to finish it students must select an answer for every ques-tion.

After each testing session, teachers report that students end up in tears. Most 4-year-olds cannot sit long enough to finish the whole test and need to be redirected to their chairs many times. District administration allows the test to be given one-on-one to kindergartners; however, pulling from the ever-shrink-

The biggest injustice here is the technology gap that has a direct effect on the achievement gap.

ing list of support staff means pulling the only available staff, the English Language Learner (ELL) teacher and librarian, to help. This test creates a domino effect that impacts the entire school.

Although our district's administration believes these tests are given on a level playing field (because in this age of technology most children are supposedly exposed to computers at a young age), our primary students often come to school with little or no computer experience. In fact, many early childhood researchers believe that responsible parenting means little or no screen time for primary school children. As a result, young students click at random. One of my colleagues reported that she often witnesses students rubbing the mouse on their faces or on the computer screens. And this data is supposed to help guide our teaching?

Widening the Gap

The biggest injustice here is the technology gap that has a direct effect on the achievement gap. Students who have regular access to computers at home are clearly advantaged, from a testing standpoint, because they have a higher likelihood of being computer literate. Meanwhile, kids who don't are being scored on both *how* to use the technology they have never had access to in addition to *what* is in the content of the test. This imbalance creates an assessment that is less valid or invalid because it measures something beyond what it is supposed to, and it penalizes students for something that they are not supposed to be tested on.

My 1st graders, Jasmine and Jayden, have figured out how to click past the dog at the end of the test to see their score. Sadly, I cannot be in two places at once to prevent it, and as a result there is little doubt that these 6-year-olds are drawing conclusions about how "smart" they are based on deeply flawed tests. To complicate things further, the data from these computerized tests are used to determine which intervention classes students should be enrolled in—or in many cases, which classes they are forced to attend in place of engaging elective courses. In primary schools, the district uses the data to track students into intervention groups, which serves to widen the achievement gap and perpetuate the racial and socioeconomic disparity between haves and have-nots. Our district's new plan to help students is heavily based on the MAP test results.

In fact, at one inservice, the students with the lowest test scores were already entered into my account as my intervention group. My professional opinion had been replaced by the test scores. I was surprised to see Julia, one of my smartest, highest readers, had been placed in the group. (I suspect she got bored with the test and decided to click randomly.) When I said that Julia was not in need of any extra help I was strongly advised by our school's literacy coach (assigned to our school one day a week) not to remove her from the group because, based on her test scores, Julia needed interventions. Of course, I moved her anyway.

These 6-year-olds are drawing conclusions about how "smart" they are based on deeply flawed tests.

This form of testing has not replaced other tests. Quite the opposite: It's given us the ability to give more tests. Milwaukee Public Schools has mandated that we administer a biweekly Dynamic Indicators of Basic Early Literacy Skills (DIBELS) test to students who scored in the bottom 20 percent on the MAP test to track their progress.

The new age of computerized high-stakes standardized testing is a frightening use of our advancing technology, but we can resist. Many parents see through the rhetoric and are choosing to opt their children out of standardized tests altogether, and a movement is brewing. Dr. Yong Zhao from the University of Oregon reports that a 6 percent opt-out rate is enough to invalidate standardized test results. However, that many opt-outs would also mean a school would not meet federal mandates for adequate yearly progress. Many involved in the opt-out movement feel that it's worth potential negative repercussions.

As educators and parents, we need to be honest about how computerized testing serves to emphasize economic disparities. We can speak out about how it takes away valuable instructional time and returns little helpful information. We need to push district administrations to reevaluate the quality and usefulness of all computerized testing and demand other more meaningful forms of assessment. And we can urge our unions to support teachers and parents who challenge the inappropriate use of tests.

Unless we stand together, erroneous computer data and educational officials detached from the realities of teaching will continue to determine our students' futures. ❧

PART 3

Testing Teaching

RANDALL ENOS

Teaching in Dystopia

Testing has a stranglehold on education

WAYNE AU

We are being tested to death.

According to Peter Sacks, author of *Standardized Minds*, adults and children in the United States took as many as 600 million standardized tests both inside and outside of schools annually in the 1990s.

And this was before Congress passed No Child Left Behind (NCLB) in 2002.

The Education Sector, an independent think tank, estimates that 45 million high-stakes standardized tests are required annually under NCLB alone, and that states would have to administer 11 million new tests in reading and math to meet that federal mandate. Rather than taking the focus off high-stakes testing, the Obama administration's Race To The Top education initiative only places more emphasis on test scores in order to gain access to federal monies.

There is no mystery to how we arrived at today's testing dystopia. The 1983 publication of the Reagan administration's report on education, *A Nation At Risk: The Imperative for Education Reform*, set the trajectory for 30 years of education policy. It sounded the alarm, alleging poor quality in education throughout the United States, and equated it with a threat to national security.

Despite the fact that it was thoroughly debunked, within a year of this report being unleashed on the United States, 45 state-level commissions on education were created, and 26 states raised graduation requirements. By 1994, 45 states implemented statewide assessments for students in kindergarten through 5th grade.

The march toward federally mandated, high-stakes standardized testing continued through to the presidency of George H. W. Bush. His Summit on Education, held with the U.S. governors, became the groundwork for his America 2000 plan, which focused on testing and establishing "world class standards" in schools.

A Broad Push to Narrow Curriculum

Even though it may have been birthed when Reagan and Bush Sr. were in office, this push for high-stakes standardized testing has always been bipartisan. Bill Clinton and Al Gore committed themselves to following through on the goals established by George H. W. Bush, maintaining the rhetoric of the

Testing is killing education. Not only is it narrowing the curriculum generally, but it also promotes bad pedagogy; and some private companies are getting rich in the process.

The logic of the zero-sum curriculum in the era of high-stakes testing is simple. If it isn't on the test, it is less likely to be taught—especially in low-performing schools and districts.

necessity of "tough standards" in our schools and pursuing a national examination system to meet those standards. By 2000, every state except Iowa administered a mandated test.

By 2008, NCLB required elementary, middle, and high school students to take more than 65 million high-stakes standardized tests a year in public schools. The problem is this: Testing is killing education. Not only does it narrow the curriculum generally, but it also promotes bad pedagogy; and some private companies are getting rich in the process.

Nationwide, the research surrounding the effects of the tests is fairly conclusive. A 2003 nationwide survey completed by researchers at the National Board on Educational Testing and Public Policy found that 43 percent of the respondents from states with high-stakes tests reported that teachers spent a great deal more time on tested areas.

Similarly, a 2006 report on a nationwide survey completed by the Center on Education Policy (CEP) found that 71 percent of the districts studied cut at least one subject to increased time spent on reading and math as a direct response to the high-stakes testing under federal mandates. As one Colorado public school teacher puts it, "Our district has told us to focus on reading, writing, and mathematics. Therefore, science and social studies...don't get taught."

Although test supporters may laud the increased time spent on tested subjects, the reality is that such increases also represent a loss, because when it comes to high-stakes testing, the curriculum is a zero-sum game: Test-induced increases in math and language arts instruction come at the cost of reductions in other subjects.

In its 2007 study, for instance, the CEP reports that federal testing mandates have resulted in an average weekly loss of 76 minutes of social studies instruction, 75 minutes of science instruction, 57 minutes of arts and music, 45 minutes of recess, and 40 minutes of physical education.

Zero-Sum Curriculum

Low-performing students and students of color feel the zero-sum curriculum particularly sharply. As the CEP reported in 2006, in some districts in California the lowest performing students have had to take extra classes in reading and math. As a consequence, those students had to completely cut science and social studies from their course loads.

In this same study, the CEP found that 97 percent of high-poverty school districts, which are largely populated by nonwhite students, have instituted policies specifically aimed at increasing time spent on reading. This compares to only 55 percent to 59 percent of wealthier, whiter districts.

In this way, instead of improving the educational experiences of low-income students and students of color, NCLB and its focus on high-stakes testing create more restrictive, less rich educational environments for the very students testing proponents claim to be helping.

Instead of improving the educational experiences of low-income students and students of color, NCLB and its focus on high-stakes testing create more restrictive, less rich educational environments for the very students testing proponents claim to be helping.

The logic of the zero-sum curriculum in the era of high-stakes testing is simple. If it isn't on the test, it is less likely to be taught—especially in low-performing schools and districts. The problem is, such logic guarantees our children are studying less about history and society, less about science, less about physical fitness, and less about art and music—let alone issues of social, cultural, or environmental justice.

To add insult to injury, the subjects being taught within our testing dystopia are ultimately being ruined because the high-stakes tests push teachers to use bad pedagogy and teach more meaningless content. For instance, in a 2003 nationwide survey, researchers found that 76 percent of the teachers in states with high-stakes testing and 63 percent of the teachers in their study from states with low-stakes testing reported that their state testing programs were increasing teacher-centered pedagogies, rote memorization of materials, and lecturing.

As one Massachusetts language arts teacher commented in response to the effect of state tests: "You know, we're not really teaching them how to write. We're teaching them how to follow a format...It's like...they're doing paint-by-numbers."

A Tough Start for New Teachers

As infuriating as it is to see how high-stakes testing negatively affects all teachers, the research about its impact on newly credentialed teachers is particularly disheartening.

Arthur Costigan, assistant professor of education at Queens College CUNY, found in his research that the tests have become the focus of the new teachers' first year of instruction, that this type of teaching has an adverse effect on their students and their practice, and that teachers developed a sense of powerlessness in the face of the amount of testing and the pressures involved.

Many of the teachers in Costigan's study felt that "a very real culture of testing has been created in the schools and districts in which they teach," and that they were "unable successfully to negotiate between a testing curriculum and personal best practice."

The culture of testing negatively affects young teachers of color as well. In one case Jane Agee, assistant professor of language and education at State University of New York at Albany, studied an African American teacher who recently gradu-ated from her teacher education program. This teacher entered the profession proudly, with the expressed goals of teaching multicultural content in her classes, teaching in ways that would help her students of color succeed, and becoming an agent for positive change in her school.

In response to the mounting pressures of the high-stakes tests, however, the young teacher gave up her more activist and equity-minded goals in order to teach to the tests.

This is one of the real tragedies of high-stakes testing. The first years of teach-ing are oftentimes precarious, as new teachers focus not only on how to manage their tremendous workloads, but also on figuring out what types of teachers they want to and can be. It is the time when they are developing their professional hab-its and their identities as teachers.

However, the tests are choking off the aspirations of our new teachers, dull-ing their sensibilities about how to best educate children before these sensibilities can even be nurtured and developed.

Marketization of Public Education

Although we may be tested to death, private corporations are making a kill-ing from our suffering: Continued compliance with the testing requirements of NCLB only means more states will offer more tests, with increased profits go-ing to select firms. Eduventures Inc., a private firm in Boston that offers its data analysis services to help companies "stay abreast of market trends, evaluate new markets and product lines, and better understand their customers" in K-12 and higher education, estimated the total value of the tests, test-prep materials, and testing services market in 2006 in the United States to be $2.3 billion.

Eduventures Inc. also estimates that the market created by test development, publishing, administering, analyzing, and reporting during the 2005-06 school year alone was worth $517 million, with 90 percent of the revenues generated by statewide testing being collected by only a few companies, which include Pearson Educational Measurement, CTB/McGraw-Hill, Harcourt Assessment Inc. and Riverside Publishing (a subsidiary of Houghton Mifflin Co.), and the Educational Testing Service. (The fact that a corporation such as Eduventures Inc. even exists is a sad testament to the growing marketization of public education.)

Amidst the avalanche of dollar signs, profits, and expanding "educational markets," two simple realities are sometimes lost. First, a handful of large cor-porations are becoming the curriculum corporation of America, as schools and districts increasingly rely on them for test-oriented textbooks, instructional programs, and test-prep materials. Through the tests, these companies are es-sentially driving our curriculum. Second, most of the monies flowing to these companies are tax dollars, earmarked for public schools, now being funneled directly into the coffers of private industry. It is a shift in the power of corpora-tions to control education that is happening under the guise of accountability and equality.

Every day, teachers enter their classrooms and try to make education meaningful for their students as well as fulfilling for themselves as teachers. Increasingly, however, our classrooms and schools are becoming testing dystopias where our abilities to effectively teach children are being distorted and marred by high-stakes testing.

The tests are choking off the aspirations of our new teachers, dulling their sensibilities about how to best educate children before these sensibilities can even be nurtured and developed.

Meanwhile, politicians on both sides of the aisle and their supporters continue to uphold high-stakes tests as the cure for what ails education. The problem is: Their cure is killing us. The tests drain precious resources from public schools. They suck the life out of the curriculum. They promote bad pedagogy. It's time to kill the tests before they kill education.

Fighting for Electives

Lessons in change

MELISSA BOLLOW TEMPEL

It was the first day of middle school for my 6th-grade homeroom students. I tentatively passed out their schedules. It took only a few moments before the questions started coming: "What is READ 180?" "Why don't I have gym?" "When do we have art?" My students looked to me for answers I was hesitant to give.

"READ 180 is a special class that will help you with your reading," I responded. "As soon as your reading improves, you can test out of READ 180. I know it's not fair you don't have gym or art, and I don't like it either." I told them I was going to do everything I could to make sure they were given a chance to take electives during the year.

When I was in middle school, we had two different elective classes each day that I really enjoyed. Cooking, sewing, art, music, gym, computer lab, wood shop, performance arts, and a choice of a foreign language were not just options; they were requirements. By the time I finished middle school, I knew how to type with my fingers correctly placed on the keyboard, bake a cake, use a power saw, sew a patchwork pillowcase, and make glass jewelry. I also knew, through experience, that I could not sing and didn't want to be in the high school marching band. I got a jumpstart in foreign language that eventually allowed me to test into fourth-semester college Spanish. It angered me to know that those classes still existed in the suburbs, where my stepdaughter was attending middle school, but that, under the best of circumstances, the electives for students at my urban Milwaukee school were reduced to art, gym, and computer class. Now most of my homeroom students had none of these. They had READ 180.

My students were enrolled in READ 180 because, based on federal mandates, the state of Wisconsin had labeled our school a Level Five School in Need of Improvement (SIFI), a.k.a. "a school with really, really bad test scores for many years in a row." READ 180 is just one of many boxed reading intervention programs popping up all over the United States and being used by districts to meet the federal requirements at a huge cost to students. The Milwaukee Public School District calls it "a research-based reading intervention program focusing specifically on students determined to be nonproficient." The Scholastic READ 180 website describes the program as a 90-minute class composed of four parts: 20 minutes of whole-group direct instruction, 20 minutes of small group direct instruction, 20 minutes of instructional software, 20 minutes of modeled and independent reading, and a 10-minute "wrap-up." Every 12 weeks the students take a computerized READ 180 assessment; if the results show they are reading at grade level, they are supposed to be exited from the program. I can't say I've researched READ 180 enough to evaluate its efficacy, but I can say from experience that scripted reading programs—especially direct instruction-based programs—do not stimulate higher level or critical thinking skills in students.

I was horrified when I realized my students would have only one class in addition to their basic academics, and that class was READ 180.

This was my first year teaching 6th-grade English and language arts, and it was my eighth year teaching overall. My students were all first-generation Mexican and Puerto Rican English language learners (ELL) and, thanks to our district's bilingual maintenance model, they were literate in both English and Spanish.

During teacher organization days at the beginning of the school year, I was horrified when I realized my students would have only one class in addition to their basic academics, and that class was READ 180. They would go from first-block literacy to second-block READ 180, then have lunch for 20 minutes, silent reading for 20 minutes, third-block science/social studies, and fourth-block math. Our school didn't have a playground or outside area; our district has a strict "no recess" policy for middle and high school students. And, even more infuriatingly, READ 180 students would not be excused from the class to go on field trips.

No Respect for Teacher Input

Administrators told me that the decision about which students would participate in READ 180 was nonnegotiable. The main criterion was scoring below "proficient" on the state standardized test, the Wisconsin Knowledge and Concepts Evaluation (WKCE), which had been administered the previous fall—10 months earlier! As their teacher, I was never asked for writing samples, class work, individual reading assessments, or my professional opinion of their reading levels. To add insult to injury, some of my READ 180 students were reading at or above grade level.

I was frustrated and didn't know where to turn. I cautiously approached a teacher I respected and asked, "Does this mean students don't get any electives?" "Yes," she said. "It's terrible, but they have to learn how to read." As a new faculty member, I didn't know who might be willing to fight this with me, and I started to feel isolated.

After seven weeks of school, the READ 180 teacher voiced concern that her students still weren't able to access the instructional software component of the program due to a licensing glitch. I emailed school board members my concerns

As a new faculty member, I didn't know who might be willing to fight this with me, and I started to feel isolated.

about READ 180, and one encouraged me to voice my frustrations at a school board meeting that focused on "innovations and school reform."

I was nervous as I spoke into the microphone, knowing that my voice would be broadcast live over public radio. "My students have been in class for seven weeks without the computers working. So they have been doing a program where the kids are having reading instead of [electives], and they are not able to use the program the way it's supposed to be used." I went on to talk more about the injustice to my students: "It is unreasonable for us, as a school and as a district, to ask students to sit all day without having a break."

The next morning when I arrived at school, the READ 180 teacher ran up to thank me, saying her software licensing problems had been fixed. For a moment I felt that what I'd said the night before had been effective, but the principal was quick to tell me that I had nothing to do with it. In fact, incorrect information about what I had said at the school board meeting quickly spread throughout the school. As a result, teachers blamed me for strict new policies introduced into our school in the following weeks. For example, a special education teacher informed me that the principal announced a "no field trip" policy for the whole school because I had brought attention to the school's low performance. I began to feel backed into a corner.

Bewildered, I went to a meeting of the Educators' Network for Social Justice, one place where I knew I'd be supported. A friend and retired principal gave me some sound advice. He told me to look for an ally at my school—someone I could talk to, someone who might help me start to build a network of like-minded faculty to work together on problems. I quickly realized that one of the assistant principals could be this person for me. Quite often, I'd walk into his office, and we'd chat about our frustrations. Having him there to listen and encourage me—even when his hands were tied and he couldn't help—got me through the year.

Since my students were not getting any arts or physical activity within their school day, I needed to decide: Do I make my students "work harder" so that they can pass out of READ 180, or do I try to incorporate more arts and movement in my class? I tried to do both by coming up with activities that would integrate classes like gym and art while still teaching reading skills.

One day I arranged for us to go to the gym. On one side of the gym I put a set of flashcards with our vocabulary words, and on the other side I put the definitions. We got into teams and ran relay races. Each time runners reached the other side of the gym, they grabbed a vocabulary word and brought it back to the rest of the team, who tried to match the word to its definition. Then we grabbed major events from the story we'd read that week, and the relay teams put the events in chronological order. My students loved these games and begged me to take them to the gym again, but with three schools sharing the space in one building, it was often unavailable.

When my students started the second quarter, I was shocked to learn that five additional students had been removed from their electives and placed in READ 180. Three were my highest readers. I will never forget the eyes of those students as they looked at me that morning after receiving their schedules.

I was beyond angry. After I took the students to READ 180 class, I marched around the building, looking for someone—anyone—who would also see the injustice I saw and help me fix it. I could hardly breathe, and I'm sure others could see the steam coming out of my ears. I was directed to the principal, who told me to talk to the SIFI supervisor, who sent me to another assistant principal. No one wanted to stand up for what was right and challenge the district. I could not believe that a school would allow this. It was my lowest point in dealing with READ 180. I felt the students had lost faith in me, because what I had naively promised—that with hard work they'd get out of READ 180—was turned on its head when students saw the "smart kids" put into the program.

> The stakes at my school were so high (improve test scores, or the district will close the school) that administrators clamped down and took power away from teachers, completely ignoring any criticism or questioning of their programs.

Lessons Learned

Looking back, I can see the broader forces affecting teachers at my school and the mistakes I made in my efforts to defend the students. The stakes at my school were so high (improve test scores, or the district will close the school) that administrators clamped down and took power away from teachers, completely ignoring any criticism or questioning of their programs. When I criticized what was going on, I was seen as attacking the plan to save the school. The teachers wanted to shake the school's bad reputation, and the administration argued that the only way to do this was through "drill and kill" for better standardized test scores. Over the course of the year, I learned that many teachers had left the school in the five years prior. Those remaining had been defeated many times, even in carefully picked battles. Most had decided to focus on what they had a measure of control over: their classrooms.

As an advocate for my students, I wanted to snap my fingers and have a new and improved schedule that included electives for the whole school. In retrospect, I could have done many things differently. I learned that there is a line of command in schools, and skipping ahead to the school board meeting before approaching the faculty was self-defeating. As a new teacher, it's important to have patience and allow for time to assess your environment, remembering that sometimes change can't be rushed. It's also important to have allies and to approach the administration as a team. Later in the year, I realized that if I had sought out teachers with seniority and status in the school, they might have helped me get what I wanted.

Through the year I talked with other teachers who were shocked at school policies, including READ 180. Taking time to seek out and form a group of allies would have been much more effective than going at it alone. We could have organized to speak collectively at staff meetings and with the administration. I also might have been able to mobilize parents by talking with them about their rights and the programs being pushed on their children.

Unfortunately, I wasn't able to claim victory against READ 180. Although a few students did test out, many remained for the duration of the school year. One of my brightest students tested "proficient" on the WKCE but, for some reason (maybe a program flaw regarding ELL students), at the end of the year she had still not tested out of READ 180.

It was a tough, discouraging year. I learned that the imposition of a standardized learning program for students leads to attempts to standardize teachers, too—and to repress those who challenge the new system. Now, more than ever, I see the need for educators to join together to rethink what we are being told and focus collectively on fighting policies that are not right for our students. ✎

Standards and Tests Attack Multiculturalism

BILL BIGELOW

Proponents of "higher standards" and more testing promise that students will learn more and schools will finally be held "accountable." In practice, their reforms are hostile to good teaching and pose a special threat to multiculturalism.

The state where I teach, Oregon, joined the national testing craze early. In the late 1990s, the Oregon Department of Education gave a glimpse of the testing onslaught to come when it field-tested its first-ever statewide social studies assessments. The tests were a maze of multiple-choice questions that lurched about helter-skelter, seeking answers about World War I, Constitutional amendments, global climate, rivers in India, hypothetical population projections, Supreme Court decisions, and economic terminology. Based on a close reading of these tests, social studies knowledge would seem to be little more than the acquisition of disconnected facts about the world.

The version of standards pressed by "accountability" proponents threatens the development of a multicultural curriculum—one that describes and attempts to explain the world as it really exists; speaks to the diversity of our society and our students; and aims not only to teach important facts, but also to develop citizens who can make the world safer and more just.

In a sense, the entire effort to create fixed standards violates the very essence of multiculturalism. Multiculturalism is a search, a "conversation among different voices," in the words of Henry Louis Gates Jr., to discover perspectives that have been silenced in traditional scholastic narratives. Multiculturalism attempts to uncover "the histories and experiences of people who have been left out of the curriculum," as anti-racist educator Enid Lee emphasizes. Because multiculturalism requires new scholarship and constant discussion, it necessarily is ongoing. Yet as researcher Harold Berlak points out, "standardization and centralization of curriculum testing is an effort to put an end to a cacophony of voices on what constitutes truth, knowledge and learning and what the young should be taught. It insists upon one set of answers." Curriculum standardization is, as Berlak indicates, a way to silence dissident voices, "a way to manufacture consent and cohesion."

"Neutral" Standards Promote Shallow Understanding

Creating an official, government-approved social studies curriculum is bound to be controversial, whether at the national or state level. Thus, according to the Portland *Oregonian*,

> Based on a close reading of these tests, social studies knowledge would seem to be little more than the acquisition of disconnected facts about the world.

from the beginning, state education officials "tried to stake a neutral ground" in order to win approval for its version of social reality: "We have tried so hard to go right down the middle between what teachers want, what parents want and what the [Republican-dominated] Legislature wants," according to Dawn Billings, a Department of Education curriculum coordinator. Not surprisingly, this attempt to be "neutral" and inoffensive means that the standards lack a critical sensibility—an emphasis on conflict and diversity of interpretation—and instead tend toward a conservative, *Father Knows Best*-type portrait of history and society. For example, one typical 10th-grade benchmark calls for students to "understand how the Constitution can be a vehicle for change and for resolving issues as well as a device for preserving values and principles of society."

Only? Is this how, say, Frederick Douglass or the Seminole leader Osceola would have seen the Constitution? Shouldn't students also understand how the Constitution can be (and has been) a vehicle for preserving class and race stratification and for maintaining the privileges of dominant social groups? For example, in the 1857 *Dred Scott* case, the Supreme Court held that enslaved people could not sue for their freedom because they were property, not human beings. Chief Justice Roger Taney declared that no black person in the United States had "any rights which the white man is bound to respect." The abolitionist William Lloyd Garrison called the Constitution an "agreement with Hell" for its support of slavery. And, in 1896, the Supreme Court ruled in *Plessy v. Ferguson* that segregation— "separate but equal"—did not violate the 14th Amendment.

Almost 40 percent of the men who wrote the Constitution, including George Washington and James Madison, owned slaves. In my U.S. history classes, we look at the adoption of the Constitution from the standpoint of poor white farmers, enslaved African Americans, unemployed workers in urban areas, and other groups. Students create their own Constitution in a mock assembly, and then compare their document to the actual Constitution. They discover, for example, that the Constitution does not include the word "slave" or "enslaved person," but instead refers only euphemistically to enslaved African Americans, as in Article 4, Section 2: "No person held in service or labor in one state, under the laws thereof, escaping into another, shall in consequence of any law or regulation therein, be discharged from service or labor, but shall be delivered up on claim of the party to whom such service or labor may be due." It's a vicious clause, which sits uncomfortably in the "preserving values and principles" rhetoric of Oregon's standards.

It is probably inevitable that school curricula will reflect the contradictions between a society's myths and realities. But while a critical multicultural approach attempts to examine these contradictions, standardization tends to paper them over. For example, another benchmark—"Explain how laws are developed and applied to provide order, set limits, protect basic rights, and promote the common good"—similarly fails the multicultural test. Whose order, whose basic rights, are protected by laws? Are all social groups included equally in the term "common good"? Between 1862 and 1890, laws in the United States gave 180,000,000 acres (an area the size of Texas and Oklahoma) to privately owned railroad companies, but gave virtually no land to African Americans freed from slavery in the South. Viewing the Constitution and other U.S. laws through a multicultural lens would add texture and depth to the facile one-sidedness of Oregon's "neutral" standards.

Indeed the "R" word, racism, is not mentioned once in any of the seven Oregon 11th-grade field tests or in the social studies standards adopted by the State Board of Education. Even if the only yardstick were strict historical accuracy, this would be a bizarre omission: The state was launched as a whites-only territory by the Oregon Donation Act and in racist wars of dispossession waged against indigenous peoples; the first constitution outlawed slavery but also forbade blacks from living in the state, a prohibition that remained on the books until 1926. Perhaps state education officials were concerned that introducing the concept of racism to students could call into question the essentially harmonious world of "change, and continuity over time" that underpins the standards project. Whatever the reason, there is no way that students can make sense of the world today without the idea of racism in their conceptual knapsacks. If a key goal of multiculturalism is to account for how the past helped shape the present, and an important part of the present is social inequality, then standards and tests like those adopted in Oregon earn a failing grade.

> **If a key goal of multiculturalism is to account for how the past helped shape the present, and an important part of the present is social inequality, then standards and tests like those adopted in Oregon earn a failing grade.**

Beyond "Facts"

Despite the publication of state social studies standards and benchmarks, throughout the country, teachers or parents don't really know what students are expected to learn until they see the tests. MetriTech, an out-of-state assessment corporation, developed Oregon's. As Professor Wade W. Nelson points out in "The Naked Truth About School Reform in Minnesota," a delightfully frank *Phi Delta Kappan* article:

> The content of the standards is found only in the tests used to assess them. Access to the tests themselves is carefully controlled, making it difficult to get a handle on what these standards are. It seems ironic to me that basic standards—that which every student is expected to know or be able to do—are revealed only in tests accessible only to test-makers and administrators. This design avoids much of the debate about what these standards ought to be.

And that debate is essential to the ongoing struggle for a multicultural curriculum.

Looking directly at the tests, their limitations and negative implications for multiculturalism become most clear. Test questions inevitably focus on discrete facts, but cannot address the deeper, multifaceted meaning of facts. For example, in the Oregon social studies field tests, one question asked which Constitutional Amendment gave women the right to vote. Students could know virtually nothing about the long struggle for women's rights and answer this question correctly. On the other hand, they could know much about the feminist movement and not recall that it was the 19th and not the 16th, 17th, or 18th Amendment (the other test choices) that gave women the right to vote.

Because there is no way to predict precisely which facts will be sought on state tests, teachers will feel pressured to turn courses into a "memory Olympics"; teachers won't be able to spend the time required to probe beneath the headlines of history. For example, in my U.S. history class at Franklin High School in Portland, students role-play about the 1848 Seneca Falls, N.Y. women's rights conference, the first formal U.S. gathering to demand greater equality for women. The original assembly was composed largely of middle- to upper-class white women. I wanted my students to appreciate the issues that these women addressed and their courage, but also to consider the limitations imposed by their race, class, and ethnicity. Thus in our simulated 1848 gathering, my students portrayed women who were not at the original conference—enslaved African Americans, Cherokee women who had been forcibly moved to Oklahoma on the Trail of Tears, Mexican women in the recently conquered territory of New Mexico, poor white New England mill workers—as well as the white middle- and upper-class reformers, like Elizabeth Cady Stanton and Lucretia Mott, who were in attendance. In this more socially representative fictional assembly, students learned about the resolutions adopted at the original gathering and the conditions that motivated those, but they also saw firsthand how more privileged white women ignored other important issues—such as treaty rights of Mexican women, sexual abuse of enslaved African Americans, and the workplace exploitation of poor white women—that a more diverse convention might have addressed.

The knowledge that my students acquired from role-playing consisted not only of "facts," although they learned plenty of these. The students also exercised their multicultural social imaginations—listening for the voices that are often silenced in the traditional U.S. history narrative, and becoming more alert to the importance of issues of race and class. However, this kind of teaching and learning takes time—time that could be ill-afforded in the fact-packing pedagogy required by multiple-choice tests. And after all of their study, would my students have recalled which amendment gave women the right to vote? If not, they would have appeared ignorant about the struggle for women's rights.

In a demonstration of its own shaky grasp of the material on which it tests students, Oregon shows that the reverse is true as well: One can master isolated morsels of fact and remain ignorant about the issues that give those facts meaning. For example, in a test question repeated throughout the seven pilot tests, the state uses the term "Suffragette," an inappropriate and dismissive substitute for "Suffragist." Someone who had actually studied the movement would know this. As Sherna Gluck points out in her book, *From Parlor to Prison*, women in the suffrage movement considered this diminutive term "an insult when applied to them by most of the American press."

My Global Studies students spend the better part of a quarter reading, discussing, role-playing, and writing about the manifold consequences of European colonialism. They read excerpts from Okot p'Bitek's poignant

> There is no way that students can make sense of the world today without the idea of racism in their conceptual knapsacks.

book-length poem, *Song of Lawino*, about the lingering psychological effects of colonialism in Uganda; role-play a trial on the colonial roots of the potato famine in Ireland; and examine how Asian economies were distorted to serve the needs of European ruling classes. But when confronted with Oregon's multiple-choice question that asks which continent was most thoroughly colonized in 1914, would my students answer correctly?

Obscuring Perspective and Undermining Educators

As these examples illustrate, in a multicultural curriculum it's not so much facts as it is perspective that is important in nurturing a fuller understanding of society. And sometimes considering new perspectives requires imagination as much as or more than memory of specific facts. For example, my history students read about the people Columbus encountered in 1492, the Taínos—who themselves left no written records—in excerpts from Columbus' journal and articles like Jose Barriero's "Taínos: Men of the Good." I ask students to write a story or diary entry from the point of view of a Taíno during the first few days or weeks of their encounter with Spaniards that draws on information in the readings, but also goes further. It's necessarily a speculative undertaking, but invites students to turn the "Columbus discovers America" story on its head, encourages them to appreciate the humanity in the people usually marginalized in tales of "exploration." In response, students have written pieces of startling insight. Sure, a multiple-choice test can assess whether students know that Columbus first sailed in 1492, the names of his ships, where he landed, or the name of the people he encountered. But these tests are ill-equipped to assess what students truly *understand* about this encounter.

Necessarily, the one-best-answer approach vastly oversimplifies and misrepresents complex social processes and entirely erases ethnicity and race as categories of analysis. One question on an Oregon Social Studies test reads: "In 1919, over 4.1 million Americans belonged to labor unions. By 1928, that number had dropped to 3.4 million. Which of the following best accounts for that drop?" It seems that the correct answer must be the first choice: "Wages increased dramatically, so workers didn't need unions." All the other answers are clearly wrong, but is this answer "correct"? Since when do workers leave unions when they win higher wages? Weren't mechanization and scientific management factors in undermining traditional craft unions? Did the post-World War I Red Scare, with systematic attacks on radical unions like the Industrial Workers of the World and deportations of foreign-born labor organizers, affect union membership?

And how about the test's reductive category of "worker"? Shouldn't students

I want the states to abandon the effort to treat teachers as cogs in a delivery system of approved social information.

be alert to how race, ethnicity, and gender were and are important factors in determining one's workplace experience, including union membership? For example, in 1919, professional strikebreakers, hired by steel corporations, were told to "stir up as much bad feeling as you possibly can between the Serbians and the Italians." And, as Howard Zinn points out in *A People's History of the United States*, more than 30,000 black workers, excluded from AFL unions, were brought in as strikebreakers. A multicultural awareness is vital if we're to arrive at a satisfactory answer to the above test question. But tests like these reward students for choosing a historical sound bite that is as shallow as it is wrong.

This leads me to an aspect of standardized tests that is especially offensive to teachers: The tests don't merely assess; they also instruct. The tests represent the authority of the state, implicitly telling students, "Just memorize the facts, kids. That's what social studies is all about—and if teachers do any more than that, they're wasting your time." Multiple-choice tests undermine teachers' efforts to construct a rigorous multicultural curriculum because they delegitimize that curriculum in students' eyes: If it were important, then it would be on the test.

At its core, multicultural teaching is an ethical, even political, enterprise. Its aim is not just to impart lots of interesting facts or to equip students to be proficient *Trivial Pursuit* players, but instead to help make the world a better place. It highlights injustice of all kinds—racial, gender, class-based, linguistic, ethnic, national, and environmental—in order to make explanations and propose solutions. It recognizes our responsibility to fellow human beings and to the Earth. It has heart and soul.

Compare that with the sterile, fact-collecting orientation of Oregon's standards and assessments. For example, a typical 49-question high school field test includes seven questions about global climate, two about the location of rivers in India and Africa, and one about hypothetical world population projections in the year 2050. But not a single question in the test concerns the lives of people around the world or any environmental conditions—nothing about increasing poverty, the global AIDS epidemic, disappearance of the rainforests, rates of unemployment, global warming, etc., or efforts to address these crises. The test bounds aimlessly from one disjointed fact to another. In the most profound sense, it's *pointless*.

Indeed the test's random amorality may reveal another of its cultural biases. Oregon's standards and assessments make no distinction between knowledge and information. The state's version of social education would appear to have no raison d'être beyond the acquisition of large quantities of data. But for many cultures, the aim of knowledge is not bulk, but rather wisdom—insight into meaningful aspects about the nature of life. Writing in the Winter 1998-99 issue of *Rethinking Schools*, Peter Kiang makes a similar point about the Massachusetts Teacher Test that calls into question the validity of enterprises such as these. He writes:

[B]y constructing a test based on a sequence of isolated, decontextualized questions that have no relationship to each other, the underlying epistemology embedded in the test design has a Western-cultural bias, even if individual questions include or represent "multicultural" content. Articulating and assessing a knowledge base requires examining not only what one knows, but also how one knows.

Students "know" in different ways, and these differences are often cultural. Standardized social studies tests nonetheless subject all students to an abstract, data-heavy assessment device that does not gauge what or how they have learned. As Kiang points out, test-makers address multicultural criticism by including individual questions about multicultural content—for example, by highlighting snippets of information about famous people of color like Martin Luther King Jr., Cesar Chavez, and Harriet Tubman. But these "heroes and holidays" additions cannot mask the fundamental hostility to multicultural education shown by standards and assessments like those initiated by Oregon.

Spelling out an alternative to culturally biased, superficial "accountability" plans would require another article. In brief, I want the states to abandon the effort to treat teachers as cogs in a delivery system of approved social information. I want departments of education to support other teachers and me as we collaborate to create curriculum that deals forthrightly with social problems and that fights racism and social injustice. I want them to support teachers as we construct rigorous performance standards for students that promote deep thinking about the nature of our society. I want them to acknowledge the legitimacy of a multicultural curriculum of critical questions, complexity, multiple perspectives, and social imagination. I want them to acknowledge that wisdom is more than information—that the world can't be chopped up into multiple-choice questions, and that you can't bubble in the truth with a No. 2 pencil. ❧

For Further Information

Several of the lessons discussed in this article are described more fully in other Rethinking Schools publications or at the Zinn Education Project site. See:

"Constitution Role Play: Whose 'More Perfect Union'?" and "The Constitutional Convention: Who Really Won?" at http://zinnedproject.org/posts/1160.

"Seneca Falls, 1848: Women Organize for Equality" at http://zinnedproject.org/posts/1445.

"Song of Lawino," in Bill Bigelow and Bob Peterson, editors; *Rethinking Globalization: Teaching for Justice in an Unjust World*. Milwaukee: 2002. pp. 50-53.

"Hunger on Trial: An Activity on the Irish Potato Famine and its Meaning for Today" at http://zinnedproject.org/posts/1422.

"Imagining the Taínos," in Bill Bigelow and Bob Peterson, editors; *Rethinking Columbus: The Next 500 Years*. Milwaukee: 1998. pp. 108-110.

Think Less Benchmarks

A flawed test does more harm than good

AMY GUTOWSKI

I'm staring at this bulging envelope on my desk. It's a big envelope, much larger than your typical letter-sized envelope—you know, a big one, like one that could fit about 15 test booklets and answer sheets. Our school's "literacy coach" just dropped it off. I put quotes around those two words because I often wonder why she was given that title.

Much of what she does has nothing to do with literacy. I think we should just call her the "test passer-outer," or something like that, because that is really the bulk of what she does throughout the school year. Positions like these have been hijacked by testing crusaders in schools and districts around the country. Originally, our district adopted ThinkLink benchmark assessments for schools identified as not adequately increasing test scores. (That was disturbing enough: "Our kids are failing, so let's make them take more tests.") Then I learned that virtually all schools were being forced to participate, regardless of their scores.

ThinkLink tests are designed to mirror the format of our state assessments. According to the district—and to the salespeople at ThinkLink—the ThinkLink "formative" assessments would help our district better predict student performance on our state's high-stakes exams. These high-stakes tests are aligned with our state's arbitrary set of standards for each grade level, standards that tend to be incredibly unrealistic and developmentally inappropriate.

There are four benchmark tests a year. Thanks to the folks at the Discovery Channel—that TV channel with the nifty little logo of the earth spinning—my 8-year-old students have four more opportunities to stop learning and fill in the bubbles. Discovery Education has added an extension to its suite of services, branching out into the assessment market and now produces ThinkLink formative assessments for districts across the country.

According to the catchy little press release from Discovery Education: "Discovery Education acquired ThinkLink Learning in April 2006, expanding the business unit's high-quality products and services to include formative assessment. ThinkLink pioneered a unique approach to formative assessment that uses a scientifically research-based continuous improvement model that maps diagnostic assessment to state high-stakes tests." So essentially, it's an expensive assessment program—our district spent roughly $400,000 on it this year—built on the assumption that repeated testing of children will help them to do better on tests. Forget about reading specialists, art, music, school psychologists, nurses, social workers, or support staff. It's ThinkLink to the rescue!

This is why the overstuffed envelope has landed on my desk. My first impulse is to chuck it in the trash. I'm sure this is the impulse of any teacher who has actually read these assessments. The first time I saw a ThinkLink benchmark, I was shocked and dismayed. It was poorly written and riddled with errors. And it was developmentally inappropriate:

> Reread the title of the story: *The Armadillo: A Shelled Mammal*. What happens when –ed is added to the word **shell** in the title?

A. it becomes a word that tells when the mammal was shelled

B. it becomes a word that tells how armadillos move

C. it becomes a word that describes the word mammal

D. it becomes a word that is the present tense of the verb shell.

Thanks to the folks at the Discovery Channel—that TV channel with the nifty little logo of the earth spinning—my 8-year-old students have four more opportunities to stop learning and fill in the bubbles.

It was all completely disconnected from the curriculum I was teaching.

I decided to call our district's director of assessment in December 2006, after our first round of benchmarks, to ask about them. It amazed me that this program was implemented so quickly. After all, hadn't Discovery Education just rolled out this new suite of assessments in April 2006? Teachers in the district were never asked whether we wanted to use such testing in our classrooms; the tests were just bought and then mandated, without any discussion. I was upset because my 3rd graders had just finished the weeklong state assessment in November (and all of the preparation preceding), and then we had to stop reading *Charlotte's Web* for two days to instead fill in more bubbles. The phone conversation was interesting.

According to the assessment director, teachers around the district *loved* the ThinkLink assessments. She said I was the only one who complained, and that teachers were amazed at the quick return of test results and data. She said that teachers told her they were learning so much about their students and their knowledge from these assessments. I was surprised by this response. I had just spoken to a teacher at another elementary school who told me that the entire staff had written a letter protesting the districtwide adoption of the additional tests. The assessment director even claimed that some principals were requesting benchmark assessments for their 1st- and 2nd-grade classrooms. (In our district, these tests start at 3rd grade and move up all the way through 9th grade, with no classroom left unscathed except kindergarten, 1st, and 2nd grades—which may very well change if this madness continues.) I could not believe what I was hearing.

Convoluted and Confusing

The benchmark testing questions were all over the place. Most of them were not at all related to what I was teaching in the classroom. For example, after reading a confusing passage about edible insects—in which there was no explanation of what "edible" means, nor any obvious context clues to help children figure out the meaning of "edible"—my students were asked:

Which of the following is nearly the opposite of edible?

A. antiedible
B. preedible
C. anedible
D. inedible.

Is this not insane?

I teach about prefixes and suffixes in my classroom, but come on, people. The questioning is so convoluted. My students are 8-year-olds who just started reading two years ago. I want my children to become independent learners and lovers of books. These tests make reading seem awful and tedious. An equally upsetting question asks children to identify an author's purpose (one of our 3rd-grade reading "standards" in Wisconsin).

My 3rd graders are often asked if a passage was written to entertain, persuade, or inform. Much of what we read in our lives does all of these. We recently finished reading *Turtle Bay*. It's a story about friends cleaning a beach so sea turtles will come and lay their eggs. The story was definitely entertaining; it persuaded my students to think about their actions (for example, littering hurts animals); and we were informed about turtles. So, in the name of "standards," my students are expected to answer these horribly misleading questions. Why has reading been reduced to this?

At the end of our conversation, the director of assessment asked me if I wanted to participate in making the tests better. I agreed to go over the initial assessment, and I highlighted grammatical errors and misplaced questions. I sent the offending booklet to her office with red marks and comments. Then she asked if I would be interested in going over future ThinkLink assessments, and at the time, I agreed. But then I began to think about it. I was never asked my opinion about these assessments in the first place, and now here I was agreeing to spend my valuable time working to make these lame assessments better? These tests were mandated in our district without critical discussion and questioning. I was also told the district would survey teachers about these assessments at the end of the school year. I have yet to see a survey.

I did not spend more of my time working to improve the flawed benchmarks.

I have, instead, decided to advocate for my students and their learning. I have been sending opinion pieces to local newspapers and magazines. I have testified at school board meetings. I stand up at staff meetings (often alone), and express my concerns. I will not be apathetic. I'm not buying into this random adoption of mandated assessments. I am tired of this antichild, for-profit agenda in our schools and classrooms.

I want to shred each booklet, page by page, especially the top page with the cute little earth logo. But I can't. I have to pass out these tests or risk my job.

Teachers must come together and speak out against the foolishness and absurdity of it all. Our students deserve more than this. The huge sums paid to Discovery Education could be put to much better use.

So here I sit, staring at the envelope full of ThinkLink tests. The envelope conjures up conflict within me. I don't want to subject my students to this nonsense. I want to resist. I want to shred each booklet, page by page, especially the top page with the cute little earth logo. But I can't. I have to pass out these tests or risk my job.

Tomorrow, when I pass out the booklets and scantron sheets, I'll explain to my students that some of the questions were confusing even to me, their teacher. I'll ask them not to worry. I'll ask them to do their best. Federal mandates put pressure on districts to gather more data, and testing companies get richer producing tests that guarantee large amounts of failure, thus ensuring future customers. It's a vicious, mean-spirited cycle. These test scores drive the way we educate our children. We spend hours at staff meetings looking at the "data" gathered from these mass-produced assessments instead of sharing ideas about meaningful learning and what really works in the classroom.

Who needs the arts? Screw recess. Let them eat tests. I'll think about this tomorrow as my 3rd graders fill in perfect little circles on their benchmark score sheets—3rd graders, who are most definitely being left behind.

About Those Tests I Gave You...

An open letter to my students

RUTH ANN DANDREA

Dear 8th Graders,
I'm sorry. I didn't know.

I spent last night perusing the 150-plus pages of grading materials provided by the state in anticipation of reading and evaluating your English Language Arts Exams this morning. I knew the test was pointless—that it has never done its job fulfilling its stated purpose as a predictor of who would succeed and who would fail the English Regents in 11th grade. Any thinking person would've ditched it years ago. Instead, rather than simply give a test in 8th grade that doesn't get kids ready for the test in 11th grade, the state opted to also give a test in 7th grade to get you ready for your 8th-grade test.

But we already knew all of that.

What I learned is that the test is also criminal.

Because what we hadn't known, what I hadn't known—this is my first time preparing 8th graders for this exam—was that it doesn't matter how well you write, or what you think. Here we spent the year reading books and emulating great writers, constructing leads that would make everyone want to read our work, developing a voice that would engage our readers, using our imaginations to make our work unique and important, and, most of all, being honest. And none of that matters. All that matters, it turns out, is that you cite two facts from the reading material in every answer. That gives you full credit on your answer. You can compose a "Gettysburg Address" for the 21st century on the apportioned lines in your test booklet, but if you've provided only one fact from the text you read in preparation, then you will earn only half credit. In your constructed response—no matter how well-written, correct, intelligent, noble, beautiful, and meaningful it is—if you've not collected two specific facts from the provided readings (even if you happen to know more information about the chosen topic than the readings provide), then you will get a zero.

And here's the really scary part, kids: The questions you were asked were written to elicit a personal response, which, if provided, earned you no credit. You were tricked; we were tricked. I wish I could believe that this paradox (you will know what that literary term means because we have spent the year noting these kinds of tightropings of language) was simply the stupidity of the test-makers, that it was not some more insidious and deliberate machination. I wish I could believe that. But I don't.

I told you, didn't I, about hearing Noam Chomsky speak last week? When the great man was asked about the chaos in public education, he responded quickly, decisively, and to the point: "Public education in this country is under

attack." The words, though chill-
ing, comforted me in a weird way. I'd
been feeling, the past few years of my
30-plus-year tenure in public education, that there was something or
somebody out there, a power of a sort,
that doesn't really want you kids to
be educated. I felt a force that wants

It represents exactly what I am opposed to, the perpetual and petty testing that has become a fungus on the foot of public education.

you ignorant and pliable, and that needs you able to fill in the boxes and follow
instructions. Now I'm sure.

It's not that I oppose rigorous testing. I don't. While you were reading and
writing away in the gymnasium, the seniors I always teach spent that morning in the village hall, reading and writing away at their Advanced Placement
English Literature and Composition Examination. I understand the purpose
of evaluation. A good test can measure achievement and even inspire. But this
English Language Arts Exam I so unknowingly inflicted on you does neither. It
represents exactly what I am opposed to, the perpetual and petty testing that
has become a fungus on the foot of public education. You will understand that
metaphor, I know, because we have spent the year learning to appreciate the differences between figurative and literal language. The test-makers have not.

So what should you do, my beautiful, my bright, my intelligent, my talented?
Continue. Continue to question. I applaud you, sample writer: When asked the
either or question, you began your response, "Honestly, I think it is both." You
were right, and you were brave, and the test you were taking was neither. And
I applaud you, wildest 8th grader of my own, who—when asked how a quote
applied to the two characters from the two passages provided—wrote, "I don't
think it applies to either one of them." Wear your zeroes proudly kids. This is a
test you need to fail.

I wondered whether giving more than 10 minutes of our every class period
to reading books of our own choosing was a good idea or not. But you loved it
so. You asked for more time. Ask again; I will give you whatever you need. I will
give you the best advice I can, advice I'm citing from a writer far more intelligent
and important than any you cited on this month's test. Do what Mr. Bradbury
said in his epigraph at the beginning of *Fahrenheit 451*: "When they give you lined
paper, write the other way."

It is the best I have to offer, beyond my apologies for having taken part in an
exercise that hurt you, and of which I am mightily ashamed. ✎

A Teacher Pushed to the Edge

SARAH KNOPP

Rigoberto Ruelas attended Miramonte Elementary as a student and returned to work there for 14 years, first as a teaching assistant, and then as a 5th-grade teacher. In 14 years, he almost never missed a day of work. But Sunday, Sept. 19, 2010, he called in sick for the next day.

His body was found a week later underneath a 100-foot-high bridge in the Angeles National Forest. Suicide is the likely cause of death, although no note was found.

Suicide rarely has a single cause and usually follows a long chain of complicated, though socially preventable, adversities. But in Ruelas' case, we know one adversity he was deeply distraught about: the Aug. 14, 2010 publication in the *Los Angeles Times* of an article called "Who's Teaching L.A.'s Kids?"

No one knows what part the article played in Ruelas' distress, but at the very least, it was a dark storm cloud over his last days.

Ruelas' brother Alejandro told KABC-TV that "he kept saying that there's stress at work" since the publication of the article. According to parents and some staff at Miramonte, the principal had been pressuring Ruelas intensely since the publication of the article to improve his students' scores. Ruelas' family is boycotting the *Los Angeles Times*.

Los Angeles Unified School District (LAUSD) officials claim they sent a memo to principals stating that the use of test score data for disciplining teachers is against the union contract, but there are reports that some principals are ignoring this.

"This guy was 100 percent teacher," said Mat Taylor, chairperson for the south area of United Teachers Los Angeles (UTLA), after spending time with the staff at Miramonte Elementary. "That's what his whole life was about. When this hit, it crushed him."

To write the article, *Times* reporters Jason Felch, Jason Song, and Doug Smith filed a public information request with the LAUSD to get test scores for the students of 6,000 3rd-, 4th- and 5th-grade teachers. LAUSD complied with the request, even though it had never before used or published student test data divided out by teacher.

Readers could click a link called "Find a Teacher" on the *Times* website and find out whether these 6,000 teachers are, according to the paper's analysis of student test data, "Most effective, more effective, average, less effective, or least effective."

Ruelas was rated "less effective," the second-to-worst category. But according to students, coworkers, and parents, nothing could have been further from the truth.

"For me, he was a good teacher," said Christian, a former student of Ruelas who is now attending high school in LAUSD. "My parents were shocked to hear this. A lot of parents had respect for him. He was always there, whether he was sick or not. He was always smiling. He was happy with the students, and friendly with the parents. He taught well. I liked being in his class."

The erosion of students' innate love of learning and self-confidence is the consequence of corporate values being imposed on human beings and their development.

Mayra Vega had stayed in touch with Ruelas since leaving the school six years ago. "He just told me two weeks ago that he was proud of me for applying to college," she said at a lunchtime meeting with classmates. "He would always help you, even if you weren't his student. He always made me feel good about myself, like when he told me to go ahead and wear my glasses at graduation. Thanks to him, I stopped confusing my '*b*'s and '*d*'s."

Vega immediately began trying to organize parents and fellow alums from Miramonte for a vigil or protest to defend Ruelas' reputation as a teacher.

According to Taylor, "He taught the toughest 5th graders. Those are the kids he wanted, even though they may be the ones who are the hardest to test."

Kristal O'Neil (not her real name), a teacher at a different elementary school who also suffered from being labeled "least effective," said of Ruelas' death: "I'm only surprised that this hasn't happened more. The issue here is that you have stripped people of their identities."

For more than 20 years, O'Neil has used her training in drama from the USC fine arts program to lead students in plays and historical dramatizations. She had a reputation among teachers and parents for succeeding with students who have special needs and creating a nurturing and inspiring learning environment in her classroom. She didn't "teach to the test."

But when the *Times* study was printed, O'Neil said she felt "like I was on public display, like a human being on the auction block or something."

O'Neil attended a protest at the *Los Angeles Times* with thousands of other union brothers and sisters, but in the end, she was so intimidated by what had happened that she remade her curriculum from whole cloth, focusing almost entirely on helping students to pass the test.

Whereas she had previously prided herself on her work with special-needs children, she now felt anxious that they would pull down her scores. "For 22 years, I couldn't wait to get up every day and go teach," she said. "I feel like someone came along and put me in prison."

The sleepless nights and crises that standardized tests impose on teachers—especially when the tests are framed, in the sensationalized manner of the *L.A.*

Times, as the only thing that matters—are only one part of the story.

Imagine kindergartners bubbling answer sheets just after they learn to hold pencils; high school students who complete all their graduation requirements but aren't able to pass the exit examination and graduate because they haven't received the remediation they need; or students being asked to take high-stakes tests in a language they haven't mastered yet.

The erosion of students' innate love of learning and self-confidence is the consequence of corporate values being imposed on human beings and their development.

Flawed Values

"Value added" is the latest catchphrase to take root among the "accountability" movement that encompasses Education Secretary Arne Duncan, billionaires Bill Gates and Eli Broad and their corporate think tanks, and the self-promoting operators of charter schools.

The "reformers" concede that it would be wrong to measure teachers by raw test scores alone because some students start so far behind. But, they say, "value-added" methods control for differences in student populations by measuring how many percentage points a student gains in a year—that is, by comparing this year's test to last's. The difference is the "value" that teachers have "added."

The problem is that there is no evidence that VAMs (value-added measures) are an effective way to rate teachers. In a briefing report issued on Aug. 29, 2010, the Economic Policy Institute surveyed current research on VAMs, concluding:

> One study found that across five large urban districts, among teachers who were ranked in the top 20 percent of effectiveness in the first year, fewer than a third were in that top group the next year, and another third moved all the way down to the bottom 40 percent. Another found that teachers' effectiveness ratings in one year could only predict from 4 percent to 16 percent of the variation in such ratings in the following year. A teacher who appears to be very ineffective in one year might have a dramatically different result the following year.

In a speech she gave to an audience of 700 UTLA members, education historian Diane Ravitch argued, "The problem with using value-added in any form is that, because it has a pseudo-scientific aura about it, and in this climate, it will dominate all other forms of evaluation."

According to the National Research Council of the National Academy of Sciences, "VAM estimates of teacher effectiveness should not be used to make operational decisions because such estimates are far too unstable to be considered fair or reliable."

Furthermore, researchers have found that the best predictor of 4th-grade test results was . . . 5th-grade teachers. In other words, we can do a better job of predicting a students test scores based on which teacher they will get next year in school than any other factor! Since children's 5th-grade teachers have nothing to do with their 4th-grade education, we can only assume that VAM is measuring something other than teacher quality.

A recent study by the National Center on Performance Incentives at Vanderbilt University researched merit pay based on students' test scores in Nashville. The study's conclusion was that merit pay didn't work.

Teachers were offered a $15,000 bonus to raise test scores of their students in math. The students whose teachers had been offered the bonus made the same gains as students whose teachers were in a control group that hadn't received the offer.

> O'Neil said she felt "like I was on public display, like a human being on the auction block or something."

This was significant because the National Center on Performance Incentives was generally understood to have a pro-accountability bent. But even supporters of merit pay couldn't prove that VAM methods were sound.

Teachers have an enormous public relations campaign ahead of us to make the truth clear: No credible research exists to back up the idea that students' test scores are a valid way to measure teachers' effectiveness.

Since the onset of No Child Left Behind, we have lost enormous ground on the argument that high-stakes standardized tests are illegitimate measures of children's progress in the first place. Rather than measuring learning, these tests measure students' socio-economic and racial backgrounds, much like the eugenicist IQ tests of the past.

To regain the integrity of learning and development, and to fight for the dignity of the work of teaching, we will have to campaign around these ideas.

Fighting Back Against Legislating VAMs

Two weeks after the *Times* article "Who's Teaching L.A.'s Kids?" appeared, the Los Angeles School Board met and voted—with just one dissent from board member Marguerite LaMotte—to accept a proposal from the newly installed Deputy Superintendent John Deasy for value-added measures on tests to account for 30 percent of teachers' evaluations. This is subject to collective bargaining with the teachers' union.

Other districts have enacted worse. In Florida and Denver, value-added may account for up to 50 percent of evaluations.

Following the LAUSD board meeting, the California state Board of Education voted on Sept. 16, 2010, to create an online database to track teachers by student test scores. The resolution was put forward by Ben Austin, whose career in the Clinton White House led him to Green Dot charter schools, where he led the takeover of Locke High School and launched the "Astroturf" group Parent Revolution. He is the author and salesman for many of the privatization and teacher-union-bashing schemes in Los Angeles.

And to add insult to injury, the Obama administration offered $442 million in grants to school districts that enacted merit pay schemes for teachers, based on their students' test scores.

The announcement was made in late September, the day before the public release of the Vanderbilt study critiquing the validity of merit pay based on student test scores. But as Ravitch noted, "Ideology trumps evidence." The irony of those riding the warhorse of "data" and having no data to back up their policy prescriptions would be funny if it didn't ruin so many lives.

UTLA held a protest at the offices of the *Los Angeles Times* Sept. 14, 2010, that was attended by several thousand teachers. With the announcements of Ruelas' death, the union is demanding that the *Times* take down the web link that rates individual teachers by name.

On Sept. 29, 2010, a public mass overflowed a South Central church and the front lawn of Miramonte Elementary. Hundreds of students, teachers, and parents came to pay their respects.

We need to channel anger over Ruelas' death into a willingness to resist the school board's effort to impose value-added measures as the most prominent component of teacher evaluations at the bargaining table. "Rigo's family wants his death to be for something," said Taylor. The process of learning and human development cannot be assigned a number value, and the people engaged in this process need to resist an attempt to commodify us. ✎

Originally published on October 1, 2010, at www.socialistworker.org.
Reprinted with permission.

Playing Smart

*Curricular activism and resisting
the script of high-stakes testing*

WAYNE AU

I became a teacher to change the world. I saw in teaching the opportunity to reach the toughest students, a way to tackle the enduring effects of poverty, racism, and other forms of oppression that continue to wrack so many of our communities.

In teaching I saw a powerful profession, in which I could develop meaningful relationships with people instead of just being another alienated automaton. To me, teaching was work that would allow me to resist the rampant injustice I saw in the world and to avoid becoming just another cog in the machine. I still see teaching this way, and this vision continues to guide me as a teacher of teachers at the university level today.

I worry about the teachers, future and present, in my education courses. Most of them are young, in their mid-20s to early 30s, and while most are working on their credentials, I also have many who are already classroom teachers returning to get their master's degrees. No Child Left Behind and its draconian test regime started 10 years ago, and in many states the testing juggernaut was already well underway.

My university students took high-stakes tests through elementary, middle, and high school. Most took high-stakes tests to get into college. They take tests to become credentialed teachers. Almost always good test takers by the time I see them, my students are members of the tested generation.

I worry about the toll that these high-stakes, standardized tests have taken on the educational consciousness of my students. The cumulative effect on their commonsense understanding of education and teaching is profound: Even if my students do question the tests and see the detrimental effects of high-stakes testing on teaching and learning, they often have a hard time envisioning classrooms that could be or should be any different. Their horizons are limited because they have mainly known and experienced high-stakes testing in their educational lives.

The conspiracy theorist in me thinks that maybe this was the intention of the test-pushers. Get one generation as the "tested generation," and we'll have a bunch of educators who cannot effectively imagine an alternative.

> **Even if my students do question the tests and see the detrimental effects of high-stakes testing on teaching and learning, they often have a hard time envisioning classrooms that could be or should be any different.**

Being handed such scripted curricula and pacing guides by the district, and then being told to teach to the tests, strikes deep at the heart of teachers and teaching.

Unfortunately, due to a combination of their own constrained vision and current educational policy, in most cases my students have this testing-is-the-only-option pedagogy reinforced when they get into classrooms. Whether they are student teachers or classroom veterans, the refrain they hear from district, state, and federal officials has been maddeningly consistent these last years: more standards, more tests, more pacing guides, more scripted instruction, more administrative threats, and more students in the classes they teach—all with fewer resources, fewer rights, and fewer protections.

Playing Dumb to Fit the Script

The current state of teaching under high-stakes testing is obvious. In my own research, as well as the research of countless others, the findings support what many classroom teachers know from their day-to-day experiences: Regimes of high-stakes testing are pressuring teachers to change both their curriculum and teaching to match whatever is on the tests.

The control of teaching by test-based accountability schemes is perhaps best illustrated through the rise of scripted reading curricula. Under such programs, administrators mandate teachers use prepackaged curricular materials that require no creative input or decision-making on the part of the teachers. Teachers in many low-performing schools and districts have been required by school leaders to use commercially packaged reading instruction programs, such as Open Court, which tell teachers exactly what page to be on each day as well as every word and line they are allowed to say while teaching reading, all in preparation for the high-stakes testing.

We can see the stringent language of such scripted curricula by looking at the *Houghton Mifflin Reading: A Legacy of Literacy*, California Teacher's Edition textbook for grade 1 as an example. The script starts from the beginning, where in the introduction Houghton Mifflin directs teachers to:

> Read aloud the first page and stop before the last paragraph. Say: *Your state is California. California has set standards for me and you to help you learn this year. Let's learn more about these standards.* Now read the last paragraph ... These pages give examples of standards...Explain that, for each story, the standards tell children what they are learning.

> Say: *When you come into school, you don't get to your classroom all of a sudden. You walk there, one step at a time. Standards are the same way. You don't have to know them all at once. You'll learn them as you go.*

From the start, not only does the Houghton Mifflin text take teachers on a scripted journey through literacy in-struction, but it also embeds an ideo-logical justification of such scripts as part of standards-based instruction.

The scripted direction continues throughout the text. In another section on phonics, Houghton Mifflin similar-ly directs teachers to:

> "There's no actual teaching required. It's like instant curriculum. You just add water."

- Say *cat*. Ask: *What sound do you hear at the beginning of cat? What letter should I write in the first box?* Write *c*.

- Ask: *What sound do you hear next in cat?* Call on a child to come to the board and write *a* in the second box.

- Ask: *What sound do you hear at the end of cat? What letter should I write in the last box?* Write *t*.

The textbook teems with similar examples of both highly scripted instruction and page-by-page directions for what each teacher must cover in what order and on what day.

Although it is true that teachers can and do resist this kind of scripting, some-times under threat of losing their jobs, this example illustrates the assumed peda-gogic incompetence of teachers today, who are considered by policymakers, ad-ministrators, and textbook manufacturers to be so unskilled and inept that they need to parrot the prewritten curriculum in order to be effective.

Such scripted curriculum programs have not just been relegated to read-ing and language arts instruction either. Julie Cwikla's research describes a case where administrators mandated the implementation of a scripted direct instruc-tion (SDI) mathematics program with the specific goals of raising test scores and providing easy evaluation of teaching. The script for this mathematics program was so rigid that, Cwikla explains, "If a student had a question, the SDI instructed teachers to repeat the script just previously read."

Being handed such scripted curricula and pacing guides by the district, and then being told to teach to the tests, strikes deep at the heart of teachers and teaching. It stifles creativity and dynamism. It disregards professional, content-area expertise and knowledge of students, communities, and cultures. It muffles the voices of teachers and students. It tells teachers not to think about their teach-ing: High-stakes test-based scripted curricula and teaching ask teachers to play dumb. As one math teacher summed up in class one evening, "There's no actual teaching required. It's like instant curriculum. You just add water."

And here lies a central contradiction within a teaching profession shaped by high-stakes standardized tests. Teachers are being held more and more "account-able" for test scores and student achievement while they are being required to take less and less responsibility for their curriculum, pedagogy, and what actually happens in their classrooms. Be tested, teach to the tests, give the tests, live and die by the tests. The powers that be will hold you accountable for teaching a lesson plan that wasn't yours to begin with, and if you break from the script, then you have failed your students and will be disciplined appropriately. It is a system that encourages teachers' submission instead of engagement, and pedagogic alienation instead of responsibility and connection to what happens in classrooms.

In this regard, policymakers' agenda for teachers is transparent. They simultaneously take authority and judgment away from teachers, while structuring teacher pay schemes and pedagogies to hold people accountable for implementing plans (formerly called teaching) over which teachers had no say in the first place. Teachers thus bear huge amounts of responsibility for student test scores, but they aren't being allowed to take responsibility for their teaching. Instead of treating teachers as professional, thinking agents of learning and change, our education policy assumes that teachers are incompetent and unqualified to engage children in learning about the world.

Playing Smart to Resist the Script

The high-stakes educational accountability movement in the United States may be forcing massive reshaping of teaching, but all is not lost. The bipartisan coalition that backed No Child Left Behind has functionally collapsed, and popular resistance to high-stakes testing continues to build among parents and teachers alike.

Research has lent credence to this discontent: For instance, a recent study by the National Academy of Sciences looked at 10 years of data and concluded that high-stakes testing has utterly failed at increasing achievement anywhere close to the levels of other high-performing nations. Further, as chronicled in the pages of *Rethinking Schools* (see "Neither Fair Nor Accurate," January 2011), we know that research finds high-stakes tests are ineffective at accurately measuring both teaching and learning.

We also know better. We know that teachers are not mindless robots programmed simply to perform the next pedagogical task on the educational assembly line. We know that, despite wrongheaded policies that push teachers in the wrong direction, teachers can take creative control of their curricular lives—and they do so in powerful ways.

For instance, for more than 10 years, Teachers 4 Social Justice (T4SJ) in San Francisco—made up mostly of K-12 public school teachers—has run a fantastic, one-day conference that now draws more than 1,000 participants locally and nationwide. It is a place where educators, students, and activists build connections, strategize for organizing, and share curriculum that is rooted in a politics of social justice and student engagement. Similar conferences and social justice curriculum fairs have since sprung up in Chicago, the Pacific Northwest, and most recently in Boston, among other cities.

The Educators Network for Social Justice (ENSJ) also provides another example. Not only do they organize an annual anti-racist/anti-bias teaching conference, but they also played a key role in shaping the textbook policy for Milwaukee Public Schools. Working with other community groups, lobbying school board members, and participating in a letter-writing campaign, the ENSJ helped halt the school district's adoption of K-8 social studies textbooks that suffered from serious shortcomings in terms of race and multiculturalism; the group subsequently got involved in the negotiation process that decided which K-8 social studies texts the district purchased.

Despite high-stakes test-based policies that squelch creativity and increase alienation from teaching, teachers want to be active participants in their own pedagogy.

What these gatherings and examples of educational organizing show is that teachers do care about what they are teaching. Despite high-stakes test-based policies that squelch creativity and increase alienation from teaching, teachers want to be active participants in their own pedagogy. They want to be engaged in the development of curriculum that is meaningful and important. Instead of playing dumb to fit the test-induced scripts, these teachers would rather "play smart" in their curriculum and instruction by engaging students in learning, paying attention to students' communities and cultures, and teach in ways that encouraging students to take up pressing social and ecological issues.

I originally became a K-12 teacher to work for a more socially just world. I thought it was important to play smart with my curriculum and my students—so we all could be actively and intellectually involved. As I work with preservice and inservice teachers today, I carry the same goals with me. I want the teachers in my classroom and the untold numbers of students who will pass through their classrooms to play smart, to see themselves as curriculum activists, and to use education to call the world into question. Given the potential created by powerful curriculum, it is no wonder policy makers encourage just the opposite. ✎

Support That Can't Support

One teacher's induction program experience

ELAINE ENGEL KESWICK

It is a cloudy Wednesday afternoon in January, and I am at a critical juncture in my teaching. As a first-year teacher, trying to hold on to my passion and initiative, my developing professional compass is spinning.

Our weekly staff meeting is coming to an end. The members of my 4th-grade cohort—all teachers on temporary assignment—stay seated at our table to finish a discussion with the principal. The day before, our principal met with us during lunch to ask if we would pilot a reading "regroup" project. Our assignment is to look at each student's level for a specific reading standard and create homogeneous skill groups across the whole grade level. To accommodate teaching these new groups, we need to find time for an additional 30 minutes of instruction in our already test-driven academic day. Our principal makes it very clear that this reading time comes in addition to the guided reading groups we already facilitate in our classrooms.

As my principal approaches the three of us, the inevitable result of the conversation is already sitting in the bottom of my stomach. Due to top-down pressure to improve test scores, the students in our school are increasingly looked at as data producers, rather than multidimensional human beings. If it is not tested, it is usually not taught. The untested subjects (social studies, science, art, music, physical education) always get the short end of the stick.

Today is no exception. Our principal proposes we use our social studies and science time for the extra reading block, arguing that our most struggling readers can't read the information from these two subjects' textbooks. Even though I expected this, it is not easy to hear. The argument makes no sense. Questions fill my mind, and disgust grabs my chest. Isn't there a different way we could build reading skills without eliminating subjects that engage students and evoke critical thinking?

On that Wednesday, I desperately need to discuss the events of the day with an experienced teacher. In fact, I am part of an induction program, Beginning Teacher Support and Assessment (BTSA)—a California state program that is meant to offer support to new teachers as they exit the credential program and begin a job in a district. But I wonder what type of support my induction program will offer. Will the induction program foster my passion, initiative, and growth as a reflective professional educator? Or will the induction program be one more agent to promote the present testing agenda?

Induction Programs in Theory

More than 80 percent of new teachers across the United States participate in some kind of induction program. At least 30 states have a required mentoring program, and the idea of having structured induction programs for new teachers is only becoming more popular. The degree of structure within the programs varies. Some are highly structured, whereas others are merely loose partnerships between mentor teachers and beginning teachers.

In my experience, our well-intentioned teacher-to-teacher induction program favors data analysis for testing progress, rather than the development of well-rounded professional educators.

Structuring an induction program for optimal support is critical. However, of equal (if not more) importance is looking at the pedagogical practices and theories illuminated within the induction programs. In my experience, our well-intentioned teacher-to-teacher induction program favors data analysis for testing progress, rather than the development of well-rounded professional educators.

BTSA is the pathway for beginning teachers to change a preliminary credential (issued as a result of successfully completing a credential program) into a clear (permanent) credential. The two-year BTSA program uses the Formative Assessment for California Teachers (FACT) system. This system requires monthly meetings and the completion of four modules each year. New teachers identify, within their classroom teaching, their areas of strength and areas where they require improvement. Through the four modules, the induction teachers focus on their weaker areas in the hopes of making progress. The modules focus on different skills and standards for the teaching profession.

An important component of BTSA is pairing each new teacher with a support provider. This guiding teacher is supposed to observe the induction teacher in the classroom periodically, offering assistance and advice. Unfortunately, my BTSA support provider is an assistant principal at a different school. I know better than to ask her questions that challenge the administration or the program itself, given the vulnerability of not only my job but also the jobs of my partner teachers. Ironically, having this mentor makes me feel more isolated than ever.

A flier for the BTSA induction program states the overarching purpose: "The goal of BTSA Induction is to support participating teachers in the process of being a reflective practitioner." This sounds positive and powerful. In today's education system, we need teachers who are well versed in reflection, who challenge themselves to reconsider their pedagogical practices to the benefit of their students' learning.

However, at least in my district, in the implementation of the induction program, the focus on reflection and professional learning can get tangled up with the strings attached to high-stakes testing. As a result, the same one-dimensional educational ideas are being passed on to the district's beginning teachers. These ideas exist within the narrow confines of the testing agenda and leave little time to reflect on the multiple aspects of teaching. My experience with the focus module of the induction program—the inquiry project—reveals this disheartening reality.

The Limited Inquiry Project

At the January BTSA meeting, shortly after we are assigned the regroup project, we inductees are introduced to Module C, our third BTSA module of the year, which is an inquiry project. I listen as a program director begins to explain the project: "A teacher inquiry, or teacher research, is when teachers explore their teaching. You examine a specific area of your teaching by asking a question and then planning specific teaching practices to examine the question, gaining further insight into the area you wanted to explore," she states.

This reminds me of my credential program. We discussed and participated in teacher inquiry. I am actually a bit excited to embark on an inquiry now that I have a classroom of my own. My mind wanders through the many questions I have had this year about the diverse needs of my energetic class of 33. I wonder how I can motivate Shane to be a positive, collaborative team member instead of a student who mumbles negative comments about every assignment and every student. I wonder how I can get Jackson to believe in himself, in spite of his low self-esteem and anger at having both his parents in jail. I wonder how I can get some of my students who come into class with an attitude of white superiority—having grown up in a privileged, predominantly white neighborhood—to become interested in learning about the history of our state from the perspective of other cultures.

I catch my wandering mind just as the woman begins to talk specifically about the inquiry question itself. "You need to make the question specific. Remember, it needs to be based on a content standard. You want to see how many more students you can move to proficiency by the end of your inquiry." I think I mishear her. I look up at the screen to see a projection of one of the module's required pages. The page has four columns. The headings are "far below basic," "below basic," "basic," and "proficient/advanced." She say, "This is where you record your data after the pretest." She flips to an identical page with a different title. "And this is where you record the data after your summative assessment. You can see how well you did, how much the students learned." I am stunned. What about all of the questions I have that don't fit the narrow limits of this inquiry? I don't know whether to laugh or cry at my naïveté about the purpose of this inquiry.

The regroup my principal requested we implement fits the requirements of the inquiry perfectly; it is based on an academic content standard, and it is focused on moving more students to proficiency. It has become clear that we don't, in reality, have a choice about our inquiry.

It is painful plowing through the tremendous amount of work necessary to complete the module when I do not believe in my project. By the time I finish my inquiry project, I have produced a 45-page document and a trifold presentation board. In fact, what I learn from my project is that if I add even more reading time to a child's day, focus that reading on a specific standard, and use sentence stems from the test to teach the kids, then students will probably get one or two more questions correct. Is this the kind of reflection my induction program is seeking?

Although the induction program speaks about promoting reflection, this "reflection" is totally linked to the analysis of data from standards-based assessments. Analysis of data does not help me to reflect on the classroom practices I genuinely want to explore.

> **What I learn from my project is that if I add even more reading time to a child's day, focus that reading on a specific standard, and use sentence stems from the test to teach the kids, then students will probably get one or two more questions correct.**

Looking to the Future

Today I write as a recent graduate of the BTSA induction program. I am happy to say I have jumped through all of the hoops and run the obstacle course. What am I left with? A 4-inch-thick binder, filled with pages of work—and a clear credential. Although accomplishing the latter is an important step for me, I lost critical time and energy in navigating the roads that led to my piece of paper, my credential.

Did I grow as a reflective educator as a result of the induction program? No. I have developed a perspective as an educator due to my own efforts to hold on to my passion and initiative, despite the induction program. I have sought out teachers who offer the perspective I need to hear in conversation and to see in action within the four walls of a classroom.

I have a lot of respect for the directors and support providers, all of whom invest much time and energy into the induction program, but I think the implementation of the induction program's goal needs to be altered.

The beginning teachers with whom I have traveled on this road are in the formative years of their careers, just as their students are in the formative years of their lives. A child only gets one chance at each grade. A score on a test lacks importance when compared with the path a student will walk for a lifetime. The same holds true for beginning teachers. We only get one chance at our first two years of teaching. The induction program ought to alleviate some of the pressure and offer opportunities for new teachers to reflect beyond data-driven instructional strategies. As new teachers, we need support to develop the other essential aspects of teaching, such as creating a positive classroom community, developing a perspective as a professional educator, and maintaining motivation within the classroom (for the students and teacher alike). As beginning teachers, we will one day be the foundation of our education system, teaching the children who will become the future of our nation. 🖎

Coming Soon to Your Favorite Credential Program: National Exit Exams

ANN BERLAK

In an Oct. 22, 2009 speech to teacher educators at Columbia University's Teachers College, Secretary of Education Arne Duncan proclaimed that revolutionary change in the education of teachers is essential if we are to solve the problems facing U.S. society and U.S. schools. Toward the end of his speech, he declared that a standardized performance-based system for assessing teachers was key to bringing about this change.

Punctuating his speech with military and corporate metaphors, Duncan declared that the supreme purpose of public schooling is to keep America competitive, and that the decline in our standing in the world order can be attributed to the fact that the institutions that prepare teachers "are doing a mediocre job." Duncan's conclusion: "Teacher preparation programs need revolutionary change, not evolutionary tinkering."

Duncan's plan to reform teacher education takes as a given the need for corporate, top-down management, a view he shares with virtually every major corporate think tank, the Heritage Foundation; the Business Roundtable; and the Broad, Gates, and Walton Family foundations. According to Duncan, the "core mission" of teacher education programs is to bring about "substantial increases in student achievement." He proposes to accomplish this by requiring credential candidates to pass a "performance-based" standardized exit exam that will measure both their competence to teach and the quality of their credential program (just as pupils' scores on standardized tests are said to measure the quality of their teachers and schools). Teacher credential programs whose candidates score well on the exam would be rewarded, while those that do not would be subject to punitive sanctions. Part of the $4.3 billion in Race to the Top funds would provide resources and incentives to construct and promote these assessments.

Near the end of his Teachers College speech, he named the particular exam he had in mind—PACT (Performance Assessment for California Teachers). Few listening to Duncan's speech had heard of PACT, but it has been a fixture in California for several years, and many teacher educators and teacher credential candidates in California are, unfortunately, quite familiar with it. This article was written in the hope that the rest of the nation might learn from and not replicate our experience.

The Lesser of Two Evils?

In 1998 the California legislature passed a law requiring teacher credential candidates to pass a state-approved high-stakes exit exam. Many credential programs in California, including San Francisco State University (where I teach in the College of Education), chose PACT, devised by members of the education faculties at Stanford University, the University of California-Berkeley, and several other institutions. The alternative to PACT was CalTPA, a system designed by the state in consultation with the Educational Testing Service. Our College of Education elected to use PACT because it purported to be qualitative, not quantitative, and to assess "authentic" teaching performance in "real-world" contexts.

If we know anything for certain about the effects of standardized testing, it's that what's not tested is unlikely to be taught.

PACT's creators and chief advocates claim PACT provides the crucial link in the chain of evidence connecting the classroom performance of individuals at the end of their credential programs to achievement of their pupils in their first year of teaching, as measured by standardized tests.[1] In academic lingo this is called "predictive validity." The assumption, then, is that PACT will identify how well various credential programs promote teaching practices and learning outcomes valued by federal and state authorities.

Like all other states, California already had an elaborate set of state-mandated entrance and exit assessments for teacher education programs. In California this included the CBEST (a test of basic literacy), CSET (a standardized test of content knowledge), RICA (a test of knowledge about teaching reading), student teaching supervision, and GPA requirements. Our programs were also assessed by an increasingly prescriptive NCATE, the national accrediting body that imposes an entirely separate and largely redundant assessment system. PACT adds another layer to what is already a complex system of assessment. Each additional test throws up yet another hurdle to becoming a teacher—hurdles that disproportionately affect people of color and those for whom English is not their first language.

How Does PACT Work?

PACT assesses two types of performance: the Teaching Event (TE) and embedded signature assignments. The signature assignments are course assignments that faculty are required to implement and score according to PACT-designated and state-approved criteria, a clear intrusion into institutions' and faculty members' prerogative to set their own criteria for assessing students.

I will focus on the TE, a 15-minute videotaped lesson taught by a candidate during the final semester of student teaching that must be accompanied by a portfolio of approximately 50 pages of teaching plans, teaching artifacts, student work samples, written reflections, and commentaries related to the TE. The guidelines and the more than 50 prompts specifying the elements of the portfolio are laid out in detail in a student handbook. Students enter the TE data (including the video recording) into a computer program. To say that the preparation for the Teaching Event consumes an inordinate amount of time and psychic energy is a serious understatement.

Scorers, trained by official state PACT trainers in two daylong sessions and then "calibrated" annually to assure scorer consistency, assess the TE video and accompanying documentation using a series of standardized rubrics. After the rubric scores for the signature assignments and the TE are submitted, a computer program transforms them into numbers that purport to represent the effectiveness of individual credential candidates, and these are forwarded to the state. Thus, in the end, this is a quantitative, not a qualitative, assessment. If the submitted numbers are at or above the cut score, the candidates will have fulfilled the PACT criteria for earning a credential.

The scorers are anonymous and must not know the candidates they are scoring. Though the scorers may be faculty members, there is no requirement that they have any particular background in teaching or expertise in the area they are assessing. (Any trained and calibrated person is qualified for the job.) Since remuneration is a central motive for engaging in the tedious, highly regulated scoring task, and scorers are paid per head, they have an incentive to score as rapidly as possible.

Education faculty members are not considered qualified to do PACT assessments unless they have been approved by PACT trainers. One professor at a state university in Southern California, who is recognized as a national and international expert in second language acquisition, was appalled by the notion that, after only two days of training, a calibrated scorer's judgments about candidates' competency to teach English language learners was considered more valid than hers. She told me that, with her 30 years of teaching and research in this discipline, she resented being calibrated to rate candidates on a questionable rubric alongside scorers who may have no knowledge or experience teaching English language learners. "PACT is a death knell for the longstanding respect for academic scholarship and expertise," she wrote.

A faculty member at another California state university wrote:

> Our faculty do not want to be involved in scoring the PACT teaching events, as it is very time consuming and tedious. We may be moving to a process that is almost exclusively scored by persons who know little about and who do not teach in our program. This is very troubling. I see institutions "farming out" the assessment of PACT to regional centers to cut costs and to score the huge numbers of

events that will need to be scored. In short, PACT seems to violate everything we know about designing assessment. What kind of assessment have we created that faculty who teach in the program do not want to score?

Many credential candidates themselves argue that the video-recorded Teaching Event is artificial and contrived, and does not represent their real teaching.

Does PACT Assess Good Teaching?

The PACT brochure proclaims: "A candidate who passes this assessment has shown he or she is a better prepared teacher who can help students succeed." What do the PACT authors mean by "succeed" and by "better prepared"? Better prepared than whom, and for what?

In his Teachers College address, Duncan proposed to "reward states that publicly report and link student achievement data to the institutions and programs where teachers and principals were credentialed," and advocated "longitudinal data systems that enable states to track and compare the impact of new teachers from teacher preparation programs on student achievement over a period of years." Since the student achievement data and longitudinal data systems Duncan refers to are inconceivable apart from students' standardized test scores, good teachers apparently are those whose students score well on standardized tests.

The rubrics or criteria used to assign PACT scores are based on state standards and are supposed to identify elements of teaching that scientific research has shown enable students to reach these standards. Teaching patterns valued by PACT are primarily aspects of explicit, systematic, direct instruction that will instill in students knowledge specified by the state-mandated standards and measured by standardized tests. PACT cannot and does not aspire to assess teachers' perseverance or their ability to think on their feet, hear and respond to feedback, learn from experience, listen to students, or promote student self-confidence and critical thinking.

Each rubric is intended to represent one aspect of a concise checklist designed to assess a component of teaching (e.g., instruction, planning, assessment). To achieve test-scoring consistency PACT assessors are trained (calibrated) to make similar if not identical inferences from their observations as the basis for assigning scores on each of the rubrics. Thus, those who construct the rubrics and train the calibrators hold the power to determine how good teaching is defined and identified.

Many of the attributes tested by the rubrics are important components of good teaching. However, if we know anything for certain about the effects of standardized testing, it's that what's not tested is unlikely to be taught. So what is not assessed by PACT? PACT does not assess most of the qualities that Duncan himself, in his Teachers College speech, lists as attributes of great teachers—namely, the ability to "literally change the course of a student's life ... light a lifelong curiosity, promote a desire to participate in a democracy, instill a thirst for knowledge, reduce inequality, and fight daily for social justice."

What's more, no one who has been specifically prohibited from interacting with a candidate personally can, on the basis of observing a videotaped 15-minute teaching segment and reading supporting evidence, identify with any certainty many of the teaching attributes most of us value highly. Nor can assessors acknowledge teaching attributes and actions they might deem as valuable but have been "calibrated" to ignore.

There's also the obvious question of whether a videotape of a small segment of instruction can actually capture authentic teaching. ("Not to mention," a teacher educator writes, "that the quality of the videos is often poor, unless we spend hours training students' video skills.") Many credential candidates themselves argue that the video-recorded Teaching Event is artificial and contrived, and does not represent their real teaching. Several reported that during the TE they were preoccupied with keeping in mind all the rubrics the assessor would be bringing to bear on the 15-minute performance, and with whether the camera was picking up their students' voices. Many credential candidates elected to plan the simplest and most technically unchallenging lessons they could think of. One reported to a faculty member that he was encouraged to teach his PACT lesson for practice the day before the videotaping.

Because of PACT timeline logistics, students usually complete lesson plans for the TE weeks before they teach it, thus discouraging contingent and learner-centered instruction. One student told me:

> I spent about 15 hours writing about the lesson I was going to videotape, citing resources, spouting theory, explaining my best practices. Then the first stormy day of the year threw everything off track. It started hailing, the kids ran to the windows as branches came crashing down and garbage whipped the windows. I had never planned so hard for a lesson in all my life, and I had never had one go that badly. It went badly because, no matter how much you plan, a lot of teaching happens in the moment. A huge part of teaching, especially for beginning teachers, is finding that feeling in your gut that says "Step in now!" or "Sudden change of plans!"

PACT's Effect on Teacher Education

Because PACT is an unfunded mandate, credentialing institutions have to pay for the video equipment and the costs of administering and scoring the assessments. Our institution did so, in part, by reducing student teacher supervision. (In his Teachers College speech, Duncan actually claimed that America's taxpayers already "generously support" teacher preparation programs, but this is certainly not true of ours.) Because supervision has been reduced, and students receive no feedback from PACT assessments unless they do not pass, the PACT regimen severely limits candidates' opportunities to engage in the reflective dialogue with experienced practitioners about their teaching that is central to learning to teach.

Most of the credential candidates' responses to PACT cited on the official PACT website are positive. However, almost all of the students at San Francisco State and at least four other California state universities found PACT a serious and significant distraction from their coursework and student teaching, as it created unnecessary anxiety and exhaustion as they tried to satisfy the requirements of what they perceived as repetitive, bureaucratized tasks. The first half of student teaching in the final semester has come to focus on preparing for the Teaching Event, to the consternation of many student teaching supervisors, master teachers, and the candidates themselves. Some students were absent from student teaching in order to complete the PACT documentation. One student told me, "I wasn't really able to take student teaching seriously until I'd completed the Teaching Event."

> **Like the frog in slowly heating water that offers no resistance and eventually is boiled, it wasn't until our department had been subjected to PACT for several years that our faculty began to recognize the effect it was having on our program and morale.**

Many students engaged in what has been called "bureaucratic ventriloquism: an inauthentic response so markedly detached from the individual's own beliefs, that the utterances themselves appear to be projected from elsewhere."[2] One talented candidate felt that "the teaching for PACT wasn't coming from me." A systematic interview study of responses from credential candidates at the University of California-Davis[3] confirmed my experience that the vast majority of credential candidates had overwhelmingly negative feelings about PACT, citing excessive writing demands, the stress of assembling portfolios while student teaching, and the toll it took on their health and personal relationships. They found PACT minimally helpful regarding classroom management and instructional strategies.

At our school, preparing students for the TE has become the focus of student teaching seminars that had formerly been devoted to examining the interface of theory and practice. Lisa, who graduated in December, reported:

> We sacrificed 90 percent of our third semester practicum class working on PACT, when we could have been discussing how to handle situations we were facing in student teaching. We sacrificed a lot to prove to the legislators in California, and everyone they answer to, that we were ready to teach. And of course PACT didn't prove that at all.

Like the frog in slowly heating water that offers no resistance and eventually is boiled, it wasn't until our department had been subjected to PACT for several years that our faculty began to recognize the effect it was having on our program and morale. We were more stressed and were working harder than ever before, not out of internal motivation, but because of the requirements PACT thrust upon us. In exchange, PACT added no information that could help us improve our credential programs, but instead diverted time and resources from programmatic commitments to prepare teachers to educate the "whole" student, promote democratic citizenship, and reduce the opportunity gap. It resulted in curriculum changes that had no justification beyond adapting to the exigencies of PACT, which was as demoralizing and disempowering to many faculty members as standardized testing has been to K-12 teachers.

Technical and logistical issues about PACT came to dominate our faculty meetings and substantive discussions, such as those about how we as a faculty should respond to the increasing focus on high-stakes testing in the schools, have virtually disappeared. One author of PACT was quoted on the official PACT website as follows: "[PACT provides a great] opportunity to talk with other faculty about expectations for candidates and what we value. A real treat to engage with faculty over substance." Perhaps prior to PACT there had been no such discussions in this author's department. But before PACT, our faculty did have discussions about issues of substance on a regular basis.

A student who graduated in December wrote:

> I tried not to let myself question PACT's usefulness while going through it because it would just make me angry and, no matter what, I would still have to do it. It was easier to just put the question of PACT's usefulness out of my mind and write, and write, and write.... PACT was just another hoop I had to jump through in order to get my teaching credential. Viewed in the most positive light: Jumping through hoops is a useful life skill, especially if I plan on working for the state for the next 35 years.

Evidently Duncan's ideal is that every certification program in the nation should conclude with a PACT-like assessment. If it comes to this, other certification programs will have to make accommodations similar to the ones we made.

The quality of teacher education programs certainly varies, and most teacher educators are well aware of the need for continuing improvement. However, imposing PACT, a system with no record of success, will surely have the same withering effects upon teacher education that high-stakes standardized testing has had on K-12 teaching.

If Duncan has his way, there will soon be no "old-timers" who can remember when teachers and teacher educators were respected as competent professionals whose role was to promote curricula and pedagogies that are relevant to time and place, and to contribute to the construction of a more just and joyful world. Perhaps as the consequences of the "accountability movement" in teacher education become even more onerous, active resistance among teacher educators will grow. We cannot, however, go it alone. We need the help of K-12 teachers and university teachers across the disciplines, and popular support as well. ❧

Endnotes

1. Raymond l. Pecheone and Ruth R. Chung, "Evidence in Teacher Education: The Performance Assessment for California Teachers (PACT)," *Journal of Teacher Education* 57.1 (2006), 22-36.

2. Peter Rennert-Ariev, "The Hidden Curriculum of Performance-Based Teacher Education," *Teachers College Record* 110.1 (2008), 105–38.

3. Irina Okhremtchouk et al., "Voices of Pre-Service Teachers: Perspectives on the Performance Assessment for California Teachers (PACT)," *Issues in Teacher Education* 28.1 (2009), 39-62.

Responses to 'Coming Soon to Your Favorite Credential Program'

Dear Editors,

I am writing in response to Ann Berlak's piece, "Coming Soon to Your Favorite Credential Program: National Exit Exams."

Berlak is angry about testing, and particularly angry about the Performance Assessment for California Teachers (PACT), which she sees as a "clear intrusion into institutions' and faculty members' prerogative to set their own criteria for assessing students" in programs of teacher preparation. Berlak makes a number of important arguments about the dangers of standardized assessment—the narrowing of the curriculum, the reduction of the immense complexity of teaching and learning to those dimensions that can most readily be measured—and other nontrivial concerns. And if you are one of the dwindling number of Americans who are happy with the way we currently prepare teachers to engage the challenges of contemporary public school classrooms...well, you can probably agree with Berlak and needn't read on.

But I am not happy with how we prepare teachers. I say this as a well-scarred veteran, like Berlak, of several decades of work as a teacher educator. I love the work and hold a deep respect for the people who do it. My dissatisfaction is not personal; it's systemic. It derives from our collective inability to respond to issues we know a good deal about, because we have been (not) dealing with them for decades. For readers who are skeptical about this assertion, I recommend the decades-long succession of reports on the "state of teacher education" from Conant (1963); Sarason (1962); Goodlad, Soder, and Sirotnik (1990); or, most recently, Levine (2006). Each of these describes the general state of practice in the field as one of incoherence—with respect to the substance and relevance of coursework, the connections between courses in a "program," and most significantly, the connections between teacher education courses and what goes on in public school classrooms. The collective inability of the field to resolve these issues is the foundation of my disagreement with Berlak's position on PACT.

One of the conditions that has allowed so much stasis in the field is the fact that teacher education programs have historically functioned in the absence of any rigorous measure of their effectiveness. Faculty may individually evaluate what candidates learn in their courses, but this information typically remains within the "silos" of those courses and is seldom shared, much less used to shape and coordinate decisions at a program level. Most teacher preparation programs also conduct some kind of survey of candidate or employer satisfaction—however, these data offer little by way of concrete and specific feedback about what graduates can or cannot do in the classroom. PACT is designed to provide a measure of what preservice teachers actually can do with the students they are teaching in the public schools. While PACT is not a perfect measure, it is an assessment process designed, like its NBTC forebear, by people who do the work of teaching and teacher education. Far from something foisted upon California's teacher educators, PACT was created through the largely unpaid initiative of a consortium of California teacher educators—including many from some of the most highly regarded teacher education programs in the state. Its enormous advantage over the pencil-and-paper (often Scantron) assessments of teacher knowledge and skill that dominate the policy landscape of teacher preparation is that is it is focused on the classroom, on actual work with kids.

The value of a measure that can give faculty in teacher education programs a common language—and a common metric through which they can gauge their own effectiveness in preparing teachers—is hard to overestimate. In the two programs that I have directed that have implemented PACT (one in California, one here in Washington State), faculty have found the data of enormous value in identifying areas in need of significant program change and improvement. One example of this is our preparation of new teachers to understand and respond to the needs of diverse learners, particularly those who are learning English. Our surveys have told us that candidates have been dissatisfied with their preparation in this area ... for years. But what PACT has done is provide us with concrete and specific feedback about what our candidates have been able to take up from their courses and implement in the classroom. The feedback has not always been pleasant. Like many of our public school colleagues, we have often caught ourselves saying, "But I covered that!" The PACT data have pushed us hard to make pervasive and coordinated changes in our program in areas that have needed change.

Berlak's description of student complaints about the workload of completing the assessment is not without substance—some of our students have complained as well. But many have also recognized the value of the assessment process and have offered these kinds of comments:

> I found the assessment task to be helpful, as it got me thinking about exactly what I was looking for instead of just grading and correcting work.

> The instruction commentary was particularly useful for me because I generally consider myself to be a very reflective teacher, but there were things in the video that I would have never reflected on if I hadn't seen them. I don't think there was any piece that was not helpful.

> The assessment portion as well as the teaching portion allowed me to see my own teaching and the results of my teaching. It was great to have hands-on material to work with and to use to improve my teaching.

There are a number of errors of fact and interpretation in Berlak's rather polemical description of PACT. For example, to say "education faculty members are not considered qualified to do PACT assessments unless they are approved by PACT trainers" seems, to me, significantly misleading. Sounds like some kind of unreasonable, authoritarian, top-down groupies trying to exclude knowledgeable professionals. What is true is that scoring PACT requires consistency if candidates are to be evaluated fairly and if the data are to be useful for making decisions about program effectiveness. So university faculty, like other evaluators, must be able to apply a consistent standard in judgments that have tremendous consequences in the lives of teacher candidates. This is the essence of PACT training, or "calibration." It means developing a common language and a consistent way of making judgments about candidate competence *relative to this assessment*. It does not necessarily displace faculty prerogatives about evaluation in coursework, nor does it necessarily displace the sophisticated clinical judgment often exercised by university field supervisors.

Another of Berlak's claims is that PACT privileges a reductionist view of teaching, emphasizing direct and explicit instruction over more student-centered pedagogies. In fact, one of the clearly articulated aims of PACT training for scorers focuses on identifying exactly these kinds of biases and guarding against their intrusion into the scoring process. Succeeding with PACT requires that candidates be clear about what they are teaching, how they will engage all of the students in their classrooms, how they will assess what students have learned, and how they will use the data they collect about student learning to improve their teaching. There are no prescriptions about the nature of instruction, about student grouping, or about curriculum. The assessment does require that candidates pay attention to the social and personal contexts of students' lives, to state curriculum standards, and to what students are actually learning. It also helps them engage in a process of continuous analysis of their teaching. Which of these would you not want *your* child's teacher to do?

To reiterate the core point here, while PACT is not a perfect instrument (as its authors readily and regularly observe), it is an important tool for improving consistency of judgments about the competence of preservice teachers and for improving the quality of teacher preparation programs. Although the concerns that Berlak and others have raised are not trivial, I think they misjudge the importance of the opportunity that PACT represents to move preservice teacher assessment out of the domain of fill-in-the-bubble testing and into the classroom. I believe PACT has pushed us to become more aware of the needs for change in our practices, and I have been struck by how responsive our faculty have been to the kind of data PACT produces about our candidates. It is significant to me that many of the challenges PACT has made more visible to us have to do with our effectiveness in preparing new teachers to understand and respond to the needs of students who are learning English, students who have disabilities, and those who are members of cultural communities that are unfamiliar to many of our candidates. In short, the PACT data have made us think hard about our effectiveness in preparing new teachers to serve *all* the kids in their classrooms. These concerns reflect values that are thematic to the work of *Rethinking Schools*, and values we share with Professor Berlak and her colleagues.

—*Charles (Cap) Peck*
Professor of Teacher Education and Special Education
University of Washington

Although it is true that the state-mandated PACT has had a profound impact on credential programs, the aim of this response is to address the claims made about the multiple subject credential (MSC) program at San Francisco State in Ann Berlak's article on PACT.

- In reference to individuals who score the PACT teaching events, the claim that "there is no requirement that they have any particular background in teaching or expertise in the area they are assessing" is not true. Contrary to this, we select individuals with a teaching background. The author was invited to attend a training to become a scorer and, by choice, did not complete the training.
- Scoring a PACT teaching event is a long, involved process. Thus, the claim that individual scorers "have an incentive to score as rapidly as possible" due to the compensation is not true. In fact, we limit scorers to a certain number of events.
- "Education faculty members are not considered qualified to do PACT assessments unless they have been approved by PACT trainers" is also not true. PACT has an established training and calibration protocol whereby individuals become qualified scorers. Due to their expertise, education faculty members are *encouraged* to become scorers.
- Although it is true that the PACT is an unfunded, state-mandated assessment, and that our MSC program struggles to meet the requirements of this legislation, it is not true that our program is funding the PACT by "reducing student teacher supervision." All teacher candidates are supervised over the course of two semesters. The high cost of supervision in the field is a challenge for credential programs in general.

I cannot allow unfounded claims about our program to be published without response. High-stakes testing places a burden on teacher preparation programs that is similar to its impact in the public schools. However, the present reality is that our candidates need to pass the PACT, in addition to other evaluative components, to apply for a credential. Our mission is to help them reach their goal.

—*Debra Luna*
Chair, Department of Elementary Education
San Francisco State University

Ann Berlak's article is an important wake-up call to teacher educators, but I fear it may be too late. Here in New York, the Board of Regents has just announced a plan for entities such as Teach for America and KIPP Academy to "train" teachers who will then be eligible for state certification and master's degrees that will be awarded directly by the state—with no university preparation. The Board of Regents simultaneously announced the need to adopt a system like PACT to serve as a high-stakes assessment required for credentials.

Seeing PACT on the horizon, I attended a session at this year's American Association of Colleges for Teacher Education conference on "What we have learned from implementing PACT." After a long, detailed, and exhausting account of the problems and limitations of PACT, including how it had consumed incredible amounts of time and technological resources, a question came from the audience about validity and reliability. The presenters stated that the outcomes correlated almost identically with field-based performance evaluations. I raised my hand and asked: "So you've explained how expensive this has been, how much time has been invested, and that it correlates very strongly with field supervisors' judgments. What, then, is the value added?"

The reply: "Yes, well, there *is* that."

There is certainly a critical need for teacher education programs to engage in systematic assessment of candidates' readiness to teach. Teacher educators are gatekeepers: We decide who is ready to teach. Having engaged in clinically rich, field-based, inclusive, and critical multicultural urban teacher education for more than 17 years, I do not want a high-stakes assessment system to replace the collaborative decision-making that is at the center of our practice. Each year there are candidates we cannot recommend for certification; these decisions are not made lightly and are based on extensive field observations and sophisticated criteria. How can any reductionist system replace collaborative deliberations with cooperating teachers, school principals, field supervisors, and university-based faculty on a case-by-case basis?

—Celia Oyler
Director, Elementary and Secondary Inclusive Learning Programs
Teachers College, Columbia University

Ann Berlak Responds

Like many of us in the field, Cap Peck would like to protect teachers and teacher education from public disrespect. He seems to think that PACT will help us accomplish this feat. If only that were so. However, if the plague of standardized K-12 testing has taught us anything, it's that standardized testing is far more likely to be used to control and degrade educational institutions and teachers. As the Race to the Top so clearly demonstrates, it's likely that under a PACT regime teacher education programs would be ranked, rewarded, and punished in terms of their students' scores on PACT.

The key question is whether PACT scores accurately and objectively measure quality teaching. That PACT assessments are neither reliable nor valid is certain to become widely apparent in the next decade.

Peck claims PACT has not displaced clinical judgment of university field supervisors. It's hard to reconcile this with the fact that too-low PACT scores prevent candidates from receiving credentials, regardless of their supervisors', teachers', and mentors' evaluations.

Contrary to Peck's assumption, I am not happy with the state of teacher education, in part because of the profession's lukewarm commitment to promoting critical thinking, social justice, and empowerment. These goals are peripheral to PACT. But I do not advocate making these goals the focus of a high-stakes exit exam based on rubrics constructed by experts. Instead, we need an assessment process that promotes democratic empowerment for students, teachers, and diverse communities.

Debra Luna, who is the chair of the department where I teach, read my article as a critique of the credential program at San Francisco State. Nothing could be further from the truth. I have great respect for the program. I wrote the article because I feared that PACT would be going national and I wanted to share my perspective on how it has been experienced by a number of credential candidates and faculty across the state. As an article about PACT in *Education Week* ("State Group Piloting Teacher Prelicensing Exam," Sept. 1, 2010) attests, my fear was not unwarranted.

It is true, as Luna claims, that all assessors have backgrounds in teaching, but they do not necessarily have particular expertise in areas they will be assessing (e.g., second language acquisition or teaching mathematics). The question of whether having a teaching background is sufficient expertise was raised by colleagues at another California university.

Luna says there is no tradeoff between paying for PACT and paying for supervision. The fact that there has been no reduction in resources devoted to supervision in our program as a direct result of PACT is irrelevant. Money that could be spent on supervision—and on stipends to cooperating teachers—is being spent on administering PACT and on paying scorers to use an unreliable and invalid assessment instrument.

Once again, I want to be clear that my article was not a criticism of any individual or program. Departments of education use PACT because it, or an equally questionable instrument, is required by law.✎

PART 4

Testing the Tests

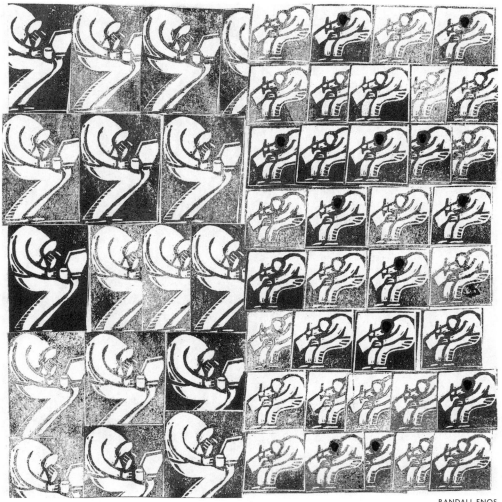

RANDALL ENOS

Neither Fair Nor Accurate

Research-based reasons why high-stakes tests
should not be used to evaluate teachers

WAYNE AU

A pitched battle raged in my hometown of Seattle in fall 2010. Then Super-intendent Maria Goodloe-Johnson and the Seattle Public Schools district fought with the Seattle Education Association over the teachers' union contract. At the heart of the dispute: Should teacher evaluations be based in part on student scores on standardized tests?

Seattle is not unique in this struggle, and it is clear that Superintendent Good-loe-Johnson took her cue from what is happening nationally. In August 2010, for instance, the *Los Angeles Times* printed a massive study in which L.A. student test scores were used to rate individual teacher effectiveness. The study was based on a statistical model referred to as value-added measurement (VAM). As part of the story, the *Times* published the names of roughly 6,000 teachers and their VAM ratings. [See article on page 96.]

In October of that same year, the New York City Department of Education followed suit, publicizing plans to release the VAM scores for nearly 12,000 public school teachers. U.S. Secretary of Education Arne Duncan lauded both the *Times* study and the NYC Department of Education plans, a stance consistent with Race to the Top guidelines and President Obama's support for using test scores to evaluate teachers and determine merit pay.

Current and former leaders of many major urban school districts, including Washington, D.C.'s Michelle Rhee and New Orleans' Paul Vallas, have sought to use tests to evaluate teachers. In fact, the use of high-stakes standardized tests to evaluate teacher performance, à la VAM, has become one of the cornerstones of current efforts to reshape public education along the lines of the free market. On the surface, the logic of VAM and using student scores to evaluate teachers seems like common sense: The more effective a teacher, the better his or her students should do on standardized tests.

However, although research tells us that teacher quality has an effect on test scores, this does not mean that a specific teacher is responsible for how a specific student performs on a standardized test. Nor does it mean we can equate effective teaching (or actual learning) with higher test scores.

Given the current attacks on teachers, teacher unions, and public education through the use of educational accountability schemes based wholly or partly on high-stakes standardized test scores and VAM, it is important that educators, students, and parents understand why—based on educational research—such tests should not be used to evaluate teachers.

Although there are many well-documented problems with using VAM to evaluate teachers, I've chosen to highlight six critical issues with VAM that are so problematic they alone should be enough to stop the use of high-stakes standardized tests for such evaluations. I hope these will be helpful as talking points for op-ed pieces, blogs, and discussions at school board meetings, PTA meetings, and in the bleachers at basketball games.

Error Rates

There is a statistical error rate of 35 percent when using one year's worth of test data to measure a teacher's effectiveness, and an error rate of 25 percent when using data from three years, researchers Peter Schochet and Hanley Chiang find in their 2010 report "Error Rates in Measuring Teacher and School Performance Based on Test Score Gains," released by the U.S. Department of Education's National Center for Education Statistics.

Bruce Baker, finance expert at Rutgers University, explains that using high-stakes test scores to evaluate teachers in this manner means there is a one-in-four chance that a teacher rated as "average" could be incorrectly rated as "below average" and face disciplinary measures. Because of these error rates, a teacher's performance evaluation may pivot on what amounts to a statistical roll of the dice.

Year-to-Year Test Score Instability

As Tim Sass, economics professor at Florida State University, points out in "The Stability of Value-Added Measures of Teacher Quality and Implications for Teacher Compensation Policy," test scores of students taught by the same teacher fluctuate wildly from year to year. In one study that compared two years of test scores across five urban districts, more than two-thirds of the bottom-ranked teachers one year had moved out of the bottom ranks the next year. Of this group, a full third went from the bottom 20 percent one year to the top 40 percent the next. Similarly, only one-third of the teachers who ranked highest one year kept their top ranking the next, and almost a third of the formerly top-ranked teachers landed in the bottom 40 percent in year two.

If test scores accurately measured teacher effectiveness, "effective" teachers would rate high consistently from year to year because they are good teachers; and one would expect "ineffective" teachers to rate low in terms of test scores just as consistently. Instead, the year-to-year instability that Sass highlights shows that test scores have very little to do with the effectiveness of a single teacher and have more to do with the change of students from year to year (unless, of course, one believes that one-third of the highest ranked teachers in the first year of the study simply decided to teach poorly in the second).

Day-to-Day Score Instability

Fifty to 80 percent of any improvement or decline in a student's standardized test score can be attributed to one-time, randomly occurring factors, according to Thomas Kane of Harvard University and Douglas Staiger of Dartmouth College in their research report "Volatility in Test Scores."

This means that factors such as whether a child ate breakfast on test day, whether a child got into an argument with parents or peers on the way to school, which other students happened to be in attendance while taking the test, or the child's feelings about the test administrator account for at

> **To reward or punish a teacher based on such scores could literally mean rewarding or punishing a teacher based on how well or poorly a student's morning went.**

least half of any given student's standardized test score gains or losses. Some factors, such as a dog barking outside an open window, can affect an entire class.

Kane and Staiger's findings illustrate that using tests to evaluate teachers ignores the reality that a host of individual daily factors that are completely out of a teacher's control contribute to how a student performs on any given test. To reward or punish a teacher based on such scores could literally mean rewarding or punishing a teacher based on how well or poorly a student's morning went.

Nonrandom Student Assignments

The grouping of students—either within schools through formal and informal tracking or across schools through race, socioeconomic class, and linguistic (ELL) segregation—greatly influences VAM test results, as 10 leading researchers in teacher quality and educational assessment highlight in their policy brief, "Problems with the Use of Student Test Scores to Evaluate Teachers," published by the Economic Policy Institute.

These researchers note that "teachers who have chosen to teach in schools serving more affluent students may appear to be more effective simply because they have students with more home and school supports for their prior and current learning, and not because they are better teachers."

Even when VAM models attempt to take into account a student's prior achievement or demographic characteristics, the models assume that all students will show test gains at an equal rate. This assumption, however, does not necessarily hold true for groups of students who historically have performed poorly on tests, for English language learners who are asked to become proficient in both a new language and a tested subject area, or for students with disabilities whose test-based rates of progress may be incomparable to any other student.

Nonrandom student assignment means teachers could be punished, dismissed, or lose tenure purely because the courses they teach or the schools they teach in have a significant population of traditionally low-scoring students who may show variable or slower test score gains.

Imprecise Measurement

High-stakes standardized tests are also unable to account for the complexities of learning (and, by extension, teaching). For instance, we know from the linguistic research of Steven Pinker and others that learning often happens in a U-shape—that making mistakes is an integral part of the learning process. When children are tested, we never quite know where on the U-shaped learning curve they might be, nor do we realize that their mistakes could be a vital part of a natural learning process. When tests are used to evaluate teachers, it is possible that highly effective teachers who push students out of their cognitive comfort zones are penalized for provoking the deep learning that requires students to make mistakes on the way to greater understanding.

Standardized tests are also too crude to account for the possibility of cognitive transfer of skills that students learn across different subjects. Using VAM, as the researchers in the above-mentioned Economic Policy Institute policy brief explain, means that "the essay writing a student learns from his history teacher may be credited to his English teacher, even if the English teacher assigns no writing; the mathematics a student learns in her physics class may be credited to her math teacher." In other words, we can never be certain which class and which teacher contributed to a given student's test performance in any given subject.

Out-of-School Factors

Out-of-school factors such as inadequate access to health care, food insecurity, and poverty-related stress, among others, negatively impact the in-school achievement of students so profoundly that they severely limit what schools and teachers can do on their own, explains David Berliner, Regents Professor of Education at Arizona State University, in his report "Poverty and Potential."

Although it is clear from the research of Stanford University's Linda Darling-Hammond and others that teachers play an absolutely pivotal role in student success, when we use high-stakes tests to evaluate teachers, we incorrectly assume that teachers have the ability to overcome any obstacle in students' lives to improve learning. Although good teachers are critically necessary, they are not always sufficient.

To assume otherwise is to think that teachers (and schools) can somehow make up for the lack of housing, food, safety, and living wage employment, among other factors, all on their own. The social safety net is the responsibility of a much broader socioeconomic network—not the sole responsibility of the teacher.

Politics, Not Reality

The reality of standardized tests is that they are too imprecise and inaccurate to measure the effectiveness of individual teachers. The sad thing is that testing experts, researchers, and psychometricians have known this for quite some time. In 1999, for instance, the expert panel that made up the Committee on Appropriate Test Use of the National Research Council cautioned that "an educational decision that will have a major impact on a test-taker should not be made solely or automatically on the basis of a single test score."

Yet two short years later, a bipartisan Congress and the presidential administration of George W. Bush passed No Child Left Behind (NCLB) and its test-and-punish approach to school reform into law.

Although the Bush administration seemed to ignore educational research as a matter of policy (as illustrated through NCLB's Reading First program and the advocacy of using phonics-only teaching methods that had little basis in research), many hoped for something different with the election of President Obama.

Unfortunately, the Obama administration has sent a clear message: When it comes to high-stakes standardized testing, the research doesn't matter.

It hasn't mattered that, according to the above cited U.S. Department of Education report, "More than 90 percent of the variation in student gain scores is due to the variation in *student-level* factors that are not under control of the teacher."

> **When tests are used to evaluate teachers, it is possible that highly effective teachers who push students out of their cognitive comfort zones are penalized for provoking the deep learning that requires students to make mistakes on the way to greater understanding.**

It hasn't mattered that the National Research Council of the National Academy of Sciences has stated that "VAM estimates of teacher effectiveness should not be used to make operational decisions because such estimates are far too unstable to be considered fair or reliable."

It hasn't mattered that even the researchers who completed the *Los Angeles Times* study acknowledged that VAM data were too unreliable to use as the sole measure of teacher performance (a point that the *Times* neglected to clearly articulate in its article).

Sadly, with Bush, and now with Obama, politics and ideology trump educational research.

One would think that all of the policy makers, politicians, pundits, superintendents, talk show hosts, documentary movie makers, business leaders, and philanthropic foundations so in love with the idea of using test score data to evaluate teachers would be equally as passionate about accuracy. People's lives are at stake, and yet the "data" underlying important decisions about teacher performance couldn't be shakier.

The shakiness of test-based VAM data illustrates that the current fight over teacher "accountability" isn't really about effectiveness. The more substantial public conversation we should be having about rising poverty, the racial resegregation of our schools, increasing unemployment, lack of health care, and the steady defunding of the public sector—all factors that have an overwhelming impact on students' educational achievement—has been buried. Instead, teachers and their unions have become convenient scapegoats for our social, educational, and economic woes.

Yes, teacher performance needs to be evaluated, but in a manner that is fair and accurate. Using high-stakes standardized tests and VAM to make such evaluations is neither. ❦

A Test Scorer's Lament

Scenes from the mad, mad, mad
world of testing companies

TODD FARLEY

Having made my living since 1994 scoring standardized tests, I have but one question about No Child Left Behind: When the legislation talks of "scientifically-based research"—a phrase mentioned 110 times in the law—they're not talking about the work I do, right? Not test scoring, right? I hope not, because if the 15 years I just spent in the business taught me anything, it's that the scoring of tens of thousands of student responses to standardized tests per year is played out in the theater of the absurd.

I'm not talking about the scoring of *multiple-choice* standardized tests; they're scored electronically, but it's not as foolproof as you'd like to believe. No, I'm talking about open-ended items and essay prompts where students fill up the blank pages of a test booklet with their own thoughts and words.

If your state has contracted that job out to one of the massive multinational, for-profit companies that largely make up the testing industry, then you've surely been led to believe those student responses will be assessed as part of a systematic process as sophisticated as anything NASA could come up with. The testing companies probably told you all about the unassailable scoring rubrics they put together with the help of "national education experts" and "classroom teachers." Perhaps they've told you how "qualified" and "well-trained" their "professional scorers" are. Certainly they've paraded around their omniscient "psychometricians," those all-knowing statisticians with their inscrutable talk of "item response theory," "T-values," and the like. With all that grand jargon, it's easy to assume that the job of scoring student responses involves bespectacled researchers in pristine, white lab coats meticulously reviewing each and every student response with scales, T-squares, microscopes, and magnifying glasses.

Well, think again.

If test scoring is "scientifically based research" of any kind, then I'm Dr. Frankenstein. In fact, my time in testing was characterized by overuse of temporary employees, scoring rules that were alternately ambiguous and bizarre, and testing companies so swamped with work and threatened with deadlines that getting any scores on tests appeared to be more important than the right scores. I'd say the process was laughable, if not for the fact those test scores have become so important to the landscape of modern American education.

I offer the following true stories from my time in testing as a cautionary tale. Although they are random scenes, they are representative of my experience in the business. Remember them when next you hear some particularly amazing or particularly depressing results from another almighty "standardized" test.

True Stories from the Field

On the second Monday of a two-week range-finding session, the project manager of a test-scoring company convenes the meeting in a large conference room. The participants are esteemed experts in writing and education from around the United States who have been invited to this leafy campus to share their expertise, but the project manager has to make an announcement they may not like.

> If test scoring is "scientifically based research" of any kind, then I'm Dr. Frankenstein.

"I have some bad news," she says.

"It seems we haven't been scoring correctly."

The room buzzes, with both a disappointment that such an assembly of experts might have erred and disbelief that anyone would doubt them.

"Says who?" a bespectacled fellow asks.

"Well," the project manager says, "our numbers don't match up with what the psychometricians predicted."

Grumblings fill the room, but one young man new to the scoring process looks confused.

"The who?" he asks.

"The psychometricians," the project manager says. "The stats people."

"They read the essays this weekend?" the young man asks.

"Uh, no," the project manager laughs. "They read their spreadsheets."

"So?" the young man says, looking perplexed.

The project manager explains. "The psychometricians predicted between 6 and 9 percent of the student essays would get 1's on this test, but from our work last week we're only seeing 3 percent. The rest of the numbers are pretty much on, but we're high on 2's and short on 1's."

The young man stares at the project manager. "The psychometricians know what the scores will be without reading the essays?"

The project manager looks down. "I guess that's one way to look at it."

"I Liked Yours Better Than Mine"

After three days of contentious and confusing training sessions, 100 temporarily employed professional scorers begin assessing high school essays. One scorer leans toward her neighbor and hands him the essay she's been reading. "Al," she whispers, "what score would you give this paper?"

The man takes the proffered essay and replaces it with the one in his hand. "What would you give this?"

For about a minute, Al and Tammy each scan the other's essay.

"I dunno. Yours seems like a 4."

"Yup. Seems 'adequate.' What do you think?"

Tammy shrugs. "I was thinking 3. It doesn't say much."

Al shrugs. "Maybe you're right … What would you give mine?"

"I think a 5."

"A 5?" Al questions. "I thought it was a 4."

"Yours has all that development and details…"

"But the grammar …"

"I liked yours better than mine," Tammy says.

"And I liked yours better than mine."

The scorers exchange essays again. Tammy smiles, patting Al's arm. "Real glad we had this talk, Al," she says. "It's been a great help." Then Tammy laughs.

Poolside Scoring

In the hot sun, at a table beside a hotel pool, two men and a woman drink icy cocktails to celebrate the successful completion of a four-week scoring project. The hotel manager brings a phone to their table. "Call for you," he says to the woman, whose face blanches when the home office tells her that another dozen tests have been found.

"I know," the woman says, "Someone has to score them. OK, read them to me over the phone." The woman turns the phone's speaker on, and she and the men listen to student responses read by a squeaky-voiced secretary several thousand miles away. One of the men waves to the bartender to bring another round and, with drinks but not rubrics in their hands, the two men and one woman score each student response via the telephone. When the voice on the phone goes silent after reading each response, the woman looks at the number of fingers the men hold in the air.

"Three," the woman says into the phone. "That's a three."

This goes on for an hour and two rounds of drinks.

"We'll Give Them Lower Scores"

A project manager for a test-scoring company addresses the supervisors hired to manage the scoring of a project. The project is not producing the results expected, to the dismay of the test-scoring company and its client, a state department of education. The project manager has been trying to calm the concerned employees, but she's losing patience. She's obviously had enough.

"I don't care if the scores are right," the project manager snarls. "They want lower scores, and we'll give them lower scores." ✏

The Loneliness of
the Long-Distance Test Scorer

DAN DIMAGGIO

Standardized testing has become central to education policy in the United States. After dramatically expanding in the wake of the No Child Left Behind Act, testing has been further enshrined by the Obama administration's $3.4 billion Race to the Top grants. Given the ongoing debate over these policies, it might be useful to hear about the experiences of a hidden sector of the education workforce: those of us who make our living scoring these tests. Our viewpoint is instructive, as it reveals the many contradictions and absurdities built into a test-scoring system run by for-profit companies and beholden to school administrators and government officials with a stake in producing inflated numbers. Our experiences also provide insight into how the testing mania is stunting the development of millions of young minds.

I recently spent four months working for two test-scoring companies, scoring tens of thousands of papers, while routinely clocking up to 70 hours a week. This was my third straight year doing this job. While the reality of life as a test scorer has recently been chronicled by Todd Farley in his book *Making the Grades: My Misadventures in the Standardized Testing Industry* [excerpted in the previous article], a scathing insider's account of his fourteen years in the industry, I want to tell my story to affirm that Farley's indictment is rooted in experiences common throughout the test-scoring world.[1]

"Wait, someone scores standardized tests? I thought those were all done by machines." This is usually the first response I get when I tell people I've been eking out a living as a test-scoring temp. The companies responsible for scoring standardized tests have not yet figured out a way to electronically process the varied handwriting and creative flourishes of millions of 3rd to 12th graders. Nor, to my knowledge, have they begun to outsource this work to India. Instead, every year, the written-response portions of innumerable standardized tests given across the country are scored by human beings—tens of thousands of us, a veritable army of temporary workers.

I often wonder who students (or teachers and parents, for that matter) picture scoring their papers. When I was a student, I envisioned my tests being graded by qualified teachers in another part of the country, who taught the grade level and subject corresponding to the tests. This idea, it turns out, is as much a fantasy as imagining all the tests are being scored by machines.

Test scoring is a huge business,

> **Our experiences provide insight into how the testing mania is stunting the development of millions of young minds.**

Every year, the written-response portions of innumerable standardized tests given across the country are scored by human beings—tens of thousands of us, a veritable army of temporary workers.

dominated by a few multinational corporations, which arrange the work in order to extract maximum profit. Scoring contracts often act as an entry point for these companies into the lucrative education revenue stream, allowing them to sell textbooks and new technology to schools. I was shocked when I found out that Pearson, the first company I worked for, also owned the *Financial Times*, *The Economist*, Penguin Books, and leading textbook publisher Prentice Hall. The CEO of Pearson, Marjorie Scardino, ranked 17th on *Forbes'* list of the 100 most powerful women in the world in 2007.

Test-scoring companies make their money by hiring a temporary workforce each spring, people willing to work for low wages (generally $11 to $13 an hour), no benefits, and no hope of long-term employment—not exactly the most attractive conditions for trained and licensed educators. So all it takes to become a test scorer is a bachelor's degree, a lack of a steady job, and a willingness to throw independent thinking out the window and follow the absurd and ever-changing guidelines set by the test-scoring companies. Some of us scorers are retired teachers, but most are former office workers, former security guards, or former holders of any of the diverse array of jobs previously done by the currently unemployed. When I began working in test scoring three years ago, my first "team leader" was qualified to supervise not because of his credentials in the field of education, but because he had been a low-level manager at a local Target.

In the test-scoring centers where I have worked, located in downtown St. Paul and a Minneapolis suburb, the workforce has been overwhelmingly white—upwards of 90 percent. Meanwhile, in many of the school districts for which these scores matter the most—where officials will determine whether schools will be shut down, or kids will be held back, or teachers fired—the vast majority are students of color. As of 2005, 80 percent of students in the nation's 20 largest school districts were youth of color. The idea that these cultural barriers do not matter, since we are supposed to be grading all students by the same standard, seems far-fetched, to say the least. Perhaps it would be better to outsource the jobs to India, where the cultural gap might, in some ways, be smaller.

Many test scorers have been doing this job for years—sometimes a decade or more. Yet these are the ultimate in temporary, seasonal jobs. The human resources people who interview and hire scorers are temps, as are most of the supervisors. In one test-scoring center, even the office space and computers were leased temporarily. Whenever I complained about these things, some coworker would inevitably say, "Hey, it beats working at Subway or McDonald's."

True, but does it inspire confidence to know that, for the people scoring the tests at the center of this nation's education policy, the alternative is working in fast food? Or to know that, because of our low wages and lack of benefits, many test scorers have to work two jobs—delivering newspapers in the morning, hustling off to cashier or waitress at night, or, if you're me (and plenty of others like me) heading home to start a second shift of test scoring for another company?

Kafkaesque Communications

Company communications with test-scoring employees often feel like they

All it takes to become a test scorer is a bachelor's degree, a lack of a steady job, and a willingness to throw independent thinking out the window and follow the absurd and ever-changing guidelines set by the test-scoring companies.

have been lifted from a Kafka novel. Scorers working from home almost never talk to an actual human being. Pearson sends all its communications to home scorers via email, now supplemented by automated phone calls telling you to check your inbox. After the start of a project, even these emails cease, and scorers are forced to check the project homepage on their own initiative to find out any important changes. Remarkably, for a company entrusted with assessing students' educational performance, messages from Pearson contain a disturbing number of misspellings, incorrect dates, typos, and missing information. Pearson's online video orientation, for example, warns scorers that they may face "civil lawshits" from sexual harassment. Error-free communications are rare. I was considering whether this was a fair assessment when I received a message from Pearson with the subject "Pearson Fall 2010." The link in the email took me to a survey to find out my availability—for the spring of 2011.

Communications at scoring centers are hardly better. For example, test-scoring jobs never have a guaranteed end date. If you ask a supervisor when a job is going to be completed, you will get a puzzling response, like "we don't know how many papers are in the system, so we can't say when we'll be done." This response persists, even though it's pretty easy to calculate how many 5th graders there are in Pennsylvania and how long it will take to grade their papers, given our scoring rate. If we are lucky, we get 24-hours notice before being told that a project is about to end and we should seek other work. Two-hours notice is more common. In general, scorers are given no information beyond what is absolutely necessary to do the job.

What is the work itself like? In test-scoring centers, dozens of scorers sit in rows, staring at computer screens where students' papers appear (after the papers have undergone some mysterious scanning process). I imagine that most students think their papers are being graded as if they are the most important thing in the world. Yet every day, each scorer is expected to read hundreds of papers. So for all the months of preparation and the dozens of hours of class time spent writing practice essays, a student's writing probably will be processed and scored in about a minute.

> **Whenever I complained about these things, some coworker would inevitably say, "Hey, it beats working at Subway or McDonald's."**

Sinister Math

Scoring is particularly rushed when scorers are paid by piece rate, as is the case when you are scoring from home, where a growing part of the industry's work is done. At 30 to 70 cents per paper, depending on the test, the incentive, especially for a home worker, is to score as quickly as possible in order to earn any money: At 30 cents per paper, you have to score 40 papers an hour to make $12 an hour, and test scoring requires a lot of mental breaks. Presumably, the score-from-home model is more profitable for testing companies than setting up an office, especially because it avoids the prospect of overtime pay, the bane of existence for companies operating on tight deadlines. But overtime pay is a gift from heaven for impoverished test scorers; on one project, I worked in an office for 23 days straight, including numerous nine-hour days operating on four to five hours sleep—such was my excitement about overtime.

Yet scoring from home also brings with it an entirely new level of alienation. You may work on a month-long project without ever speaking to another human being, never mind seeing the children who actually wrote the papers. If you do speak to another person, it's at your own expense, since calling the supervisors at the test-scoring center takes time, and might cut into the precious moments you spend scoring (especially when you have to wait 15 minutes for someone to answer, as happens routinely on some projects).

The piece-rate system also leads to some sinister math; I have often wondered how much money I lose for every trip to the bathroom, and debated taking my laptop there with me. And because you are only guaranteed employment until the papers run out, you are in a race against all your phantom coworkers to score as many papers as you can, as fast as possible. This cannot be good for quality, but as long as the statistics match up and the project finishes on time, the companies are happy. I did receive some automated warnings from Pearson that I was scoring too fast, while simultaneously receiving messages on the Pearson website to the effect that, "We're way behind! Log in as many hours as you can and score as much as possible!"

No matter at what pace scorers work, however, tests are not always scored with the utmost attentiveness. The work is mind-numbing, so scorers have to invent ways to entertain themselves. The most common method seems to be staring blankly at the wall or into space for minutes at a time. But at work this year, I discovered that no one would notice if I just read news articles while scoring tests. So every night, while scoring from home, I would surf the internet and cut and paste loads of articles—reports on Indian Maoists, scientific speculation on whether animals can be gay, critiques of standardized testing—into what typically came to be an 80-page, single-spaced Word document. Then I would print it out and read it the next day while I was working at the scoring center. This was the only way to avoid going insane. I still managed to score at the average rate for the room and perform according to "quality" standards. While scoring from home, I routinely carry on three or four intense conversations on Gchat. This is the reality of test scoring.

There is a common fantasy that test scorers have some control over the grades they are giving. I laugh whenever someone tells me, "Make sure you go easy and give the kids good grades!" We are entirely beholden to and constrained by the standards set by the states and (supposedly) enforced by the test-scoring companies. To ensure that test scorers are administering the "correct" score, we receive several hours of training per test, and are monitored through varying quality control measures, such as random "validity" papers that are prescored and that we must score correctly. This all seems logical and necessary to ensure impartiality—these are, after all, "standardized" tests. Unfortunately, after scoring tests for at least five states over the past three years, the only truly standardized elements I have found are a mystifying training process, supervisors who are often more confused than the scorers themselves, and a pervasive inability of these tests to foster creativity and competent writing.

Scorers often emerge from training more confused than when they started. Usually, within a day or two, when the scores we are giving are inevitably too low (as we attempt to follow the standards laid out in training), we are told to start giving higher scores, or, in the enigmatic language of scoring directors, to "learn to see more papers as a 4." For some mysterious reason, unbeknownst to test scorers, the scores we are giving are supposed to closely match those given in previous years. So if 40 percent of papers received 3's the previous year (on a scale of 1 to 6), then a similar percentage should receive 3's this year.

I also question how these scores can possibly measure whether students or schools are improving. Are we just trying to match the scores from last year, or are we part of an elaborate game of "juking the stats," as it's called on HBO's *The Wire*, when agents alter statistics to please superiors? For these companies, the ultimate goal is to present acceptable numbers to the state education departments as quickly as possible, beating their deadlines (there are, we are told, $1 million fines if they miss a deadline) and proving their reliability so they will continue to get more contracts.

As Farley writes, "Too often in my career the test results we returned had to be viewed not as exemplars of educational progress, but rather as numbers produced in a mad rush to get things done, statistics best viewed solely through the prism of profit."[2] It seems to me that what the companies would tell us, if they were honest, would be something like, "Hey guys, your scoring doesn't really matter. We just want to give the same scores as last year, so that there's no controversy with

> I imagine that most students think their papers are being graded as if they are the most important thing in the world. Yet every day, each scorer is expected to read hundreds of papers.

I have often wondered how much money I lose for every trip to the bathroom, and debated taking my laptop there with me.

the state and we get more contracts and make more profits—so no matter what you learned in training, just try to forget it." States and local governments, meanwhile, play their own version of this game, because it looks good for them when politicians can claim that test scores are going up. Witness the recent controversy in New York City, where the percentage of students passing the math exam rose from 57 percent in 2006 to 82 percent in 2009, before plummeting back down to 54 percent in 2010 (along with a 43 percent passing rate in English) after the standards were reviewed.[3]

As test scorers, we never know what the numbers we are assigning to papers mean, or where we fit in this elaborate game. We are only responsible for assigning one score, on one small part of a test, and we do not even know whether the score we assign is passing or failing—that information is never divulged in training. We never hear how the students fared. Whether Marissa will be prevented from going to 7th grade with her friends because one of us, before our first cup of coffee kicked in, decided that her paper was "a little more like a 3 than a 4," we will never know. Whether Marissa's school will be closed or her teachers fired (to be reborn as test scorers next spring?) remain mysteries to the test scorers. And yet these scores can be of life-and-death importance, as seen in the suicide of beloved Los Angeles middle school teacher Rigoberto Ruelas, Jr. Upon learning that he ranked as "less effective" on the *Los Angeles Times'* teacher performance rating scale—based solely on test scores—Ruelas took his own life.[4]

Even if the scoring were a more exact science, this would in no way make up for the atrocious effect on creativity wrought by the mania for standardized testing. This impact has now been documented. According to one study, creativity among U.S. children has been in decline since 1990, with a particularly severe drop among those currently between kindergarten and 6th grade.[5]

Although test scorers and students might be separated by age, geography, race, and culture, we share one bond: Standardized testing puts us to sleep. In the face of the crushing monotony of the hundreds of rote responses fostered by these tests, scorers are left to fight their own individual battles to stay awake. In any test-scoring center, by far the most essential job is done by the person whose sole responsibility consists of making coffee for hundreds of workers, many of whom will consume four to six cups a day to survive. In my mind, I see a hideous symmetry between test scorers' desperate attempts to avoid dozing off, and the sleepy, zombie-like faces of the students as they prepare for and take these tests.

Of course, these students only exist in my imagination. Just as test scorers are never allowed to know the effects of our scores on students, we never get a chance to meet them, to see how they have developed as writers, thinkers, or human beings, or to know what life in their communities or families is like. All we see is a paper on a screen. And after reading hundreds of monotonous papers each day, it's not uncommon to start to feel a bitter distaste for the undoubtedly beautiful youth of America and the seeming poverty of their creative thought.

I remember reading, for 23 straight days, the responses of thousands of middle schoolers to the question: "What is a goal of yours in life?" A plurality devoted several paragraphs to

We are entirely beholden to and constrained by the standards set by the states and (supposedly) enforced by the test-scoring companies.

explain that their life's goal was to talk less in class, listen to their teacher, and stop fooling around so much. It's asking too much to hope for great literature on a standardized test. But, given that this is the process through which so many students are learning to write and to think, one would hope for more. These rote responses, in themselves, are a testament to the failure of our education system, its failure to actually connect with kids' lives, to help them develop their humanity and their critical thinking skills, to do more than discipline them and prepare them to be obedient workers—or troops.

Although we test scorers might be prone to blame these children for the monotony of their thoughts, it's not their fault that their imaginations and inspirations are being sucked out of them. No points are given for creativity on these tests, although some scorers have told me that, until recently, a number of states did factor creativity into their scores. Ironically, scorers are often delighted to see papers that show individuality and speak in their own voice, and often reward them with higher scores, though, judging by the papers I've read, it appears as if students often explicitly are told not to be creative. Yet even if creativity were considered, it would not likely do much to change the overall character of the writing—and education—engendered by an emphasis on standardized testing. As Einstein put it, "It is a miracle that curiosity survives formal education."

An entire education policy that thrives on repetition, monotony, and discipline is being enacted, stunting creativity and curiosity under the guise of the false idol of accountability. What is more, this policy has a differential impact, depending on students' race and class. As Jonathan Kozol explains,

> In most suburban schools, teachers know their kids are going to pass the
> required tests anyway—so No Child Left Behind is an irritant in a good school
> system, but it doesn't distort the curriculum. It doesn't transform the nature of
> the school day. But in inner-city schools, testing anxiety not only consumes about
> a third of the year, but it also requires every minute of the school day in many of
> these inner-city schools to be directed to a specifically stated test-related skill.
> Very little art is allowed into these classrooms. Little social studies, really none of
> the humanities.[6]

Seeing the results of this process is demoralizing to test scorers, and you can feel it in the scoring centers. Even though you can move about freely, use the bathroom when you need, and talk to one another, the room I was in this spring was almost always completely silent. On every project, as the weeks go by, the health of many scorers deteriorates, making me curious as to whether the relentless, soul-crushing monotony of the papers has an actual physical impact on those forced to read them.

The Testing Game

To be fair, these papers aren't a total wash. There is often wisdom in them, even on standardized tests. The chasm between rich and poor is at times felt in the writing itself, as some students come from unimaginable privilege, while many more endure heartbreaking experiences in foster homes. The papers are also a testament to the persistence of racism, describing teenagers kicked out of stores or denied service or jobs because of the color of their skin. And it would be wrong to think of test scorers as a down-and-out bunch—many of us do this job in order to avoid having to get other ones that would keep us from our creative endeavors, or from traveling or pursuing other life-enriching possibilities. A number of test scorers I've met over the past three years are authors, artists, photographers, or independent scholars, and it's common to see postings for book releases and other events featuring the work of test scorers on bulletin boards in the break room.

In the error-filled Pearson training video, Marjorie Scardino says, "Most of the people who work at Pearson work with a passion and an intensity, because they think know are doing something important." But I've never gotten the sense from my coworkers that they "think know" what they're doing is helping kids or the education process. If the Obama administration asked test scorers whether the solution to this country's education system would be more standardized testing, I think most of them would laugh. Unfortunately, the joke is on us, as the Obama administration pushes for even more high-stakes standardized testing. I didn't know whether to laugh or cry when all workers at my test-scoring center were asked to fill out a form allowing the company we were working for to get a tax break for hiring us. This tax break came via the Obama administration's Hiring Incentives to Restore Employment (HIRE) Act, which was supposed to provide subsidies for companies "creating jobs." Never mind that we were all going to be hired anyway, because this is seasonal employment. Or that this money was subsidizing temporary jobs with no health care and no hope for transitioning into long-term employment—jobs which, in a better world, would not exist.

While these companies brazenly collect what can only be described as corporate welfare checks, hundreds of thousands of teachers are being laid off as governments cut funding to education. Maybe next year, some of them will get paid $12 an hour (or $10, if they flood the market) to score tests taken by students stuffed into even bigger classes, and help "impartially" decide which schools will be shut down and which of their colleagues will be laid off. Equally bad, the fanaticism surrounding accountability via testing, which claims it will result in higher-quality teachers, is doing nothing of the sort. Referring to the test-intensive No Child Left Behind Act, Kozol says, "By measuring the success of teachers almost exclusively by the test scores of their pupils, it has rewarded the most robotic teachers, and it's driving out precisely those contagiously exciting teachers who are capable of critical thinking who urban districts have tried so hard to recruit."[7]

As a friend of mine was saying his goodbyes to the coworkers in his room at the end of this year's scoring season, his 70-year-old supervisor, a veteran test-scoring warrior, uttered the words I imagine many test scorers hope to hear: "I hope I never see you here again." This is a measure of the cynicism with which many test scorers approach the industry, recognizing that it is fundamentally a game, which too many people are forced to play—but "hey, it beats working at McDonald's or Subway!" Yet amid all the hopes of escaping the industry, these test-scoring companies are successfully expanding and are now hoping to get their hands on billions in "school turnaround" money handed out by the Obama administration and state governments. Pearson, for example, has "formed the K-12 Solutions Group, and . . . is seeking school-turnaround contracts in at least eight states...[claiming it] could draw on its testing, technology and other products to carry out a coherent school-improvement effort."[8]

> Even if the scoring were a more exact science, this would in no way make up for the atrocious effect on creativity wrought by the mania for standardized testing.

The big test-scoring companies will undoubtedly be called on to furnish their supposed "expertise" in developing and scoring the new generation of more complex tests envisioned by Secretary of Education Arne Duncan. In 2010, the Obama administration gave two groups of states $330 million in grants to develop these new national tests, with the stated aim of assessing more critical thinking skills and providing better feedback to students and teachers. But rather than addressing the problems outlined above, it seems more likely that this move will only transfer the absurdities in current state tests to a national level, with the danger that they will take on an even greater legitimacy. In fact, given that Duncan's proposal involves even more tests, it is likely to make matters worse.

If scoring is any indication, everyone should be worried about the logic of putting more of our education system in the hands of these for-profit companies, which would love to grow even deeper roots for the commodification of students' minds. Why would people in their right minds want to leave educational assessment in the hands of poorly trained, overworked, low-paid temps, working for companies interested only in cranking out acceptable numbers and improving their bottom line? Though the odds might seem slim, our collective goal, as students, teachers, parents—and even test scorers—should be to liberate education from this farcical numbers game. ❧

This article was originally published in the 12/01/2010 issue of Monthly Review *(www. monthlyreview.org). Reprinted with permission.*

Endnotes

1. Todd Farley, "Making the Grades: My Misadventures in the Standardized Testing Industry," *San Francisco: Polipoint*, 2009.

2. Todd Farley, "Standardized Tests Are Not the Answer: I Know, I Graded Them," *Christian Science Monitor*, October 28, 2009.

3. Sharon Otterman, "Confusion on Where City Students Stand," *New York Times*, August 28, 2010.

4. Alexandra Zavis and Tony Barboza, "Teacher's Suicide Shocks School," *Los Angeles Times*, September 28, 2010, http://articles.latimes.com.

5. Po Bronson and Ashley Merryman, "The Creativity Crisis," *Newsweek*, August 10, 2010.

6. Matthew Fishbane, "Teachers: Be Subversive (Interview with Jonathan Kozol)," *Salon.com*, August 30, 2007.

7. Ibid.

8. Sam Dillon, "Inexperienced Companies Chase School Reform Funds," *New York Times*, August 9, 2010.

Fuzzy Math

MEREDITH JACKS

As a public school English teacher, I observe standardized testing season each year with a sort of grim fascination. So this is it, I think, as I pace around my silent classroom, peering over kids' shoulders at articles about parasailing. Line graphs tracking the rainfall in Tulsa. Parts of speech. Functions of x. These are the 34 questions that will determine some aspect of my students' futures—as well as our school's yearly progress report, my own teacher report card, and soon, possibly, my salary. I wince at my young charges' careless mistakes. I see eyes rove. I know who came in yawning, who's feeling sick, whose brother is back in jail. So many variables (input) producing a single-digit score (output). Functions of x.

Last month, several weeks after those long quiet mornings, I got another glimpse inside the testing industrial complex. Instead of reporting to my own school and teaching my 8th-grade writing classes, I reported to the gymnasium of a middle school uptown, along with 100-odd other New York City teachers, to score 5th-grade New York State math exams. I was there in place of a colleague, a special education teacher—as are the vast majority of the educators pulled out of schools to grade the state tests—who had already spent most of the prior week scoring reading tests and begged me to take her spot in "the warehouse." (I should note that most standardized test scoring is done not by teachers, but by temp workers—who must possess at least a four-year college degree and are paid a low hourly rate.)

I arrived on the Upper East Side that Tuesday morning in a chilly May downpour, already on my second cup of coffee. Students with overstuffed backpacks jostled into the school's double doors ahead of me, squealing about the rain. Inside, I headed toward the open gym door, where I could see 20 round tables, bedecked in red and blue plastic tablecloths. Clusters of damp-haired teachers were settling into the folding chairs, chatting quietly, leafing through newspapers. They were mostly young, in their 30s—some older and distinguished looking—with bright eyes, sensible footwear, books. This was no temp crew; these seemed like people who should be off teaching children. I took my seat among them.

After a spirited welcome sermon from the site manager, we scorers had to be trained. This involved several steps, starting with deciphering three pages of guidelines with stipulations like:

> In all questions that provide response spaces for two numerical answers and

The Department of Ed has never plucked me from my classroom and asked me to do that kind of precise, intense thinking—for three full days— about how kids *learn best*.

require work to be shown for both parts, if one correct numerical answer is provided but no work is shown in either part, the score is zero. If two correct numerical answers are provided but no work is shown in either part, the score is one.

A series of boxes labeled "Holistic Rubric" informed us that a two-point response "may reflect some misunderstanding of the underlying mathematical concepts," while a one-point response "demonstrates only a limited understanding" thereof. Semantically, we were in the deep end.

Around me sat dozens of focused teachers, brows furrowed, eyes and lips and pencils moving silently through the subclauses. Rereading, circling, raising hands to ask "What if..." questions. I wondered, "What if all this brainpower could be devoted to the subject of actual teaching and learning?" Not that it never is; not that we don't all pour tremendous energy into our own classrooms and schools. But the Department of Ed has never plucked me from my classroom and asked me to do that kind of precise, intense thinking—for three full days—about how kids *learn best*. I was struck by the sight of us all, serious and alert, poring over these scoring guidelines like legal briefs. What could these minds do if given a different task?

When we finished reading, we were asked to peruse several scored sample problems (three-pointers, two-pointers, one-pointers, zeroes), then to try scoring a few sample questions on our own. At that point, and from then on, we were encouraged to cross check with our neighbors, to debate, and together to refer back to the rubric. Throughout the day, I found this social aspect of the grading process to be crucial; in fact, it may be the only thing guaranteeing any consistency in the final scores. In teams of two, four, sometimes eight, we were able to find some consensus about whether a child's response fulfilled the task in a much more consistent way than we might have achieved alone. (It's interesting to consider how often students are prohibited, or at least discouraged, from engaging in that type of collective thinking, in favor of silent individual work. Even in some "cooperative learning" classrooms, student collaboration still feels teacher-driven or scripted. But that's another story.)

However, despite its relative perks, our social working process was vital precisely because of one scary fact: So much about these tests is subjective. I alluded earlier to the "input variables" that make standardized exams a less-than-reliable measure of a child's intelligence—what subject matter appears in the passages, how the questions are worded, the amount of sleep or breakfast a child had that day. But last week I saw how subjective things are even on the output end. Was that a decimal or a stray mark? Is this a four or a nine? We dutifully passed tests around the table, weighing students' responses against the sample questions, squinting at crossed-out work, shaking our heads.

"But he *got* it!"

"But he wrote *add* when he meant *multiply*."

"But he *did* multiply!"

Our table was especially diligent; we spent 20 minutes debating a question on one of our last tests for the day and, after getting conflicting opinions from three site coordinators, ended up calling the question in to the city testing headquarters. (Final verdict: full credit.) The higher-ups' response made us realize that we may have scored several other students' answers too harshly, so we asked the site manager to reopen the

Despite its relative perks, our social working process was vital precisely because of one scary fact: So much about these tests is subjective.

boxes of tests we had turned in. The other round tables in the gym were empty—it looked like an extremely boring prom had just ended—as we unshouldered our bags and sat back down to make sure we hadn't denied any children their rightful points.

The results of our search: Three other students' responses got bumped up to full credit, and we found two full tests and one half test that hadn't been checked at all.

So much focus and energy and intelligence in that room. So much riding on those numbers. And even a table of overachievers couldn't get through day one without a few glaring mistakes and a whole lot of gray. 🐾

Apologies to Sandra Cisneros

How ETS' computer-based writing assessment misses the mark

MAJA WILSON

At 27 years old, I was quickly becoming an English teacher stereotype: Frizzy hair escaped my hastily secured bun, and my eyes had gone slightly wild from reading pile after pile of student papers.

It was exam time during my first year of teaching high school writing courses. I'd been determined not to turn the mandatory finals into a multiple-choice test, so I'd assigned a final revision and had given an in-class reflective writing assignment during the exam hour. But I had only one work day to read and grade the papers and reflective writings, calculate and submit semester grades, and prepare for my next round of courses. After toiling alone in my classroom, I had moved my piles of papers to the teachers' lounge in an increasingly futile attempt to preserve my sanity.

Another teacher appeared, weighted down with her own stack of exams. "It's a lot of work, isn't it?" she empathized. She understood! But as she turned and began to feed her stack of papers into the Scantron machine on the counter, my wan smile faded. "Sometimes I have to run these through two or three times to make sure there are no mistakes," she said, shaking her head, clearly not noticing that my eyes were now boring into the back of her skull.

Five years later, I still haven't given students in my writing courses a multiple-choice final exam. I'd like to chalk up my resistance to idealism and strength of character, but it's partly an issue of logistics. I've got to keep the students occupied for an entire hour and a half. How many multiple-choice questions can *you* devise about the steps of the writing process? Secretly, though, I've held out hope; if technological progress can send a probe to Mars and pack 15,000 of my favorite songs into an iPod, why can't it devise a way to grade student writing?

Free Trial from ETS

The truth is, the technology to grade student writing has been around for a while. In the late 1990s, the Graduate Management Admissions Test (GMAT) began using Educational Testing Service's (ETS) e-rater, a computer-based grading program, to score applicants' essays along with one human reader; even my state's standardized testing program was considering a computer grading program the following year.

But when it comes to technology, I'm usually a bit behind the times. So I didn't begin to seriously consider computer writing assessment until I received an email offering a free trial of ETS's Criterion—a web-based grading program.

I'd had no idea how widespread computer grading systems already were; in

2004, Criterion was scoring and responding to 10,000 student essays a week, according to article in *AI* by Jill Burstein, a researcher at ETS who developed Criterion. ETS's website claimed that "hundreds of thousands of students" were now using Criterion.

I quickly registered for my free trial, and browsed Criterion's website while I waited for the email confirming my guest password. ETS pointed out that its grading tools "only process information; they cannot read and analyze it." When someone sits down to grade a paper, the first thing they do is *read* the paper; how can a computer program claim to evaluate writing when computers can't "read"? Although Criterion's promises of accurate scores and "immediate feedback" for students appealed to my dream of organizing my file cabinets on teacher work days, I remained skeptical. If I were to embrace ETS's Criterion, I needed first to compare it with what I wanted for my students and what I knew about writing pedagogy and assessment.

> When someone sits down to grade a paper, the first thing they do is read the paper; how can a computer program claim to evaluate writing when computers can't "read"?

Reading involves a complex set of interactions among language, experience, emotion, and thought that I suspected were at the heart of writing assessment. For example, today I finished reading *The Year of Magical Thinking* in which Joan Didion chronicles her thoughts and memories during the year following her husband's death. In the last chapter, this sentence—which recalls a trip Didion took with her husband to Indonesia and Malaysia—caught in my throat: "Some of the islands that were there then would now be gone, just shallows." My entire being responded to the metaphor of loss in the image of the disappearing islands, as I layered Didion's story of grief and my own experiences of loss onto those 14 words. Many a grammatically correct sentence had failed to inspire or move me like this one had; my assessment of its power rested firmly on the experiences and ideas that I brought to the reading as well as the images and rhythms of language Didion had built in earlier chapters. Simply put, my assessment depended on my ability to read. Without the ability to read, what *can* Criterion do?

How Criterion "Reads"

Criterion uses formulas to compare a student's performance to exemplars, or pre-scored student papers. It then rates the student's work based on these comparisons. For example, if the sentence length ratios and instance of repetitious words in Emily's essay match the data gathered from the set of pre-scored C- essays, Emily will receive a C- for style. And how does Criterion define "Style"? According to Burstein, Criterion finds errors in "Style" by looking for "the use of passive sentences, as well as very long or very short sentences within the essay. Another feature of potentially undesirable style that the system detects is the presence of overly repetitious words."

In other words, when e-rater looks at Didion's last chapter, it isn't interested in grief or loss or metaphor. It isn't interested in what Didion wrote in chapter two about her fear of her daughter's death and how this fear—combined with her husband's death and my own losses—create a hum underneath the sentence about disappearing islands. Criterion bypasses the reading process by analyzing and responding to the surface of the writing.

I was leery of Criterion's reliance on pre-scored essays because I've often been pleasantly surprised at a student's unique approach to a writing assignment—an approach that may break my preconceived visions of quality. Last week, Tyler wrote a run-on sentence that blew my mind; if it hadn't moved me so deeply, my green pen (Is green the new red?) would have had a field day with it. But Tyler was illustrating his tendency to zone in and out of the world around him and the world of his mind, resulting in a kind of muddy image-soup that could only be captured in a half-page sentence. It is absolutely true that—like Criterion—I have images in my head of previous students' work when I read new papers. But I like to think that my mind isn't as rigid as a computer; I can leave the exemplars behind when I'm swept away on the current of beautiful writing that doesn't fit the mold. My ability to read—with all the complex interactions involved—allows me this freedom.

Despite my suspicions that e-rater couldn't grade as well as a human being, research from links on Criterion's website suggested that human readers and Criterion's scoring program agreed on scores *more* often than humans agreed with each other. The logic was dizzying; e-rater scored more like humans than humans did? But the human readers against which e-rater were compared had been trained to use the same scoring rubric used by Criterion. I'd become suspicious of the rubric's ability to capture what I value about students' writing. When I used rubrics, I struggled to narrow my reactions to students' writing into the language and categories of the rubrics. Some writers clearly followed directions too well, writing horribly boring but mechanically correct and organized essays that scored high, while some writers took huge risks, producing engaging and often beautiful work that scored low because the rubric didn't value the risks and unique approaches they'd taken. I wondered if the researchers' implication that e-rater scored more like humans than humans did had been inverted. Did e-rater grade like a human, or had rubrics forced humans to grade like a computer?

And to be honest, I was less interested in Criterion's claim to grade student writing and more interested in its promise to give "immediate feedback," not only on grammar and mechanics, but also on style, organization, and development.

Feedback was critical to my teaching of writing; if I did nothing but grade, I'd have plenty of time to organize those files. But I wanted for my students the kind of feedback I'd experienced from interested readers I'd had all through-out my life—from my father, my friend Sarah, and from the participants in writing workshops I'd taken as an adult.

> I like to think that my mind isn't as rigid as a computer; I can leave the exemplars behind when I'm swept away on the current of beautiful writing that doesn't fit the mold.

None of these readers had based their reactions on criteria based on the surface of my work. Instead, they'd let my words roll around in their minds and then told me how they had been affected. When I tried to provide this kind of feedback for my students, I not only saw their writing improve, but I also saw them investing in the writing process with a commitment I'd never seen when I focused on grad-ing. Like Linda Christensen, who describes her refusal to grade students' papers in "My Dirty Little Secret" (*Rethinking Schools*, Vol. 19, No. 2.), I'd decided to give full credit for a paper once the student had revised and we were both satisfied with it, no matter how many revisions it took.

I saw the benefits of this decision with Jessica, who came to my class con-vinced that she was a horrible writer. She handed in a short piece of descriptive writing about her favorite place, her couch, and she told me that she hated it and that I should just throw it out after I failed it. I wasn't engaged at all in her piece until I read one line that Jessica wrote about how she sat with her grandmother on the couch every day. I pointed out this line to Jessica, telling her how much I liked it and how it made me wonder about her grandmother and how they'd come to see the couch as a kind of common ground. Perhaps she really wanted to write about her grandmother, using her favorite place on the couch as a frame for describing their relationship. Later that week, Jessica handed in another draft of the paper, this time smiling as she handed it in. After I read it out loud to the class—anony-mously, as she'd requested—she raised her hand and proudly and loudly demanded her paper back so that she could show it to her grandmother.

Testing Criterion

How would I test Criterion's feedback? My guest username and password had ar-rived, and as I considered the empty textbox into which I was invited to type an essay, I briefly considered submitting one of my student's papers. But then I thought of Sandra Cisneros' "My Name" from *House on Mango Street*, a wonderful model for narrative and descriptive writing used by writing teachers all over the country. Every time I read "My Name" to my students—and I always read it out loud because I love to play with the rhythm Cisneros creates—my students and I find different things to love. Last year, Maria lit up when I read, "It is the Mexican records my father plays on Sunday mornings when he is shaving, songs like sob-bing." She began to talk about the Mexican music her own father played, and how those songs had always felt vaguely sad.

This year, when I read it, Tom stopped me after this passage about Esperanza's namesake, her grandmother: "I would've liked to have known her, a wild horse of a woman, so wild she wouldn't marry. Until my great-grandfather threw a sack over her head and carried her off. Just like that, as if she were a fancy chandelier. That's the way he did it." Tom, the class clown, frowned and called out, "He didn't really carry her off! That's crazy!" Ayame said, "It's a metaphor! It means she really didn't want to marry." When Tom protested that she shouldn't have agreed to marry him, the class was off onto a heated conversation about gender and culture that I hadn't planned but wasn't about to shut down.

Since "My Name" ends as Esperanza fantasizes about the names she could choose for herself, "Esperanza as Lisandra or Maritza or Zeze the X. Yes. Something like Zeze the X will do," I often invite my students to consider the names that might fit them better than the names they've been given. And sometimes, we simply read it, savor it quietly and meditatively, and begin to write about our own lives. I wondered what feedback Criterion would give a writer such as Cisneros. I typed "My Name" into the blank textbook and clicked "Submit."

Criterion delivered perfectly on its first promise; it created a printout of responses about grammar, mechanics, style, organization, and development in less than 30 seconds. But Criterion was not overjoyed by Cisneros' writing; the first thing that struck me about the feedback was that it offered no praise. Praise is important in my own feedback because it helps students become better writers. When I sit down to write, about 90 percent of what spills out is not suitable for public consumption. Part of becoming a good writer is the ability to recognize the 10 percent with potential and the courage to purge the rest. When I praise parts of my students' papers, I am pointing out the standards they have set for themselves. But Criterion cannot recognize what writers do well. It only defines and describes deficits, and its feedback to Cisneros merely pointed out "mistakes" in "My Name"—repetitious word use, use of fragments, and problems with organization and development. What would happen to "My Name" if Criterion's immediate feedback had shaped it?

"Improving" Cisneros

Criterion had highlighted words and phrases that might need work, and directed me to the *Writer's Handbook*—provided by Criterion via links. With profuse apologies to Cisneros, I set out to revise "My Name" in the hopes of finding out what effect Criterion might have on our students' revision and writing.

I began by examining Criterion's comments on Cisneros' grammar. It highlighted "A muddy color." "My great grandmother." and "Esperanza." Criterion pointed out that these were fragments, requiring a subject and a predicate. Although changing the fragments to complete sentences changed the rhythm of "My Name," I tried to preserve Cisneros' syntax. For example, "My great grandmother." became "I would have like to have known my great grandmother, a wild horse of a woman." In the Mechanics section, Criterion had highlighted "the one nobody sees," pointing out an extra article. This suggestion wasn't a mandate, so I left the extra article intact. So far, so good.

Incorporating Criterion's comments about style proved a bigger challenge. First, I replaced Cisneros' word repetitions. I also took the program's advice and combined short sentences into long ones. The second, third, and fifth sentences became one streamlined sentence: "In Spanish, my name, which is Esperanza, has a muddy sound and means too many letters, sadness, and waiting."

Organization and development caused me the most consternation. Criterion asked if the first three sentences were the introduction, then directed me to the *Writer's Handbook* for suggestions on how to "capture the *reader's interest, provide background information about your topic, and present your thesis sentence.*" I settled on "general background" and wrote about how examining the meaning of one's name in different languages may lead to insights. The new improved introduction set me up nicely for my next task: to write a clear thesis statement that would "organize, predict, control, and define the essay."

The sentence about the records played by Esperanza's father—highlighted and identified as the thesis—surely didn't meet the criteria for a good thesis. It was back to the *Writer's Handbook*, where I learned that perhaps I needed to define the terms used and prepare the reader for the points that would be made later. To reorganize the rest of Cisneros' writing into supporting material with strong topic sentences, I had to think long and hard about the point of Cisneros' loosely associative narrative. But I managed to make all of these associations clear in the end.

By the time I got around to taking Criterion's suggestion to transform the end of "My Name," it was easy to write a conclusion that "reminds the reader about your thesis, stresses the importance of the ideas you have developed, and leaves the reader with thought-provoking ideas." It was time to resubmit the essay to Criterion:

> Names mean different things in different languages. While many people never consider the origin of their names, comparing the different meanings of one's name can lead to interesting insights. An insight is some kind of deep understanding one comes to about an issue—global or personal. When I began to reflect on the meaning of my name in different languages, I not only began to understand personal truths about my family legacy, about the nature of gender and culture, and about myself, but I discovered a plan to grow in the future.
>
> The negative associations I have with my name in Spanish reflect my family's legacy and make me question if I should accept this legacy. In Spanish, my name, which is Esperanza, has a muddy sound and means too many letters, sadness, and waiting. The muddy sadness that I associate with my name in the Spanish language reminds me of the Mexican records my father plays on Sunday mornings when he is shaving, songs similar to sobbing. Why were the songs so sad, and how did this sadness affect me and my family?

Praise is important in my own feedback because it helps students become better writers.

The sadness of this legacy began because Mexican men don't like their women strong. This caused sadness for my great grandmother, for whom I am named. While my great grandmother was a wild horse of a woman when she was young, my great grandfather forced her to marry him against her will and she spent the rest of her life looking out of the window, the way that so many women do, waiting. I wonder if she was sorry because she couldn't be all the things she wanted to be, or if she made the best of her life. In Spanish, the name Esperanza is made out of something soft, like silver, but I don't want to be soft, like my great grandmother was forced to become. I don't want to inherit her place by the window, a sad place that was dictated by her culture and her gender.

I am not sure that my name fits me. When I think about the meaning of my name in English, I am torn between the culture of my family and the culture in which I find myself here in the United States. My name in English means hope. While I hope that my life in the United States will be different than my grandmother's life, I do not like everything about the culture here. I know this because I do not like the way the other students at school pronounce my name. At school they pronounce my name strangely, as if the syllables are made out of tin and hurt the roof of their mouths. My reaction to the way they say my name shows that I am not altogether comfortable here. Still, my dislike of my name in Spanish and my grandmother's role shows that I am not comfortable with my family's culture.

Perhaps I don't fit in anywhere and must create my own identity. If I were to name myself, I would choose a strong sounding name. With this strong name that I chose for myself, I would reclaim my identity, which is lost between two worlds right now. I would choose a name such as Lisandra or Mirtza or Zeze the X. Yes, the strong sound of Zeze the X will do. Those who are struggling with their own identity would be wise to consider the meaning of their name in different languages and to rename themselves, as I have done.

New and Improved?

My rewrite avoided most of Criterion's criticism. When Criterion highlighted my introduction and asked if it provided background information, I was able to answer affirmatively. In addition, my essay was 270 words longer, and ETS research said longer was better. I was also pleased that I'd managed to turn Cisneros' essay into five paragraphs; according to ETS, Criterion was based on a "five paragraph essay strategy for developing writers."

But did my revisions make "My Name" a better piece of writing? I did what Criterion couldn't do and re-read Cisneros' original work and my own revision. This reading rendered the question ridiculous. True, Cisneros' work wasn't an argumentative, expository piece. Was *my* test fair? A halfhearted disclaimer on Criterion's website simultaneously claimed not to "stifle creative writing" and to be better suited to grade writing done for standardized tests. But Criterion also claimed to be able to grade and respond to narrative and descriptive work, which Cisneros' piece certainly was.

I also questioned the distinction between "creative writing" and expository and argumentative writing. Much of my own argumentative writing relied on what I considered to be creative descriptions and narrative, and I found that my students argued and informed more effectively when they adopted creative approaches to their investigations and writing. Most of the argumentative and informative writing I enjoyed reading in *The Atlantic Monthly* or in bestsellers such as Bill Bryson's *A Short History of Nearly Everything* demonstrated this creative, reflective, and layered approach. Distinguishing between creative writing and other kinds of writing represented a kind of delusion that allowed Criterion to get away with reshaping all writing into the five-paragraph essay—a form I'd never enjoyed reading, writing, or teaching—simply because it is easier to grade.

> **The five-paragraph essay, along with the computer programs developed to evaluate it, separated thought from language.**

But I didn't dislike the five-paragraph essay just because I found it boring. I disliked it because I mistrusted its intentions. The five-paragraph essay, along with the computer programs developed to evaluate it, separated thought from language. The thought embodied by the words no longer mattered, as long as the thesis sentence was in the right place and the three main points were captured in topic sentences and the conclusion was safely summative. Teaching the five-paragraph essay turned writing into a formula to be memorized and spit out again and again. It turned students into factory workers who cranked out essays that all looked alike. It turned me into a quality-control manager slamming my template down in perfect rhythm over every essay and looking for deviations from the norm. This process didn't honor my own mind as a teacher or my students' minds as writers.

But the standardization of writing pedagogy and assessment doesn't just encourage formulaic teaching and writing; it creates a pyramid scheme with students and teachers at the bottom and corporations such as ETS at the top. Corporations make a fortune every year telling overburdened and underpaid teachers how to teach—and selling products to help students pass the tests. ETS, with its commitment to standardized testing and its subsequent development and marketing of Criterion, are poised to capitalize on this phenomenon.

If the considerable time and effort that has been put into computer grading systems that produce standardized writers had been put into reducing instructors' loads, perhaps we wouldn't be so desperately looking to testing corporations for solutions to problems that they have created. But the corporations that profit from the perception of our incompetence can't let that happen. If they trusted teachers to teach, and if they trusted students to think and question, they'd be out of a job.

Will resisting Criterion's claims thwart ETS's attempt to turn writing from an art to a test-taking skill? Maybe, maybe not. But for the sake of Cisneros and all of the students in my class whose writing has the power to change all of our lives, I'm not buying into this one. ✎

On White Preference

JAY ROSNER

In 2003, the United States Supreme Court supported affirmative action when it ruled on two of the University of Michigan's affirmative action plans. It found the undergraduate program unconstitutional but upheld the law school's policy.

In the cases, the white complainants argued that it was fundamentally unfair that Michigan accepted black applicants with lower SAT scores (or LSAT scores at the law school) than some whites who were rejected. But an analysis of the SAT that I conducted revealed something startling: Every single question carefully preselected to appear on the test favors whites over blacks. These data have the potential to reframe the affirmative-action debate, especially if they spark advocates to ask the iconoclastic question: What's wrong with admitting some black students with lower SAT scores, when every question favors whites?

On the October 1998 SAT, for example, every single one of the 138 questions (60 math and 78 verbal) favored whites over blacks. By favoring whites, I mean that a higher percentage of white than black students answered correctly every question prescreened and chosen to appear on that SAT. I call these "white preference questions." This is not a quirk of one particular SAT form. SAT forms are designed to very strongly correlate with one another. And the pattern I've identified is a predictable result of the way the tests are constructed. Latino test-takers are similarly affected, faring only a bit better than blacks.

I don't believe that the Educational Testing Service (ETS)—the developer of the SAT and the source of this October 1998 test data—intended for the SAT to be a white preference test. However, the "scientific" test construction methods the company uses inexorably lead to this result. Each individual SAT question ETS chooses is required to parallel the outcomes of the test overall. So, if high-scoring test-takers—who are more likely to be white—tend to answer the question correctly in pretesting, it's a worthy SAT question; if not, it's thrown out. Race and ethnicity are not considered explicitly, but racially disparate scores drive question selection, which in turn reproduces racially disparate test results in an internally reinforcing cycle.

Here's a verbal question that illustrates the SAT's skewed test construction process:

> The actor's bearing on stage seemed _____ her movements were natural and her technique _____ (A) unremitting ... blase; (B) fluid ... tentative (C) unstudied ... uncontrived (correct answer) (D) eclectic ... uniform (E) grandiose ... controlled

This looks like a typical SAT verbal question. Yet this question differs from others in one important respect: According to ETS, "8 percent more African Americans than whites answered this question correctly." I call this a "black preference question." I don't know why blacks did better here, but nearly all SAT questions capture something about race that can't be determined until pre-testing. Because it favored blacks—who score lower on the test overall—this "actor's bearing" question, which was pretested by ETS in 1998, did not favor high scorers and therefore was rejected for use on the SAT. I have identified several other examples—including a black preference SAT math question—that were rejected.

My considered hypothesis is that every question chosen to appear on every SAT in the past 10 years has favored whites over blacks.

My considered hypothesis is that every question chosen to appear on every SAT in the past 10 years has favored whites over blacks. The same pattern holds true on the LSAT and the other popular admissions tests, because they are developed similarly. The SAT question selection process has never, to my knowledge, been examined from this perspective. And the deeper one looks, the worse things get. For example, although all the questions on the October 1998 SAT favored whites over blacks, approximately one-fifth showed huge 20 percent gaps favoring whites. Skewed question selection certainly contributes to the large test score disparities between blacks and whites.

Supporters of affirmative action can take solace in the broad cross-section of higher education, labor, and business institutions that filed amicus briefs favoring the University of Michigan in the Supreme Court cases. But defenders of affirmative action in university admissions have shied away from confronting the term "preferences" and from vigorously attacking the assumption of test neutrality. It is essential that we document the plethora of powerful white preferences throughout the admissions process, ranging from disparities in family wealth and income to unequal K-12 education—and, we now know, biases in SAT question selection. Affirmative action, at the very back end of this entire process, serves as only a partial corrective to the considerable white preference that precedes it. ✎

For more on the Michigan cases, see www.thenation.com. This article was originally published in The Nation, *Vol. 276, Issue 14 on April 14, 2003.*

Testing What Matters Least

What we learned when we took the Praxis Reading Specialist Test

MAIKA YEIGH, ANDIE CUNNINGHAM, AND RUTH SHAGOURY

We clutched our printed-out paper tickets in one hand and driver's licenses in the other, passing both to the grim attendant who directed us to our seats. In case these documents had changed in the 15 seconds it took to walk to our assigned seats, she checked them again and instructed us to leave them on the desk for her continued access. We felt like we were about to embark on some weird plane trip. As it turns out, it was quite a trip—into the bizarre world of standardized testing for adult professionals, in our case, the Praxis test for reading specialists.

We are three professors of literacy in a teacher education program that leads to a reading endorsement. Our graduates are reading specialists, literacy coaches, and district language arts specialists—but only if, in addition to the coursework and practicum experience that make up our National Council for Accreditation of Teacher Education (NCATE) certified reading program, they also pass the Praxis Reading Specialist Test. Like any students approaching a high-stakes test, the adults we work with are anxious about the Praxis, a two-hour, 120-question, multiple-choice, gatekeeper test for their chosen positions as literacy leaders.

From their reports, we had become increasingly concerned about what seems to be a very narrow focus of this professional test. We decided it was time for us to embark on a journey into the two-dimensional world of the Praxis test.

We discovered that, at best, the Praxis test measures the least important aspects of professional knowledge. At worst, it reinforces harmful ideas about the profession: that reading specialists and literacy coaches should "know their place," not buck the system, and certainly not encourage their colleagues to critique the standardized tests that dominate our profession.

A Political Subtext

The Praxis test we took showed no understanding of the intended use of standardized tests, and even reinforced misuse of large-scale testing results. A telling test item asked what the reading specialist should do with state assessment results. One answer option was for the specialist to put the results into teacher mailboxes. Another choice was to use the results to group students for instruction. There was no answer that implied that standardized assessment scores should be used *as just one piece* of collected data regarding student learning. As test takers, we were forced to choose which wrong answer seemed the least offensive, or guess what was in the test maker's mind. How could this be a thoughtful way to evaluate a potential reading specialist's understanding of the role of standardized testing data?

As we took the Praxis test, a disturbing subtext emerged from the questions. The exam implied that the main function of a reading specialist is to do the bidding of the building administrator and the school district—that the position is not one of decision-making but of implementation and enforcement. Test questions communicated no expectation that reading specialists and literacy coaches should rely on their own understanding of the reading process or look to students in making decisions. One test question scenario, for example, involved a school that scored significantly lower on a standardized reading achievement test than others in the district; the reading specialist was asked by the superintendent to recommend how to restructure the reading program in the low-performing school. As test takers, we were asked what steps would be most important for the reading specialist to take. The choices were all top-down options that assumed following the superintendent's request without question. We recall one possible answer was to evaluate the adequacy of the licensure and certification of the teachers in the low-performing school; another was to compare the students' scores to state and national norms. There was no option for educating the superintendent about the needs of the school, the teachers, and the children rather than "fixing" the problem. Once again, there was no answer we were comfortable choosing.

At worst, it reinforces harmful ideas about the profession: that reading specialists and literacy coaches should "know their place," not buck the system, and certainly not encourage their colleagues to critique the standardized tests that dominate our profession.

Rather than doing their administrators' bidding, the role of the literacy leader is to support teachers in their daily work—planning, modeling, team-teaching, and providing feedback in collaboration with teachers, creating a community of teachers empowered to discuss children's needs and plan together. By omitting any reference to such a crucial role, the Praxis test implies a different stance, one we find troubling.

By contrast, the International Reading Association (IRA) recommends that the reading specialist's role in assessment includes evaluation of the school's literacy program on a broad basis.[1] Specifically, the reading specialist should focus on individual student strengths and needs and be able to communicate these to various stakeholders and paraprofessionals.

> By breaking reading instruction down into isolated facts for the purposes of a standardized test, the creators of the Praxis test measure what matters least.

Measuring What Matters Least

A majority of the test items on the Praxis exam fit the definition of "easily measured." We found a clear preference from the test makers for questions that test terminology: *Schwa, cloze, digraph, homonym, SQ3R,* and *lexile* were all test items on the exam. Certainly, these are terms that should be familiar to literacy specialists, but the sheer number of terminology questions raised their importance. For example, one question went something like this:

> You have a student who struggles to read "banana, "lemon," and "some." This child could be helped with a word sort on:
>
> a. digraphs
> b. schwas
> c. diphthongs
> d. morphemes

By breaking reading instruction down into isolated facts for the purposes of a standardized test, the creators of the Praxis test measure what matters least.
In an attempt to see if the candidate knows what a schwa is, its importance is elevated to a teaching strategy. (For the uninitiated, the definition of schwa, from Macmillan's dictionary, is "a vowel sound used in unstressed syllables, for example, the sound of 'a' in 'above.'") We can think of no reason to teach a young, struggling reader to find schwas—or find any research to support such a task. Nonetheless, on each of our versions, there were at least three questions that included the term "schwa."

We also found an emphasis on isolated terminology that must be some test writer's pet strategy. "Say-it-fast-break-it-down" and "narrow reading" were terms included on the test. These are not mainstream—or particularly useful—activities for working with young readers. But they are easy to measure!

One of the major influences on the field of literacy has been the proficient reader studies, which focus on the process good readers use, instead of the deficit model of "fixing" poor readers.[2] This research has shifted instruction to an emphasis on comprehension strategies, as well as what all readers bring to the text. This field-changing body of work stresses a student's culture and background knowledge, and was noticeably missing from the Praxis exams we took. Instead, the more easily tested "literal and higher-order" hierarchy was included in test item after test item.

Not Measuring What Matters Most

The test failed to address or attempt to measure some of the most important standards created by IRA/NCTE for the preparation and certification of reading specialists (2003). There are five standards by which our teacher education program is measured in this area: Foundational Knowledge; Instructional Strategies and Curriculum Materials; Assessment, Diagnosis, and Evaluation; Creating a Literate Environment; and Professional Development. Within these five standards are descriptors of well-rounded literacy leaders' actions,

These test-maker assumptions oppose the standard itself, which states that the reading specialist should support the teacher in finding relevant and interesting reading material.

work, and strategies that cannot be measured using a one-dimensional assessment.

Let's look more closely at the fourth standard as an example:

> Creating a Literate Environment: Assist the classroom teacher and paraprofessionals in selecting materials that match the reading levels, interests, and cultural and linguistic background of students (*standard 4.1*).

One facet of creating this literate environment is the ability to support teachers and paraprofessionals in the selection of materials that match the needs, backgrounds, and interests of students. This is a complex skill that requires building relationships with colleagues and students, making keen observations and judgments, and exercising a deep multicultural sensitivity.

Supporting family literacy is an important endeavor for many of our inservice teachers, including those who work with families that are not native English speakers. Recently one student, inspired by Jennifer Allen's book swap project, documented in *Becoming a Literacy Leader*,[3] created a book library for her families whose native language was Spanish. She wrote a successful grant to purchase picture books written in Spanish and created a mini-library that parents could access. She kicked off her project with a family literacy night at which she showed parents the books, demonstrated the checkout system, and taught parents how to picture-read with their children. She also worked with teachers to support students bringing these texts into their classrooms during the reading block. This inservice teacher obviously meets the standard of "creating a literate environment"—yet it is impossible for a standardized test question to capture the depth of this project.

Instead, the Praxis test questions imply reliance on a basal reader, with the reading specialist's role to facilitate its use. The suggestion is that a basal reader is the preferred vehicle for accessible literature. For example, one item asked whether reading specialists should judge textbooks according to curriculum objectives, students' reading levels, students' performance on standardized tests, or the classroom teachers' preference in reading textbook format. We still aren't sure what the intended "right" answer is. Although textbooks may be part of the reading diet in a classroom, the omission of any questions about reading workshop instruction, use of book clubs, or how reading specialists might promote use of trade books within classrooms reinforces the message that purchased reading textbooks are the norm—and the expectation.

These test-maker assumptions oppose the standard itself, which states that the reading specialist should support the teacher in finding relevant and interesting reading material. A wealth of reading materials "match the reading levels, interests, and cultural and linguistic backgrounds of students." How well a potential reading specialist knows appropriate reading material—and can make it accessible to teachers and students—is indeed worth measuring. Not surprisingly, we found no mention of assessments other than high-stakes standardized tests on the exam, even though the IRA/NCTE standard 3.1 states that reading specialists should "compare and contrast, use, interpret, and recommend *a wide range of assessment tools and practices*," [emphasis added]. Miscue analysis, for example, is a widely accepted assessment tool that the test ignored. Portfolios—another respected method—failed to make the test as well.

But how can 120 multiple-choice questions possibly encompass the complex tapestry that literacy specialists are expected to weave every day? Why break down the complexity to sound bytes that distort the real world of schools, classrooms, children, and teachers?

Fundamentally, the Praxis test ignores the role of reading professionals in modeling a love of reading and demonstrating how reading and writing can be utilized in the world. Readers read for real purposes: critically interrogating the world, questioning assumptions, probing for implied values, and even challenging bogus assessments of achievement—like this test!

A Call to Action

Currently 15 states require the Praxis Reading Specialist Test, and the number is growing each year. Our conclusion is that this exam does nothing to help prepare these critical education specialists. If anything, it miscommunicates what it means to be a reading professional to test takers. Based on our experience, the test directly contradicts the professional standards that we embrace.

Why are we allowing the testing industry to usurp our responsibility to assess and evaluate teachers who have gone through the rigors of an advanced professional program? What is the rationale for lining the pockets of the testing industry? The test costs $85 to take, with a required additional registration fee of $50. And that's the minimum; if you need your scores expedited or want to check them online before 30 days, there are hefty additional fees. And many teachers take it more than once before they achieve a passing score.

It isn't just reading specialists who face these needless and damaging standardized tests. We recently spoke with colleagues at our institution from teacher education, educational leadership, and counseling psychology programs about our Praxis test experience. Chagrined, they realized that they hadn't thought to take the tests that their students must take to apply for licensure or endorsement. They also realized they didn't know enough about either the content of the exam or the intersection between their coursework and the required tests.

We believe it is time to take back our professional responsibility. Our next step is to initiate dialogue with colleagues nationwide and craft resolutions through our professional organizations (such as NCTE) to oppose continuation of this testing requirement. And we hope this kind of grassroots effort will have an impact on others who work in our schools and communities. In the long run, we can't stop the damaging effects of standardized testing on the children until we examine the impact it is having on teachers as well as on the larger culture of schools.

Why break down the complexity to sound bytes that distort the real world of schools, classrooms, children, and teachers?

Endnotes

1. International Reading Association, *Standards for Reading Professionals*, 2003. www.reading.org/downloads/resources/545standards2003/index.html.

2. David Pearson et al., "Developing Expertise in Reading Comprehension," in A. Farstrup and J. Samuels, eds., *What Research Has to Say About Reading Instruction*. Newark: International Reading Association, 1992.

3. Jennifer Allen, *Becoming a Literacy Leader*. Portland, Maine: Stenhouse, 2006.

PART 5

Resisting and Responding to High-Stakes Testing

RANDALL ENOS

Responding to Test-Driven Reform

BARBARA MINER

In response to the standards and testing movement, several approaches are emerging. Some argue that progressives should concentrate on using the rhetoric of "high standards for all" to reopen the discussion on "opportunity to learn standards"—that is, providing sufficient resources and "opportunities to learn" before instituting across-the-board expectations for results. Others emphasize the importance of legal action and filing suits against high-stakes tests on civil rights grounds.

Many progressive educators emphasize a stance of active resistance and, where appropriate, of boycotting the tests and adopting a "just-say-no" approach. A number of parents, teachers, and students have been organizing along these lines.

As Monty Neill of FairTest argues, "Should you go along with the dominant definition of reform, or do you fight it if you think it is an educational disaster? And I think it is an educational disaster."

In addition to active test resistance, Neill highlights two other important tasks: demanding better and more authentic methods of public accountability and developing high-quality classroom-based assessments that can help teachers improve teaching.

Theresa Perry, professor of Africana Studies and education at Simmons College in Boston, argues that many African American educators and parents are leery of a "just-say-no" approach and worry that the African American community can't wait forever for better assessments to come along. She underscores the need to help African American students pass the tests, and to use the tests to redress the chronic problem of low expectations and substandard curriculum for many African American students.

"Fundamentally, the only way you can gain access to opportunity is by passing through the gatekeeping tests," she says. "Unless the tests are going to go away tomorrow, the real issue is, how do you …help poor kids pass the test?"

"The tests are flawed, but what is the alternative?" she continues. "And are white progressives willing to take a stand in their local community to equalize outcomes?"

Michael Apple, an education policy professor at the University of Wisconsin-Madison, stresses the importance

> **Many African American educators and parents are leery of a "just-say-no" approach and worry that the African American community can't wait forever for better assessments to come along.**

of a dual stance. Although it's important to recognize that the tests are not going to go away anytime soon, he says, one must still point out "how these things have worked historically. That is, they exacerbate social problems, they blame the same students, teachers, and parents who have been blamed before, and they serve as an excuse not to equalize material resources."

Apple cautions that progressives who are opposed to high-stakes tests must be careful not to allow themselves to be painted as anti-reform and as defenders of the status quo. "The idea is to think strategically," he says, "and not to form a rejectionist front that allows your enemies to position you in a way that is less powerful."

The late Asa Hilliard, former professor of urban education at Georgia State University, argued, "For the segment of the community that doesn't have power, the worst thing they can do is drop out of the game and not take the test," he said. But, he added, after helping kids pass the test, "you have to then turn right around and challenge the tests."

Asked for what's the best way forward, Hilliard summed up the problem this way: "I don't think there's a magic solution. The problem is, the people who are advocating high-stakes tests believe that they have the solution. And they are going to make consequences based on that." ✎

High-Stakes Harm

Teaching students to read tests

LINDA CHRISTENSEN

Tests today are high stakes. Based on these numbers, students are retained, placed in summer school and remedial classes; schools are reconstituted, and teachers' and principals' salaries rise and fall. Students, especially those who "fail" the tests, internalize the failure, and question their ability and their intelligence. They learn to blame themselves, and some come to believe they will not succeed because they are not capable enough. As my daughter said after receiving a 3 (not competent) on an oral Spanish test, "Maybe I don't have what it takes." The test took away the experience of animated conversations with her host family in Cuernavaca as well as her ability to navigate Mexico City. Instead of questioning the validity of the measurement tool as an "authentic assessment," especially compared to her experience in Mexico, she questioned herself.

So while critical teachers might stand back and say we don't want to have anything to do with tests, you better believe that we can't just go on with business as usual. The question for anyone who cares about kids is how do we retain our critical stance on assessments while preparing students for them? Can we "teach the tests" without compromising what we know to be true about teaching and learning?

My friends at low-achieving elementary schools have been counseled to acclimate students to tests by redesigning their regular curriculum so that students can get accustomed to multiple-choice questions. But in an activist classroom, that's not easy. How can a role play about an important historical or social issue be reformatted into a multiple-choice activity? How does an a, b, c, d answer format encourage students to imagine themselves an interned Japanese American or a Cherokee Indian facing government-ordered removal? Teachers are also asked to mimic the more "authentic" assessments in fairly inauthentic ways. A kindergarten colleague was asked by the 3rd-grade teachers to prepare students for the state six-trait analysis scoring guide by giving them 1-6 scores on everything from lining up at the door to tying their shoes and counting.

Clearly, this isn't the kind of teaching we want to happen in our classrooms. To achieve real gains in student knowledge and skill, we must continue to give students a rich curriculum with varied opportunities to use their learning in real world activities. This material will generate growth that may or may not be reflected in test scores, but will increase the likelihood of students seeing themselves as readers, writers, historians, scientists, mathematicians, and thinkers.

However, I live in a state that has filled our classrooms with tests—multiple choice and work samples. As a teacher and mother who has patched up the wounds test scores left behind and as the victim of a school that was reconstituted in part due to low test scores, I am a firm advocate in fighting against the over-assessment

> The question for anyone who cares about kids is how do we retain our critical stance on assessments while preparing students for them?

of students. But I also believe we must seize the opening to help our students critically analyze these exams and the motives that put them into practice, as well as teach them how to improve their skills and scores. Thus, we need to teach students to critique the tests as well as coach them on how to increase their performance.

Talk Back: Questioning the Assumptions of the Test

A social justice curriculum equips students to question what is often taken for granted. Tests have become as much a part of the curriculum as books. (In fact, these days there seems to be more money for testing, test preparation, and test scoring than for the books we need to teach. A good question might be: "Why are we spending so much money on testing when we need books?") In critical classrooms, we can make testing the object of our curiosity.

Begin by questioning the origins and purpose of these tests. I ask students: Who made them? What are the tests supposed to measure? What information will be generated from the scores? Who will have access to that information and how will it be used? For example, in Oregon, students take multiple tests. One might think that these tests will be used to help teachers more accurately assess their students' abilities or progress to improve instruction. But because the tests are given during the school year—from February to April—and the scores aren't returned to the schools until after the school year has ended, one has to question the legitimacy of that claim.

If we really want to know how well students are doing in school, why can't we ask teachers, students, or parents? Why don't we look at student work? Portfolios? Dave Hamilton, an award-winning science teacher, wrote the following in the *Oregonian*:

> [T]ests given by classroom teachers are almost never high stakes. Teachers typi-
> cally use an average of test scores (never a single test score) as only one indicator
> of student achievement. They also rely on written work such as papers and other
> assignments, class participation, and special projects. Compared to the state's
> single test score, teachers have a wealth of information on which to assess student
> achievement ... [T]eachers are the *only* people with the intimate knowledge of
> student achievement over time needed to make such judgments.

Another way to scrutinize the tests is to find statistics generated from these exams. In my school district, the local newspaper happily prints scores and rates schools, but our research and evaluation department also has broken the scores down by gender and race. Have students examine the statistics. Which school in the district usually receives high scores? Which ones don't? Is there a pattern? Are the scores related to parents' income? Race?

This one is tricky because I don't want to leave the students with the idea that race and income are indicators of intelligence or the only factors determining academic achievement. It is important to examine the questions to see how the content might favor one race or one gender or one income bracket. *FairTest Examiner* is a good resource for this information on the SATs. They reported how students of color scored higher, for example, on passages that feature multicultural readings. [See also Jay Rosner's article, "On White Preference," in this book.]

> **The SAT/ACT scores become a brand of shame students carry long after they bubble in the last answer.**

Sometimes you can find these selections in your own city or state assessments. Ruthann Hartley, a former colleague from Jefferson High School, was furious after she administered the state reading test. According to Hartley, a disproportionate number of questions examined a passage and chart from *Consumer Reports* on frequent flyer benefits. Hartley noted, "This is a problematic item for teenagers, but especially for low-income students who don't travel. Passages like this raise the question of what is being tested. If students answer incorrectly, is it because they can't read or because they don't have the background knowledge?"

Students might also question how the test results are used. Who benefits if they get high scores? Are students placed in honors or remedial classes? Given scholarships? Special programs? Are teachers' or principals' salaries tied to the results? Have students interview school and district administrators and department chairs about how students are placed in honors classes or gifted and talented programs. Are test scores the only criterion?

Asking students to become investigators prior to exam time can help put the tests in a social context, but more than that, it diminishes the size of their opponent. Students see behind the Wizard of Oz curtain and realize that no geniuses are laboring to construct these tests. The test-item creators are not people who have scrutinized the great order of the universe and then created these 20, 40, or 60 reading and math problems to determine which students will succeed in life and which ones will fail. [See also Dan DiMaggio's chapter, "The Loneliness of the Long Distance Test Scorer," included in this book.]

Investigating the Origins of the SAT

While my junior and senior students weren't saddled with the Certificate of Initial Mastery (CIM) reading, writing, and math tests—which Oregon 3rd, 5th, 8th, and 10th graders currently take—they were having their behinds kicked by the SATs. After their encounters with these grueling tests, they fumed at me and their math teachers. "Those tests might as well have been written in Greek!" Shameka said after the exams ruined her Saturday. For my students, an investigation of the history of the SATs was as critical as teaching them how to improve their scores. The SAT/ACT scores become a brand of shame students carry long after they bubble in the last answer. If they score low on the test, they doubt themselves and wonder if they are as capable as the kid who scored higher.

To help students understand the origins of the exam and help them put the score in perspective, my class reads a chapter from David Owen's book *None of the Above* called "The Cult of Mental Measurement." In this essay, Owens describes the racist past of the SATs and also points out how race continues to be a factor in these kinds of standardized tests today. Students are outraged by their discoveries. (For example, the founder of the SATs, Carl Campbell Brigham, published in the same eugenics journal that Adolf Hitler wrote for.) But even without this gem of a chapter to use, getting students to investigate the origin and use of tests in their school district or state is a good place to start. (See Bill Bigelow's "Testing, Tracking, and Toeing the Line: A Role Play on the Origins of the Modern High School" in this volume to help students develop a critique of the historical motivation behind the testing industry.)

Examining the Tests

Once students have gained a critical edge on the tests, we can help them improve their performance by examining both the content and the format of the tests themselves. The more they know about how the questions are put together as well as the vocabulary of the material, the better prepared they are to meet the challenge.

In my senior English class, students demystified the SATs and used their knowledge to teach others about their discoveries. We started by analyzing each of the verbal sections of the SATs. We examined the instructions, language, and "objectives" of each section. We took apart the analogies and figured out the kinds of relationships they paired. (We used *The Princeton Review: Cracking the SAT* to help us wade through and prepare. David Owens wrote the foreword.) We looked at how the language and culture of the SATs reflected the world of upper-class society with words like heirloom, inheritance, conservatory, and regatta.

After examining each section and taking the tests a few times, I asked students to construct their own tests using the culture, content, and vocabulary of our school—from sports to dance to awards. Pairs of students worked together developing questions that the entire class examined; then we put together the Jefferson Achievement Tests (JAT).

JAT

Each question below consists of a related pair of words or phrases, followed by four lettered pairs of words or phrases. Select the lettered pair that best expresses a relationship similar to that expressed in the original pair.

1. Tony : Play ::
   a) Broadway : Annie
   b) Oscar : Tom Hanks
   c) Brandon : soccer
   d) Howard Cherry : sports

(The correct answer is d. The "Tony" is an award given for a play. At Jefferson, the "Howard Cherry" is an award given for sports.)

After examining each section and taking the tests a few times, I asked students to construct their own tests using the culture, content, and vocabulary of our school.

2. New Growth : perm ::
   a) press : straight
   b) weave : long
   c) corn row : braid
   d) nails : fill

(The correct answer is d. When you get "new growth," it is time for a perm. In the same way, if you wear acrylic nails and your nails grow out, you need to get a fill.)

4. *Red Beans and Rice* : play ::
   a) corn and tortillas : run
   b) song : dance
   c) mozzarella : cheese
   d) sonata : musical

(The correct answer is c. *Red Beans and Rice* is the name of a play; mozzarella is the name of a kind of cheese.)

5. Dancebelt : boxers ::
   a) shoes : socks
   b) student : teacher
   c) leotard : leg warmers
   d) prison : freedom

(Although this one changes form from concrete nouns to abstract nouns, I like the humor and use of Jefferson's dance legacy in the answer—d. As a male dancer explained, a dance-belt secures a male dancer's privates during dance. Comparing the dancebelt to boxers is like comparing prison to freedom.)

After completing the test, students took the JAT up to Ruth Shagoury's education classes at Lewis & Clark College. My students asked the pre-service teachers to imagine that the JAT was a high-stakes test that will determine their future—what college they get into, scholarships, etc. After the tests, students discussed the issues of testing and language. In this way, my students had a real audience whose future teaching practice was hopefully enlightened by their work.

Obviously, our JAT is not an exact equivalent of the SAT, but developing their own analogies from Jefferson's culture helped students understand the mechanics of the exam. It also made them see that if they were the test makers, using their culture and their vocabulary, they could also devise a test that could be used to exclude some and include others.

Perhaps the most important lesson of the unit came when students asked,

"Why would someone want to devise a test to keep students out of a college they want to enter?" Indeed.

Teaching students to examine the history and motives of local and state tests and preparing them for the big day(s) is no substitute for fighting to end the encroachment of assessments in our classrooms. Although the work I've proposed may raise student scores by a few points and help students question the tests' legitimacy as well as their results, our bigger work as teachers and parents is to engage in the battle to stop testing that makes young people, like my daughter, question their ability. ✎

An Untold Story of Resistance

African American educators and IQ testing in the 1920s and 1930s

ALAN STOSKOPF

It was not until I was long out of school and indeed after the [first] World War that there came the hurried use of the new technique of psychological [IQ] tests, which were quickly adjusted so as to put black folk absolutely beyond the possibility of civilization.

—W. E. B. Du Bois, 1940[1]

The words of W. E. B. Du Bois still haunt us. We are now experiencing another onslaught and "hurried use" of tests in our schools. How African American educators fought against their uses in the past has important implications for today's resistance to high-stakes testing.

We have grown accustomed to the constant refrain of schools needing to institute "world-class standards" and be held accountable through externally based, high-stakes exams. Research and experience demonstrate that this version of "education reform" will negatively impact all students, especially students of color from lower income backgrounds. We also know that the best assessments originate in the classroom and are an ongoing part of a student's reflection of her or his progress. Few people realize that current critiques of testing and the calls for more authentic forms of assessment have been built in part upon the pioneering work of African American intellectuals in the 1920s and 1930s.

An appreciation of what these educators accomplished begins with race. The underside to the "Roaring '20s" was the era's violent racism and xenophobia. Jim Crow ruled. In the South, an apartheid-like caste system enveloped daily life. In the North, African Americans faced discrimination in housing, employment, the courts, and schools. The Ku Klux Klan reached its peak of popularity and claimed members in most states. Lynchings of African American men were a familiar occurrence. Fears of racial impurity propelled the passage of the Immigration Restriction Act of 1924. (This act set draconian quotas based on race and nationality. It blatantly favored people of northern and western European ancestry and was not substantively revised until 1965.)

Even the liberal New Deal Era of the 1930s did not fundamentally alter striking social inequalities wrought by racism. As an economic depression en-

The use of these tests in this fashion reflected a eugenic ideology of human worth, where some individuals and groups were born to be superior and others fated to be inferior.

gulfed the entire nation, the Roosevelt administration initiated a variety of public works projects aimed at providing relief to ordinary Americans and structural reform to unregulated private enterprise. The aid and reform were not as dramatic as supporters or critics of the New Deal claimed. African American communities were the hardest hit and received the least amount of relief.

These racial divisions were especially evident in schooling. By the early 1920s, standardized IQ tests were being used to track millions of students into separate educational curricula. Lewis Terman of Stanford University first developed these tests for schools. The questions on the test were based on a small norm-referenced sample of white, middle- and upper-class children and adults. Terman—like most other white educational researchers of the day—believed these tests objectively measured aptitude and could be used by school systems to rank, order, and sort the school-age population of the United States. The use of these tests in this fashion reflected a eugenic ideology of human worth, where some individuals and groups were born to be superior and others fated to be inferior.

African American children were routinely channeled into either low tracks or separate vocational schools based upon low scores on IQ tests. The resources, curricula, and instruction African American students received reflected the lower academic expectations white school officials had for them. Unsurprisingly, this institutional racism contributed to high rates of failure and poor school performance among many African American students. White teachers of African American students frequently assumed it was the "low mental level" of the race that accounted for their problems in school.[2]

The mainstream academic community had given legitimacy to these attitudes in the 1920s. The use of testing for racial tracking purposes had been supported and promoted by distinguished educational theorists. Carl Brigham, assistant professor of psychology at Princeton University, wrote one of the most influential racist interpretations of the IQ test at the time. His book, *A Study of American Intelligence*, was widely read by policy makers, educators, and the general public. And those giving testimony before the House immigration hearings frequently referred to it. The book provided a "scientific" rationale for the racist quotas established in the 1924 immigration act.

Brigham later became a dean at Princeton and went on to develop the Scholastic Aptitude Test (SAT). In *A Study of American Intelligence* he wrote:

> According to all evidence available then, American intelligence is declining, and will proceed with an accelerating rate as the racial admixture becomes more and more extensive. The decline of American intelligence will be more rapid than the decline of the intelligence of European groups, owing to the presence here of the Negro. These are the plain, if somewhat ugly, facts that our study shows.[3]

His book had a monumental impact on public policy and schooling. This book, along with numerous other educational publications in the 1920s, provided the intellectual rationale for inferior schools and diminished educational expectations for African American students.

Although Brigham's ideas represented a dominant educational ideology of the 1920s, these beliefs did not go unchallenged. African American social scientists and educators helped to lead that challenge. They exposed the false assumptions and faulty methodology of those who claimed the tests proved "Negro inferiority." In doing so, they opened up a more expansive vision of intelligence and learning.

The wellspring for resistance began in the black colleges of the era. African American men and women established these institutions in the mid-19th century when they were denied admission into white universities. The situation had not changed greatly by the 1920s. By 1940, there were more than 100 black colleges in operation. Though inadequately funded, understaffed, and with limited facilities, these colleges nonetheless played a vital role in training the men and women who provided counter arguments to the use of tests for tracking and racial ranking.[4]

This was not an easy thing to do in the early 20th century. Most of the academics generating studies on IQ testing were trained in doctoral programs in psychology. Only a few northern universities accepted African American students into doctoral psychology programs. Black colleges in the 1920s were just beginning to offer doctorates in this field. It was even more difficult for African American women to get graduate-level training in psychology in that era.

Despite these challenges, the black colleges offered a unique educational environment, one that nurtured a different view of human potential. White researchers in the area of human development throughout the 1920s usually focused on the differences among human beings. Educators at these black colleges stressed the inherent similarities.[5]

African American scholars who graduated from these schools also challenged the accepted myths that most of their white counterparts held as scientific truth. These included:

Test scores proved that African Americans and other "lesser strains" were innately inferior to northern European whites.

Environmental conditions had little to do with performance on IQ tests. Intelligence was essentially fixed and unchangeable.

Exceptionally intelligent children were rarely found among African Americans.

Children of mixed white and black ancestry had a higher intelligence than "pure Negro" blacks. (This was known as the "mulatto hypothesis" at the time.)

Better educational opportunities made little difference in helping children succeed.

Horace Mann Bond (1904-1972) was one of the first educators to challenge these myths and Brigham's interpretations of IQ test scores. Bond wrote a scathing critique of *A Study of American Intelligence* in *Crisis*, the official magazine of the NAACP. Bond, like other African American intellectuals of the era, found it very difficult to get published in the white-controlled press. Publications like *Crisis* and *The Journal of Negro Education* were crucial in circulating the ideas of African American writers.

In 1924, Bond published an article titled "Intelligence Tests and Propaganda." At the time, Bond was the director of the school of education at Langston University in Oklahoma. Although he wasn't formally trained as a psychologist, Bond demonstrated a remarkable insight into the construction and use of these tests. In the article he dismissed the claim that these tests were objective. Instead, Bond called them "funds for propaganda" and encouraged each African American student to:

> ... be in possession of every detail of the operation, use, and origin of these tests, in order that he might better equip himself as an active agent against the insidious propaganda which seeks to demonstrate that the Negro is intellectually and physically incapable of assuming the dignities, rights, and duties which devolve upon him as a member of modern society.[6]

Bond went on to model what he hoped inquiring students would do with this kind of research. In particular, he questioned Brigham's thesis, which was widely shared by psychological testers, that African Americans from the North who scored consistently better on IQ tests did so because they were a "higher strain of Negro." Bond drew attention to the fact that African American children, on average, received relatively better education in northern schools than their counterparts in the South.

Bond offered a small study he conducted among college freshmen at Lincoln University to refute Brigham's thesis. The number of African American students from northern and southern states was about evenly divided at the school. Bond administered IQ tests similar to the ones used on U.S. Army recruits and subsequently analyzed by Brigham in *A Study in American Intelligence*. Bond discovered that students from the South did not do as well on these tests as northern students. Unlike Brigham, Bond's study demonstrated that the resources, preparation of the teaching staff, and curricula were worse in the Jim Crow schools of the South. Bond wrote that academic performance of these students at Lincoln did improve when they were given better opportunities. He wrote:

> ... when placed in the same environment, given the same treatment, taught by the same staff, it is found that these men from the poorer Southern schools are just as quick in grasping and making the best of the new college surroundings.[7]

Other African American educators at this time, such as Howard Hale Long of Paine College, raised similar objections to Brigham's work. Their writings and Bond's research did not receive any outside foundation funding, nor were they widely reported. Yet Bond highlighted some of the underlying causes for variations in test scores between different groups of students. Since his time, hundreds of better-funded research studies have confirmed his essential premises.

In 1927 Bond wrote another article in *Crisis*. In that essay, Bond attacked the myth that IQ test scores proved African Americans had no people of "exceptional intellect." Bond's tone was impatient and filled with sarcasm as he referred to IQ testing as a "major indoor sport among psychologists."[8] He wondered why white psychologists emphasized the need for a rapport between white testers and white children but did not think it necessary to emphasize the same approach with African American children. He also wondered why normed samples were always based on white middle- and upper-class students.

> **Bond drew attention to the fact that African American children, on average, received relatively better education in northern schools than their counterparts in the South.**

Bond and his research team decided to alter the rules of the game. They were determined to create a positive and reassuring environment for the students chosen to take the test. They also wanted to include students from a variety of economic backgrounds. They selected 30 school children from Chicago for the study and provided a comfortable testing situation in a small group setting. They provided encouragement and emotional support to the students before administering the tests. The students came from working-class, middle-class, and professional family backgrounds.

The results of the test shattered long-standing beliefs in the testing community. Bond found that 63 percent of the children scored above 106, whereas Terman found in his sample of white youth that only 33 percent did so. Bond added, "Mr. Terman states that only 5 percent of white children may be expected to equal or exceed an IQ of 122; no less than 47 percent of our subjects exceeded this score."[9] Bond was not making the case for a reverse racial superiority. He argued that economic class, parental emphasis of reading at an early age, and a stimulating school environment would boost scores for all children.

By 1930 most research into differences in intelligence had moved away from racial explanations. Although racist social attitudes and polices were still entrenched in the larger society, a few prominent white colleagues had joined African American researchers. The published works by anthropologist Melville Herskovits and psychologist Otto Klineberg in the 1930s supported Bond's findings. They were some of the first white social scientists, along with Franz Boas and Margaret Mead, to write and speak out against the racial myths that infused the research on intelligence testing.

Also, in the 1930s African American intellectuals were beginning to receive more opportunities to publish and gain resources for extensive research studies. The playing field was hardly equal, but these scholars took advantage of the small openings that appeared. This can be seen in the work of Martin Jenkins (1904-1978). Jenkins did his undergraduate work at Howard University and, in 1935, was the first African American to receive a Ph.D. in psychology from Northwestern University. He built upon the work of Bond and others in the 1920s to do major studies of school children in Chicago.

Jenkins confirmed what people like Bond and Long had been saying in the

1920s. He found that a greater percentage of African American students scored higher on IQ tests when they had elevated economic and educational backgrounds. Furthermore, these scores were represented evenly throughout various age and grade levels, as long as students maintained higher levels of economic and educational support. No evidence supported the thesis that African American students who performed well on the tests did so because of alleged white ancestry. Jenkins conclusions were clear:

> The findings of this study suggest that the differences in test performance of white and Negro children found by so many investigators are not due to inherent racial factors. In home background, in developmental history, in physical development, in school progress, in educational achievement, in interests, in activities, and in social and personal characteristics Negro children of superior intelligence [high scores on IQ tests] resemble other American children of superior intelligence.[10]

Jenkins was able to cite numerous studies by both black and white educators in drawing his conclusions. Also, white scholars such as Mellville Herskovits and Otto Klineberg had begun to cite him and other African American scholars. New ground was being broken. In 1939, Jenkins was one of the first African American researchers to have his findings about race and IQ included in an educational journal that was not restricted to primarily African American audiences. Previously, articles of this kind had to be co-authored with a white scholar if they were to be accepted in publications such as *The Journal of Educational Psychology* or *The Journal of Social Psychology*.

Many other African American scholars also spoke out and wrote against the racist use of IQ tests. Herman Canady, Charles St. Clair Price, and Charles Johnson were only some of the names.[11] They represented varying interests in approaching questions of race and IQ testing. Yet almost all entered their research with a basic assumption that students were similar in their capacity to achieve when provided with adequate learning environments and social opportunities.

The legacy of these efforts is with us today. Progressive education rests on some of the foundation blocks laid by people like Bond and Jenkins; many of today's educational programs have sprung from their contributions. The need for early intervention programs in reading, the importance of using multiple assessments to monitor student learning, and the need to create school cultures that foster high expectations for all students are beliefs that have been drawn from their work. They make up the canon of good education. When African American educators were writing in the 1920s, however, scholars often considered their ideas to be radical, flying in the face of established dogma.

Also, we know that discredited ideas from the past can have a remarkable power to persist. It is a terrible irony that Charles Murray and Richard Herrnstein's *The Bell Curve*, the modern day equivalent of Carl Brigham's *A Study in American Intelligence*, is more well known than the writings of Bond or Jenkins. And it is a scandal that *The Bell Curve* recycled some of the arguments debunked by African American intellectuals back in the 1920s but still managed to become a best seller in the 1990s.

Brigham recanted his views in 1930 because he realized that the findings of Bond, Jenkins, Long, Klineberg, and others undermined the credibility of his work. Brigham concluded in his article in *The Psychological Review*:

> This review has summarized some of the most recent test findings which show that comparative studies of various national and racial groups may not be made with existing tests, and which show, in particular, that one of the most pretentious of these comparative racial studies—the writer's own—was without foundation."[12]

It is a terrible irony that Charles Murray and Richard Herrnstein's *The Bell Curve*, the modern day equivalent of Carl Brigham's *A Study in American Intelligence*, is more well known than the writings of Bond or Jenkins.

No such recantation has ever come from Herrnstein, now deceased, or Murray.

Although some policy makers and academics still embrace it, *The Bell Curve* has also been denounced by a range of scholars and lay people—quite a different reaction from when Brigham published *A Study in American Intelligence*. When *The Bell Curve* was published, many white educators joined African American scholars in writing and speaking out against the assumptions, methodology, and policy conclusions found in the book. Early forgotten graduates of Howard, Lincoln, Virginia Union, and numerous other black colleges had laid the intellectual foundations for these critiques much earlier.

As things change, they remain the same. Jim Crow no longer rules American society. Terman and Brigham's views of on race and intelligence would exist on the margins of today's educational research. But we also know that attitudes and practices of the past can be reworked and institutionalized in other ways. In fact, the echoes of the past are loudly heard in the reliance on high-stakes tests to shape educational policy. Except now the tests are not purporting to be sorting devices based on a racial ranking according to IQ scores but instead on student, teacher, and school performance. The schools and students who do poorly on these exams will once again be those who do not have access to better resources. The tracking and unequal funding that were institutionalized in the 1920s will be only further entrenched in the current incarnation of high-stakes testing.

The past efforts of African American educators can be instructive for the educational climate we are living in today. Black colleges helped nurture an alternative paradigm to intelligence and learning that enabled African American educators to question the dominant assumptions of the day. Today we need educational spaces in our communities that encourage similar alternative views to established policy. In the 1920s and 1930s African American educators struggled against incredible racial barriers. Their ideas deserved a wider circulation. Today, we have greater opportunities to build coalitions with various groups of people to press for a rethinking of what is accepted as dogma.

When schools mimicked the policies of exclusion in the wider society, African American intellectuals demanded a higher standard of democratic justice for the nation's youth.

Equally important is the contribution these educators made in keeping alive the promise of American democracy. When schools mimicked the policies of exclusion in the wider society, African American intellectuals demanded a higher standard of democratic justice for the nation's youth. Through moral outrage and intellectual rigor they helped set in motion a movement of ideas that defined education as the liberation of human potential. Those ideas were needed then. We must not forget them today. ✎

Endnotes

1. As quoted in, Robert V. Guthrie, *Even the Rat Was White: A Historical View of Psychology* (2nd edition) (Boston: Allyn &Bacon,1998), p. 55.

2. David Tyack, *The One Best System* (Cambridge: Harvard University Press, 1974), p. 219.

3. Carl Brigham, *A Study in American Intelligence* (Princeton: Princeton University Press, 1923), p. 210.

4. Guthrie, p. 123.

5. Ibid., p. 125.

6. Horace Mann Bond, "Intelligence Tests and Propaganda," *The Crisis*, vol. 28 (2), June 1924, p. 61.

7. Ibid., p. 63.

8. Horace Mann Bond, "Some Exceptional Negro Children," *The Crisis*, vol. 34 (8), October 1927, p.257. c

9. Ibid., p. 259.

10. Martin D. Jenkins, "A Socio-Psychological Study of Negro Children of Superior Intelligence," vol. 5 (2), April 1936, pp. 189-190.

11. See bibliography of V. P. Franklin, "Black Social Scientists and the Mental Testing Movement, 1920–1940," in *Black Psychology*, 3rd ed., pp. 222-24.

12. Carl Brigham, "Intelligence Traits of Immigrant Groups," *The Psychological Review*, XXXVII (1930), p. 165.

Teaching is Not Testing

*A community-led struggle to find an alternative
to California's graduation exam*

TINY (AKA LISA) GRAY-GARCIA

The stores were small. Low roofed, and peeling paint. The storefront signs were oddly sized, lettered in a handmade cursive font, and prone to losing their neon. Through the steam rising from the sun-baked asphalt in front of my car, I spotted a large block of faded red brick fronted by an aging marquee: Richmond High School.

"We are hard-working students—we are simply asking that this test be more fair, that there be alternatives to the exit exam or that it be given in the students' first language 'cause one size doesn't fit all," said Maria C., 16, Richmond High School student and member of Youth Together, a youth justice organization. Maria spoke in front of Richmond High school in September 2005 at a press conference on the mandatory high school exit exam that California students have to pass before they can graduate and receive their diploma.

As I adjusted my microphone so it would register her soft-spoken voice over the din of cars rushing by, I reflected on the possibility of a collaboration between Youth Together and Justice Matters, a research and policy institute that works for racial justice in education, where I am communications director. I thought that combined forces might affect policy on the exit exam.

Youth Together was founded in 1996 by five nonprofit organizations: small and large, radical and established, to address racially based violence on school campuses and eventually foster campus-based leadership for high school youth on issues of social justice. In 2003 they began working on the impact of the California High School Exit Exam (CAHSEE) on low-income students of color in the San Francisco Bay area. These same students, many of whose first language was not English, were very low-income and most were failing the exit exam in large numbers.

California is one of 25 [Note: that number is now 28—eds.] states that require an exit test for a high school diploma. However, the state has not addressed the lack of resources and other educational inequities that exist for low-income students of color and that determine whether they have been prepared to pass the exit exam.

In terms of the impact of the exit exam, the numbers of California students affected were staggering: 46,700

> **Although economic self-sufficiency is one important purpose of education, we disagreed with the prevailing thinking that individual earnings and national economic growth are the only valid goals for our school system.**

seniors had not passed the test as of March of 2006. Of these, 20,600 were designated as limited English learners and 28,300 were very low-income. In addition to a huge outcry from educators, advocates, and thousands of youth across California, a report from the state's own sanctioned research team, Human Resources Research Organization (HUMRRO) acknowledged the impact of the exit exam on the students who would be denied diplomas in 2006. HUMRRO recommended implementing multiple methods of assessing English and math skills to more accurately determine a student's real-life academic ability.

The 2005-06 school year was an urgent time for groups concerned about the exit exam because it was the first year that high school seniors who did not pass the test would be denied a diploma.

A New Collaboration

A month after Youth Together's press conference, Justice Matters formalized a collaborative campaign with Youth Together in Richmond, one of the cities in the West Contra Costa Unified School District (WCCUSD). Our goal was to turn around what was happening to learning in the district as a result of rigid and narrow approaches to curriculum and teaching practices that have been implemented as accountability strategies in the post-NCLB world of high-stakes testing.

After the press conference on the streets of Richmond, our staff of researchers, advocates, and educators began a series of brainstorming sessions that included student leaders from Youth Together as well as West Contra Costa School Board Trustee Dave Brown, who seemed to be truly concerned about the needs of students in his district. Our driving question was: How could we address the crisis of unresponsive, narrow student learning in this district in a way that would also get at the testing issues that immediately faced these youth?

The exit exam's constitutionality and related issues were already being challenged in the courts in two separate class action suits brought forth by Public Advocates and the firm Morrison and Foerster; although these were cases with statewide implications, the majority of the plaintiffs in both actions were students in West Contra Costa and Oakland.

There are a total of 35,000 students in West Contra Costa Unified School District. Of those, 14,000 attend schools that receive federal Title I money (which goes to schools with a high number of low-income students). Because these schools receive federal funds, they are the most severely affected by federally mandated multiple testing requirements. Of the 14,000 students in these schools, 12,600 are children of color.

Seeking the voices and scholarship of parents, students, educators, and community members in the district, Justice Matters and Youth Together began organizing a series of community events and actions aimed at identifying the problems faced in that district from the perspective of the folks experiencing it firsthand. The first one was a Community Town Hall on Student Learning held in Richmond in December 2005.

"What you don't need a diploma for is to go to jail," Diana Ponce, mother of children attending Downer Elementary School in Richmond, called out to the crowd of more than 40 families.

The Phone Call

After we assessed the findings from the community, Justice Matters staff members began to ask ourselves how we could take the input we had heard about frustrating learning experiences—and the looming threat of denied diplomas for that year's seniors—and develop a policy that would begin to address all of these issues. And then an opportunity arose from an unexpected corridor.

It was almost 6 p.m. on another wet Friday night in February. As the uncharacteristic California rains pounded on our windows and our spirits, Program Director Olivia Araiza received a phone call from West Contra Costa Trustee Dave Brown. Within seconds the small staff remaining in the office watched as Olivia's face registered first disbelief and then shock.

After a few more minutes of suspense, Olivia emerged from "The Call." Her entire face wrapped around a growing smile. She told us about Dave's decision to put forth a school board resolution to offer a diploma to seniors who had met all of their other graduation requirements and who completed an alternative to the exit exam. "And," she explained, "he wants the alternative to focus on success in life after high school."

A small door of access was opened.

Toward a Lifetime of Success

Another series of meetings ensued between Dave Brown, Justice Matters staff members, and youth leaders from Youth Together to craft a resolution. We hoped that our proposal, if implemented, would create a template for change that could ripple across the state. Our resolution read:

> Whereas the West Contra Costa Unified School District (WCCUSD) Board of Education believes that all students who pass the requisite high school courses and demonstrate readiness for success beyond high school will have satisfied all state and local requirements for a fully-accredited diploma; and

> Whereas the WCCUSD Board of Education believes that academic achievement is far too complex to be accurately measured by any one method and that the California high school exit exam is only one of many viable ways for students to demonstrate their ability to be successful after high school...

In less than two weeks our collaborative proposal was done. We called it the "Senior Year Demonstration."

The Senior Year Demonstration proposed a structured process for students to demonstrate knowledge and skills through portfolios, action research, and exhibitions. As we developed this alternative, we grappled with fundamental questions.

> The media actually reported and documented student voices calling for educational justice and the end of high-stakes testing.

We first had to figure out what values this alternative should reflect. We knew we stood in opposition to those who seemed only to want to create assessments that measured a narrow set of academic skills. The alternative could measure anything, as long as it could be connected to the idea of success after high school.

We decided not to confine the idea of success after high school to a student's ability to obtain lucrative employment. Although economic self-sufficiency is one important purpose of education, we disagreed with the prevailing thinking that individual earnings and national economic growth are the only valid goals for our school system.

We wanted the alternative to be a force for broadening the discussion about the purpose of education, reminding people that education can and should help build a more just society and foster the growth and health of our communities, families, and interior lives. We decided that the Senior Year Demonstration should allow students to demonstrate their readiness to: 1. build a stronger democracy; 2. contribute to their family and community; as well as, 3. pursue a career. Students would be asked to use the state academic standards to demonstrate their knowledge, but only insofar as they were demonstrating their readiness in the core areas we had selected.

Our next question was: How should students show their knowledge? We believe that assessments should enhance students' ability to show what they know. We gathered ideas for accomplishing this from the practices of innovative high schools such as such as Anzar High School in California and Central Park East Secondary School in New York. We designed the Senior Year Demonstration to allow students to demonstrate their knowledge through portfolios, and also through presenting exhibitions to the school and local community where they could incorporate theater, art, science experiments, and more.

We also saw learning as a community venture. Students would be asked to help each other prepare their demonstrations. Community members would be recruited as additional resources. And community members would be invited to witness students' final exhibitions.

Something interesting started to happen in discussions of the Senior Year Demonstration, whether these discussions happened within our planning group or with board members and district staff. These conversations would turn to how the Demonstration reflected their values and aspirations for what all of high school should look like. For example, one district official said, "Many of the ideas addressed . . . should be included in how we do business on a day to day basis."

Ultimately, the board resolution itself included the idea that the Demonstration not only serve as an alternative to the Exit Exam, but that it be used to change what high school is about:

> BE IT FURTHER RESOLVED, that the WCCUSD Board of Education call upon the Superintendent to work with students, teachers, staff and parents to infuse the values and approaches of the Senior Year Demonstration within the high school curriculum.

Teaching is Not Testing

Justice Matters communications staff began creating a media campaign to support the exit exam alternative. Our goal was simple: to ensure that low-income students and families of color in the district, the ones directly affected by the racist, classist exit exam, were

Caramel, honey, white, and dark chocolate arms and multilingual voices rose in unison to join us in the march into the school board meeting.

"heard"—that their voices, their scholarship, and their solutions were portrayed and recognized with dignity throughout the region.

The first step toward this goal was to author the "story" from the first-person perspective of the students and families affected and to work in tandem with our independent media contacts such as the *San Francisco Bayview*, an independent, radical black newspaper; and *POOR Magazine*, an online and radio news service that gives media access to low- and no-income youth and adults on issues of poverty and racism. We hoped that these stories would establish a frame for our campaign that was rooted in our community's voices.

Justice Matters staff met with students and families—in our view, the experts on the situation—to work on their media message. We also called in outside "experts" and research studies to support our position in the media. All members of the press and school board members received "Multiple Measures Approaches to High School Graduation," published by the School Redesign Network at Stanford University. This report summarizes the research about the negative consequences of exit exams and explains how, unlike California, most states that have exit exams also include alternative measures of student performance, using the examination as only one indicator of graduation readiness.

The proposal went before the WCCUSD school board for a vote on April 10, 2006. We held a pre-vote press conference on the lawn outside the hearing room. The media turnout was huge and included radio, TV, and print: CNN, NPR, and many local channels. The media actually reported and documented student voices calling for educational justice and the end of high-stakes testing.

"I have completed all my classes, I got good grades, and yet I still can't get a diploma," said Trina M., a 17-year-old high school student in the district. Young African American women like Trina maintained the camera's gaze. Her sentences were quoted in their entirety on ABC, NBC, and CBS television local affiliates.

The voices at the press conference were enhanced by choreographed visual aids announcing the same clear message: Teaching is NOT Testing! This shout for justice was plastered on buttons, banners and signs held and worn by youth, families, educators, and advocates who stood together in front of the cameras.

¡Sí Se Puede!

As per our plan, just as the press conference ended, a march of more than 400 students from the district ascended the street to meet up with us on the lawn. "¡Sí Se Puede!" (Yes we can!) they shouted. Caramel, honey, white, and dark chocolate arms and multilingual voices rose in unison to join us in the march into the school board meeting.

As the two-hour meeting progressed, hundreds of students, parents, teachers, and advocates spoke in favor of the proposal, while only a handful of mostly white administrators, businesspeople, and residents of other parts of the county spoke in opposition.

Some of these speakers directed comments at the students. Opponents' remarks were peppered with references to the students' future lack of employability as "janitors and plumbers." Nonetheless, the students continued to stand together in handmade orange t-shirts with the acronym CAHSEE written in black with a slash through its center.

School board members, one by one, responded to a warning from State Superintendent Jack O'Connell that passing the resolution would break the law and put district money at risk. "We are not a diploma mill. We don't just give them away," lectured one board member. "You need to earn them."

And then it was time. The final vote was counted. The school board defeated the resolution 4-1. In the moment following the vote, Justice Matters staff, Youth Together leaders, parents, educators, and community members stood up simultaneously. We had not planned this "stand" beforehand. Our signs denouncing CAHSEE were raised in the air. The hot air from the room rose around us in the silence of grief that followed. We walked out. Together.

Small slivers of afternoon sun peeked through the rain clouds above. Through teary eyes I asked one of the youth leaders from Youth Together, 16-year-old Wendy O., who had spoken so eloquently in favor of the proposal, if she felt discouraged. "Oh no," her brown eyes sparked fire into mine. "This is just the beginning."

Notwithstanding the "defeat" of the proposal, as Wendy said, it was just the beginning, the beginning of a similar landmark fight that Youth Together would launch on two more districts in the Bay Area—Berkeley and Oakland— in the ongoing struggle to defeat the unjust exit exam. As of the writing of this article, the Oakland effort concluded in a unanimous school board vote in favor of dropping the exit exam. Unfortunately, because Oakland schools have been taken over by the state, although the board's vote was a powerful symbolic gesture, it lacked the power to actually kill the exit exam.

For Justice Matters staff it was also a powerful beginning. A beginning of a long-term fight to make learning accessible, relevant, and meaningful in West Contra Costa County through an ongoing effort of parents, students, and conscious legislators. ✎

None of the Above

*Defiant teachers show they have
had enough of high-stakes testing*

AMALIA OULAHAN

[*No No. 2 pencils were harmed
in the making of this movement.*]

Instead of watching students fill in test bubbles last school year, teachers around the country have risked their jobs and career prospects by refusing to hand out standardized assessments. Their actions administered new life into a stirring antitesting movement. The real test, though, will be how the antitesting movement can harness the momentum generated by these actions.

Connecting local actions to build a strong national movement has proven difficult. To begin, every state has its own test and alternatives to testing. Another factor is the vulnerability of teachers in a fight against the district, a fight in which public support might be limited at best.

It's not clear that federally mandated standardized testing will inspire mass civil disobedience. Nonetheless, national organizers say individual acts of protest can expose the most pressing problems with standardized testing and inspire broader activism, perhaps coalitions across state borders.

"The actions and civil disobedience highlight the damage being caused to the kids," says Monty Neill, deputy director of the antitesting organization FairTest, which works to connect allies in all states.

"The success of each action depends on what can happen with the people around the particular teachers," says Neill. "We don't have the personnel in these localities."

According to Neill, FairTest tries to support teacher boycotts without compromising its policy-related goals. But, despite this challenge, Neill says civil disobedience has unique potential to express the issue's urgency. "When protests get media attention, it raises the signals in the public mind that some people feel so strongly about this they're willing to risk their jobs," says Neill.

David Wasserman, a teacher from Madison, Wis., is one educator who did just that. In October 2007, Wasserman boycotted the Wisconsin Knowledge

"I think boycotts certainly could stop testing in its tracks, if teachers all decided to do what I did," Chew says. "But, teachers are obviously dedicated people who do not want to be out of the classrooms taking an action that jeopardizes their careers, families, classes."

and Concepts Exam (WKCE) being given at Sennett Middle School. Although he received support in an editorial from the Madison *Capital Times*, Wasserman eventually gave the WKCE to avoid being fired.

"Giving tests is not why I'm a teacher," says Wasserman. "We're taught to engage in best practice, and nowhere does that doctrine include this type of assessment. Long-term, over-generalized standardized knowledge or fact recall just doesn't come up."

Wasserman continues antitesting work in Wisconsin and says he's optimistic about the future.

Resistance in Seattle and North Carolina

In Seattle, veteran educator Carl Chew refused to administer a test he felt had a negative impact on his students. Chew boycotted the Washington Assessment of Student Learning (WASL) in April 2008 and was suspended from his middle school for the duration of the test. Unlike some younger teachers, Chew could take advantage of his life situation in his stand against the district.

"I'm 60, retired from my first job," Chew says.

"The idea that they could fire me was not a happy one. But, on the other hand, it wasn't one I felt could mortally wound me."

Chew was supported during his suspension through e-mails, letters, and phone calls from around the country and offers to strategize from the union. Yet Chew was left wondering about his boycott's effectiveness and where all the attention will lead.

"I think boycotts certainly could stop testing in its tracks, if teachers all decided to do what I did," he says. "But, teachers are obviously dedicated people who do not want to be out of the classrooms taking an action that jeopardizes their careers, families, classes."

Doug Ward, a North Carolina teacher, put his career in jeopardy when he carried out a boycott. Ward's rural school district fired him after he refused to administer the state's test for students with severe disabilities. He co-taught in a special education classroom at Cullowhee Valley School, a rural school in the mountainous section in southeastern North Carolina. Ward worked with severely disabled students for three years, and says his frustrations with mandated high-stakes tests included having to give a different test each year.

"I constantly dealt with issues of my kids being treated as second-class citizens because they have disabilities," says Ward. "Everyone else from the state on down said, 'That's OK, we'll just let those kids fail,' and the bottom line is that my students were basically guaranteed to fail this specific test because it was way above their level."

Ward, who describes his boycott as "a lone wolf thing," has secured a new teaching position on a Native American reservation near his former district. It's a job where he's been told to give exams without protest. Ward calls state administrative attitudes "black-and-white": Testing is the law, and the law must be followed. Ward is working around this attitude by connecting with local antitesting parent groups.

Despite consequences, Ward says he maintains his faith and continues advocating for the rights of students with severe disabilities. He and his co-teacher at Cullowhee Valley taught social justice history, and their students tied historic struggles to disability inclusion in their own school.

> **Opponents' remarks were peppered with references to the students' future lack of employability as "janitors and plumbers."**

"The students were able, when exposed to texts and discussions about African Americans and 1930s Mississippi, and events in Jena in 2008, to connect that to how people with disabilities are segregated most of the time," says Ward. "They learned that it was important to start a movement to get treated equally."

Students Get Involved

When students in New York City decided to start their own movement by boycotting a May 2008 practice test for their state social studies exam to be given in June, school administrators cracked down. About 150 middle school students in the Bronx's Intermediate School 318 handed in blank practice-test booklets and signed petitions. Their social studies teacher, Doug Avella, had to fight for his job. Even after interrogation by school administration, students say their instructor did not instigate their action.

Sam Coleman, a founding member of the New York Collective of Radical Educators' (NYCoRE) "Justice Not Just Tests" group, met the IS 318 students after the boycott.

"The students said this was something like the 23rd test they'd been given this year. They had projects to work on, and they felt this was absurd," says Coleman. "They recognized what they learned was more important than the test."

Urban students are strong advocates against testing, Coleman says, speculating that the school's demographic—a student body of poor minority students—elicited the especially harsh reaction to the boycott.

One problem with organizing IS 318 students is their teacher's vulnerability.

"An educator refusing to give the test can be spun in the news, but high school students who explain why will be listened to," Coleman says, adding that small numbers of educators boycotting can "get easily swept away" or go unnoticed.

In other areas, a few larger boycotts have demonstrated the effects of larger movements. Internationally, in May 2008, the British Columbia Teachers Federation voted to take job action against standardized testing in 2009.

In February 2008, teachers from DuPage County's Carol Stream Elementary District 93 threatened to refuse testing their English language learning students. Their opposition came after Illinois discontinued an alternative test for students who were learning English, and received some media attention. However, the teachers eventually decided against boycotting and, after settling for a few provisions for English language learners, gave the test to all students. Their agreement to give the test with some accommodations for English-learners can't be seen as an endorsement of high-stakes testing as a cure-all to problems in public education.

Culturally Relevant Resistance

Another U.S. educator used similar civil disobedience tactics in 2008 to make a statement about curriculum in her classroom. Teacher Karen Salazar refused to use standardized curriculum at Jordan High School in Los Angeles' Watts neighborhood. Despite school administrative orders, she taught what she calls "culturally relevant material." Her students, who she says are "exclusively black and brown," read material including *The Autobiography of Malcolm X*, the lyrics of Tupac Shakur, the poetry of Langston Hughes, and discussed local social conditions. Although Salazar's action was not directly connected to testing, she relates to antitesting advocates. "Either way, it's an imposed curriculum that doesn't speak to the needs of our students," she says. "The standard curriculum, these tests, they're really the same thing devoid of humanity."

Salazar is part of the teacher-activist group, The Association of Raza Educators (ARE), an organization of Latino/a teachers and allies working for community involvement and social justice teaching. Salazar's protest also incorporated new media to spread the message and elicit support, including launching a wiki page and producing numerous YouTube broadcasts.

"Alternative media is so valuable. We write a press release, send it out through links and our listserv, and we'll get thousands of clicks in one night," says Jose Lara, an ARE organizer who worked with Salazar and her students. "We have worked with people in San Francisco, Chicago, New York, to share ideas and see what actions they've been doing. That's how we've found other social justice educators will support us."

Salazar says successful organizing comes from the grassroots.

"It's important for people to network, but until we're able to organize our own communities, we're not able to organize in others," she says, adding that in an ideal world students, parents, and community members would be the policy makers.

Salazar says her students are their own best advocates, and she's committed to preventing "co-opting of their language," and misuse of terms like "social justice" and "culturally relevant" in education.

Beyond action taken in the classroom, protesters say that parents' right to opt their children out of tests may be the most immediate way to fight standardized testing in schools. Although it is not possible to opt out in every state, antitesting activism is possible in every district.

Juanita Doyon is one parent who has already joined the cause. When her children failed parts of the WASL exam, she began thinking about difficulties the test posed for students without the advantages her kids had. This concern launched her 20-year antitesting activist career. She and another mother formed the activist group Mothers Against WASL, and Doyon even ran for state superintendent of public instruction in 2004 on an antitesting platform.

"My organization pushed for the right for parents to view the test and question the scores," said Doyon. "We are looking at alternative ways of getting the diploma; we may start looking at schools that accept transcripts and award a diploma for a fee."

"The standard curriculum, these tests, they're really the same thing—devoid of humanity."

When the WASL became a high school graduation requirement, Mothers Against WASL supported students held back after failing the test and their increasingly outraged parents and teachers.

"I think all of the issues of teacher, parent, and student rights are connected," says Doyon. "It's centered around the control of curriculum. When we go to these standardized lessons, we lose our variety and the strength of our country. Eventually, we become standardized as people."

Antitest organizing presents a balancing act to everyone involved with education. U.S. teacher unions stay poised between "opposing" standardized testing and acting against them, despite their potential to be essential antitesting allies. Teachers boycott on behalf of their students, but often risk their jobs in the process. And parents, who boycotters say could end testing through opting students out of tests, have to consider the consequences—some substantial—if they decide to hold their children from taking high-stakes tests.

Teachers' acts of civil disobedience have drawn new attention to the ineffective tests-and-punish approach to improving academic achievement. Their acts stand as a challenge to teacher unions, parent organizations, teacher-parent coalitions, teacher social justice groups, students, and individuals of conscience to continue the momentum.

Taking a Stand for Learning

Chicago teachers speak out against a "really bad test"

GREG MICHIE

Ask Curie High School English teacher Martin McGreal what's wrong with the Chicago Academic Standards Examinations—better known as the CASE—and he doesn't mince words. "It's an indefensible test," he says flatly. "It's not a valid assessment, and it's a huge waste of instructional time."

Fellow teacher Umbreen Qadeer is equally blunt. "I feel guilty that I actually allowed my students to believe that this test was any sort of measure of their intelligence," she says.

I know the feeling. During my nine years as a Chicago public school teacher, one of the few things I truly dreaded was watching my 8th graders suffer through the Iowa Test of Basic Skills (ITBS) each spring. And when the ITBS became a "high-stakes" event in 1996—used as the measuring stick to determine whether my students would move on to high school—the scene was even grimmer.

Occasionally, I would talk with other frustrated teachers about boycotting the tests or staging a walkout. I attended meetings of a grassroots group called Teachers for Social Justice, where we brainstormed ways to fight the growing reliance on test scores as the singular means of assessing students, teachers, and schools. But come April, I'd always be right back where I'd been the year before: tail between my legs, passing out No. 2 pencils and bubble sheets.

Not so for McGreal, Qadeer, and 10 other English and social studies teachers at Curie, a 3,300-student high school on Chicago's Southwest Side. In September 2002, the members of the group—calling themselves Curie Teachers for Authentic Assessment—sent a signed letter to Chicago schools' CEO Arne Duncan (who later became U.S. secretary of education under President Obama) that laid out a detailed, convincing critique of the CASE, a series of exams administered each January and June to freshmen and sophomores in Chicago public schools. The letter concluded by stating matter of factly that its authors "will not be administering the CASE this year."

Taken alone, that may not sound like such a bold statement. But in the context of recent Chicago school reform, it's a printed bolt of lightning. Classroom teachers' voices have traditionally been ignored in the dialogue about what's best for the city's students and schools, and with the accountability push that began in the mid-1990s—led by Chicago Mayor Richard Daley and then-schools' CEO Paul Vallas—that silencing became even more pronounced. After George Schmidt, then a teacher at Chicago's Bowen High School, published portions of the CASE in his *Substance* newspaper in 1999 in an effort to highlight the test's weaknesses, the board sued him for more than $1 million and then fired him. The message was clear: Teachers were expected to toe the line.

In large measure—and with gritted teeth—we did. But pockets of resistance bubbled up, and with the 2001 election of Deborah Lynch, a strong advocate for classroom teachers, as head of the Chicago Teachers Union, the tide appeared to be turning. The Curie teachers' public stance against the CASE was further indication that it had.

> **Come April, I'd always be right back where I'd been the year before: tail between my legs, passing out No. 2 pencils and bubble sheets.**

Selling Students Short

Skeptics might fear that the group's actions suggest a willingness to lower the bar for their struggling students. But the "Curie 12" say just the opposite is true. Their letter to Duncan outlined a principled argument, rooted in a belief that the CASE ultimately impedes quality instruction and sells students short. It does a poor job of assessing higher-order thinking skills, the group believes, while validating memorization and rote learning.

"For me, the spirit in which the test was created was to hold teachers accountable," says Willie Watson, one of the 12 who submitted the letter. "But it's offensive to me as a professional. I'm being held to standards that are not as high as those I place on myself."

Daniel McGinn, who helped draft the letter to Duncan, agrees: "The CASE is based on the model that every English classroom in every school will be doing the same thing at the same time. But you can't teach English that way."

"You can't teach children that way," adds Qadeer.

McGreal, a 10-year teaching veteran and the group's official spokesperson, is quick to point out that he and his coworkers are not protesting all standardized testing, nor are they against genuine efforts to hold teachers accountable for their work. They just want to get rid of the CASE.

"Tests are supposed to be tools for us to gauge where we're going with our students' educations, to find out where the weaknesses are, and to make adjustments," McGreal says. "With the CASE, that doesn't happen. There's no feedback. You spend eight days taking an exam, get the scores back, and that's it."

The teachers met with board officials to discuss their concerns, but they made little headway. Mike Vaughn, a spokesman for Chicago Public Schools, says the board is "always interested in teachers' input and in working with teachers. We're looking for ways to make [the Curie teachers] more comfortable with the

"Tests are supposed to be tools for us to gauge where we're going with our students' educations, to find out where the weaknesses are, and to make adjustments," McGreal says. **"With the CASE, that doesn't happen. There's no feedback. You spend eight days taking an exam, get the scores back, and that's it."**

exam. But they're in the minority. The majority of teachers have given us positive feedback on the CASE." According to Vaughn, the board has no plans to discontinue or replace the exam. He is uncertain what actions might be taken should the teachers follow through with their protest.

Whatever the potential ramifications, the Curie 12 say they aren't backing down. In fact, their immediate goal is to get teachers from other high schools to join them. "This is totally about teacher activism to me," says Katie Hogan, a second-year English teacher. "How can I teach my kids to stand up for what they believe in if I'm not doing that myself?"

"It's about changing the system from within," agrees Lori Huebner, another member of the 12. "As teachers, that's our responsibility."

Other group members, while just as determined, are more modest. "We're not really trying to change the world," says Qadeer. "Just one really bad test."

Maybe so. But for students in Chicago high schools—and for teachers everywhere fighting to be heard—that would be a pretty good start. ✎

Testing, Tracking, and Toeing the Line

A role play on the origins of the modern high school

BILL BIGELOW

What we don't teach in school can be more important than what we do teach. When we fail to engage students in thinking critically about their own schooling, the hidden message is: Don't analyze the institutions that shape your lives; don't ask who benefits, who suffers, and how it got to be this way; just shut up and do as you're told.

Several years ago, my wife and teaching partner, Linda Christensen, and I began teaching a unit on the history and sociology of schooling. In the unit, our 11th-grade students at Jefferson High School in Portland, Ore., wrote and shared stories about their own school lives—both good learning experiences as well as times they encountered unfairness or abuse. We invited students to probe the hidden curricula in their own classes, including ours, asking them to reflect on what they were learning about authority, bosses, and democracy; solidarity and resistance, people's capacity to stand up for themselves and each other; knowledge, what kind is valued and where it comes from; and self-respect. Our class traveled to a high school in a wealthy Portland suburb to compare the hidden curriculum there with that at Jefferson, a school serving a predominantly working-class, African American community.

Roots of Modern Schooling

To explore some of the historical roots of the modern high school, I wrote a role play that I hoped would allow students to question aspects of schooling they often take for granted, such as tracking ("ability grouping"), standardized testing, guidance counseling, student government, the flag salute, bells, required courses with patriotic themes, and extracurricular activities like athletics and the school newspaper. These now commonplace components of high school life were introduced in the early years of the 20th century, a time of growing union militancy and radicalism, and large-scale immigration from southern and eastern Europe, accompanied by vastly increased high school enrollment.

Underlying the new reforms was a consensus among leading educators that social class stratification was here to stay, and that high schools should abandon a single academic curriculum for all students. Charles Eliot of Harvard, for example, argued that classes were "eternal," with an elite "guiding class" at the top and on the bottom, a "thick fundamental layer engaged in household work, agriculture, mining, quarrying, and forest work." Schools, the educational establishment concluded, must be "realistic" and train children for specific roles in the social hierarchy. Intelligence testing would allegedly ensure students' accurate placement in differentiated curricular tracks. Simultaneously, as one school board president complained, "Many educators have failed to face the big problem of teaching patriotism. ...We need to teach American children about American heroes and American ideals."

Instead of just lecturing about the profound changes in schools occurring in the early years of the century, I wanted students to encounter them as if they were members of different social classes and ethnic groups, learning of proposed reforms for the first time. Through argument and negotiation, students-as-different-social-groups would need to decide whether they supported the then-new reforms in public education.

In the activity, I portray a gung-ho superintendent, newly arrived in "Central City," determined to modernize—i.e., stratify and "Americanize"—the curriculum. Each student portrays an individual in one of five social groups: corporate executives, members of the Industrial Workers of the World (IWW), middle-class people, Hungarian immigrants, and black activists. Everyone is posed a series of questions about their views on schooling and is invited to advise the superintendent at a community meeting. In preparation, each group has a chance to consult and build alliances with any of the others. Through participating in the role play I hoped students might see firsthand that the school reforms were not simply benign, value-free changes, but were deeply political, benefiting some people at the expense of others. (For more on this activity, see the section "An Explicit Critique of Tracking" in "Getting Off the Track: Stories from an Untracked Classroom," in the Rethinking Schools book, *Rethinking Our Classrooms: Teaching for Equity and Justice, Vol. 1.*

Materials Needed

Enough for all students: copies of "Superintendent's Statement," "School Reform Meeting Questions," and "Mental Ability Test." Enough role sheets so that each student has a role (pp. 202-09).

Suggested Procedure (Also see "Suggestions for a Successful Role Play," in *Rethinking Our Classrooms, Vol. 1.*)

1. Write on the board: "Place: Central City, U.S.A.; Time: Early 1920s." Also list the names of the five social groups. (Note: "Central City" represents numerous Midwestern and Eastern U.S. cities; I set the role play in the early 1920s because this is when standardized testing took off, but the social and educational trends described in the role play began earlier, in the beginning years of the 20th century.)

2. Divide the class into five groups, of roughly equal numbers. Distribute a different role sheet to students in each of the groups: i.e., all the members of one group portray Hungarian immigrants, etc. Ask students to read these carefully, and, in their role, to think about the kind of schooling they want for their children. Encourage them to mark important sections. After they've finished reading, you might ask them to write a brief interior monologue—their inner thoughts—on what kind of education they hope for their children; or they might write on their fears. Afterward, ask them to read these to others in their group. The goal here is simply to prompt students to internalize the information in their role sheets, and to encourage them to imagine these individuals as real people. Ask students to make placards or name cards indicating their social group.

"What does knowing the color of emeralds have to do with your intelligence?" an inquiring immigrant or black activist might ask.

3. Tell students that Central City has hired a new superintendent who is proposing a series of reforms in Central City high schools. To each student, hand out the "Superintendent's Statement" and the "School Reform Meeting Questions." As mentioned, the teacher plays the superintendent. Before my "speech," I generally ask a student to introduce me as Superintendent Quincy P. Aldrich or another similarly aristocratic sounding name. I read the statement aloud, with a good dose of pomp, stopping along the way to emphasize a point and to make sure students understand each proposed reform. (Note that the four tracks—feebleminded, dull, etc.—come from a quote by Lewis Terman of Stanford, who suggested that these categories of students would never change. I tell students that if they don't like those designations, perhaps they'd prefer the tracks suggested by Professor George Strayer of Teachers College: bright, slow, backward, and deficient. Clearly, I am hoping to provoke students by using these terms. For public consumption, the educational elite preferred designations such as college, general, commercial, and vocational.) I assure the gathering that all tracking will be based on scientific evidence, and I have a sample test to prove it. Students always want to see the test, so at this point I distribute the "Mental Ability Test," (developed by Lewis Terman, p.202). "What does knowing the color of emeralds have to do with your intelligence?" an inquiring immigrant or black activist might ask. I encourage students' critical questions, but don't respond to them all, as I want to conserve their defiant energy for the community meeting. After the superintendent's proposal on guidance counseling, I emphasize that this is especially important considering the increased number of females in school these days: "Why, suppose a girl were to score high on a science test. It would be senseless to place her in a chemistry class. There are few if any female chemists in the country. It would be more sound to place her in an advanced domestic science course, which will help prepare her for the actual challenges she'll face in her life." After my presentation, I tell people that I don't want to argue about the reforms I've proposed, that right now all I want are questions about my speech, and later, in the community meeting, they'll have a chance to argue all they want. Generally, students in several of the groups will pay no attention to this plea and will

argue anyway. Again, at this stage it's good to get their critical juices flowing, but not to exhaust their arguments.

4. In preparation for the community meeting, in their small groups, students should discuss the "School Reform Meeting Questions" and, at least tentatively, decide what they think. These opinions may change based on their negotiations with other groups.

5. After they've had a while, probably 15 minutes or so, to discuss the questions, I say something like: "Choose half your group to be 'traveling negotiators.' These people will meet with individuals in other groups to discuss the questions. This is your chance to find people who agree with you about the superintendent's reforms, or to convince others. Remember, there is power in numbers; the more united you are in the community meeting, the more likely it is that the superintendent will be convinced—or forced—to agree with you. One rule: Travelers can't meet with other travelers, otherwise people left sitting in their groups will be left out."

6. This is the part I enjoy the most. As students dart around the classroom arguing points and finding allies, I listen in (as teacher, not superintendent), sometimes prodding people to meet with other groups or raising points they may not have considered. There is no "correct" amount of time to give this phase, but I don't want students' enthusiasm to wane, so I call a halt before they're talked out, perhaps 20 minutes or so.

7. Students should return to their small groups to prepare a presentation, however informal, on the various questions. I ask each group to choose a member to write on the board their response to question 1, on the purpose of schooling.

8. I seat the entire class in a circle (people should remain seated with their social group, each indicated with a placard) and begin the meeting by asking each group to respond to the question on the purpose of schooling. Again, there is no right and wrong way to run the meeting. The aim is to encourage the most spirited and democratic participation possible. As superintendent, I'm able to provoke people, point out contradictions, and raise questions. By the way, sometime during the community meeting I remind them that this is only an advisory meeting, that there is a school board, elected citywide, to decide educational policy. I'm just seeking "input." We wouldn't want to give students the false impression that all social groups affected by school reform actually had any say-so.

9. After the meeting, it's important that students have a way to distance themselves from their roles so the debriefing discussion is not simply a continuation of the community meeting. Sometimes I ask students to write about who they think "won" in real life, and to think about how things work in our high school today, to get clues on whose vision of schooling prevailed. Students might write a critique of the superintendent's position or of the position of one of the groups, including their own. Alternatively, they might remain in character to write an interior monologue on how they feel about their child's future in Central City Schools. Afterwards they might read these to the class.

10. Discussion questions include:

> Sometimes I ask students to write about who they think "won" in real life, and to think about how things work in our high school today, to get clues on whose vision of schooling prevailed.

- Who do you think "won" in real life?

- Which of the reforms do you think were adopted in U.S. schools?

- If a majority of the groups opposed the superintendent's plan: If most of you opposed the reforms, why were they put into effect? What power did the different social groups have? What power didn't they have?

- Which of the alliances you built might not have happened in real life? Why not?

- Which of the superintendent's proposals do you see in our school today?

- Draw students' attention to the five purposes of schooling that a member of each group wrote on the board: Which of these do you personally find most appealing? Why?

- Which of these seems closest to the kind of schooling you've had? Which of these do you think guides the way our school is set up today?

- What did the "intelligence test" measure? What didn't it measure?

If you haven't already done so, it might be valuable to have students write about their personal experiences with standardized testing and/or tracking. ❦

Useful Background Materials

Paul Davis Chapman, *Schools as Sorters*, New York University Press, 1988 (especially Chapter 5, "The Use of Intelligence Tests in Schools: California Case Studies").

David Tyack, *The One Best System: A History of American Urban Education*, Harvard University Press, 1974.

Joel Spring, *The American School, 1642-1985*, Longman, 1986 (especially Chapter 7, "Education and Human Capital").

Robert S. Lynd and Helen M. Lynd, *Middletown*, Harcourt, Brace, 1929 (especially part II: "Training the Young").

Jeannie Oakes, *Keeping Track: How Schools Structure Inequality*, Yale University Press, 2005 (Chapter 2, "Unlocking the Tradition").

Samuel Bowles and Herbert Gintis, *Schooling in Capitalist America*, Basic Books, 1976, (Chapters 5 and 6, "The Origins of Mass Public Education" and "Corporate Capital and Progressive Education").

Mental Ability Test

Stanford University Test 1 Information

Draw a line under the ONE word that makes the sentence true, as shown in the sample.

Sample:

Our first president was:	Adams	Jefferson	Lincoln	<u>Washington</u>
1. Coffee is a kind of	bark	berry	leaf	root
2. Sirloin is a cut of	beef	mutton	pork	veal
3. Gasoline comes from	grains	petroleum	turpentine	seeds
4. Most exports go from	Boston	San Francisco	New Orleans	New York
5. The number of pounds in a ton is	1000	2000	3000	4000
6. Napoleon was defeated at	Leipzig	Paris	Verdun	Waterloo
7. Emeralds are usually	blue	green	red	yellow
8. The optic nerve is for	seeing	hearing	tasting	feeling
9. Larceny is a term used in	medicine	theology	law	pedagogy
10. Sponges come from	animals	farms	forests	mines

© *1920 by World Book Co. From Paul Davis Chapman*, Schools as Sorters, *New York University Press, 1988.*

Superintendent's Statement on Reforming the High Schools

I've inherited a 19th-century school district in a 20th-century city. It's time for some changes. The following proposals are based on reforms that are sweeping the nation, reforms developed by the finest universities. Up until now we've run pretty much on the "common school" system. We've assumed that all students are the same, that all should be trained to be president of the United States. Well, my friends, not all our students are going to be president. In 1890, when fewer than 10 percent of 14- to 17-year-olds were in high school, this probably made sense. But by 1920 more than a third of all teenagers were in high school, and not all these kids are well served by such a difficult academic curriculum. Nor is our society as a whole well served by such a system. As the revered Stanford educator Lewis Terman reminds us, we have both "gifted and defective" children in school, and they need to be taught differently. It's too bad, but as Ellwood Cubberley, dean of education at Stanford, points out, in our schools we have "many children of the foreign-born who have no aptitude for book learning, and many children of inferior mental qualities who do not profit by ordinary classroom procedure."

Therefore, I propose segregating students into four tracks, each with a different curriculum: Track No. 1: **Feebleminded**; Track No. 2: **Dull**; Track No. 3: **Average**; and Track No. 4: **Superior**. This will allow us to adapt a given course of study to students' individual needs. As suggested by one California school administrator, the lower tracks will naturally train students for "definite hand occupations as opposed to brain occupations."

There will be no guesswork in placing students in different tracks. They will be placed scientifically, on the basis of test scores. A system of guidance counseling will assist students in the interpretation of test scores, and to help them plan a personally rewarding and socially useful occupation.

Many of the people entering Central City schools are immigrants. These immigrants are worrisome for a number of reasons. Instead of identifying themselves as Americans, they see themselves as Hungarians or Italians. Some of them identify with the working class against the owners, or even with radicals, people who want to overthrow our form of government. In order to ensure that all children become loyal Americans, I'm proposing the following: To encourage students to learn about democracy, all schools will have student councils, and every day all students will pledge allegiance to the flag. In all classes we will teach that our system of government is the best in the world. Through clubs, athletics, school assemblies, school newspapers, and the like, we will encourage students to identify not with their social class or radical group, but with their school. We will teach them to be patriotic to their country and patriotic to their school.

School Reform Meeting Questions

Be prepared to explain the following in your presentation at the school reform community meeting.

1. In one or two sentences, describe what you see as the purpose(s) of schooling.

2. Do you support the superintendent's plan for "tracking?" Why or why not? If you don't support the plan, how do you propose to deal with the variety of social backgrounds and skill levels in Central City high schools?

3. Do you support the superintendent's plan for increased testing and guidance counseling? Why or why not?

4. Do you support the superintendent's curricular and extracurricular proposals? Why or why not? Do you have any other suggestions? ✎

Corporate Executive

You are an executive with a large and prosperous corporation. There are a lot of problems in the country, problems that pose serious challenges to public education. In your eyes, the schools have not been meeting these challenges very successfully. For example, before 1900, fewer than one out of every 10 kids between the ages of 14 and 17 was enrolled in high school. This is a real problem because people who are not in school become juvenile delinquents, turn to crime, or worse, join radical groups like the Industrial Workers of the World (IWW). And besides, there simply aren't enough jobs to go around for everyone who wants one.

Also, many of those entering schools are immigrants. They don't speak much English and haven't learned anything of what it means to be an American. Instead of identifying themselves as Americans, these immigrants see themselves as Hungarians or Italians. Some identify with the working class against the owners, or even see themselves as radicals. In Lawrence, Mass., in 1912, a massive strike involving 30,000 workers—teenagers, men, women, almost all immigrants—led by IWW radicals, defeated the mill owners. In 1919, workers in Seattle staged the first citywide strike in U.S. history, and there were huge strikes in the steel, coal, and meatpacking industries. What is this country coming to? You need to make sure that the children of immigrants identify themselves as loyal, responsible Americans—and that they don't identify with one social class against another.

Besides all the immigrants arriving in Central City, there are lots of people leaving the farms to come to the city. These immigrants and farmers aren't used to the factory ways of the city. They aren't used to being prompt, working by the clock, doing repetitive work, obeying orders from a boss, etc.—all skills and attitudes needed to succeed as factory workers. Their children are not ready to meet the challenges of modern life. You want the schools to turn out good factory workers—but also serve the needs of your children, who are certainly not going to be factory workers. Up until now, the high schools in Central City have been "common schools" with one curriculum for all students. With few exceptions, everyone took the same subjects in the same classes: boys with girls, bright kids with dull kids. The problem is that in earlier times, very few people went to school, so if you had a high school diploma, it meant something—you could get a good job in the business world. These students tended to be from upper-class or middle-class families. But now, with all these farm kids and immigrants entering the schools, there's no way that all of them are going to get these high-paying jobs. You need to figure out a way for the school system to train the future bankers as well as the future factory hands in the same classrooms—or at least in the same schools. ✎

Hungarian Immigrant

Let's get one thing straight: You didn't move to the United States to take any-body's job. At the turn of the century, conditions were tremendously difficult in Hungary. You owned a little plot of land, but when wealthy farmers began buying machinery to harvest their crops, you simply couldn't compete. You could either starve or move. When labor contractors began showing up, they promised good jobs and high wages if you would travel to the United States—a real land of milk and honey. The traveling conditions in Europe, on the ship coming over, and within the United States were difficult beyond belief. But finally you arrived in Central City, home of Miller and Jones, a giant manufacturer of railroad cars. Instead of milk and honey you found grease and grime.

Even though in Hungary you were a skilled farmer, here you were called "un-skilled labor." Your pay was low, but at least work was steady—for a while. But then you realized that you were guaranteed nothing. Often you'd work only six months out of the year and be laid off the rest of the time. Needless to say, during these periods there were no unemployment benefits. As an unskilled worker, you had no security. At times your friends would not be hired back by Miller and Jones; the company would hire younger, stronger workers to take their places. With no formal education, no access to additional training, and no big bank account, you have little hope of escaping this life of poverty.

There may be little hope for you, but there is hope for your children. In America, education is free. You've been told that a high school diploma guar-antees a young person a decent job. Just because you are an unskilled laborer doesn't mean that your children will suffer the same fate. They might be teach-ers, clerks, shopkeepers, or even doctors or lawyers. That's why you will sacrifice anything to send your children to school. They will be in the same classes with the sons and daughters of bankers and businessmen, architects and artists. They will read the same books, write the same essays, and solve the same equations. In school, rich and poor will mean nothing. Your children are smart. There will be no limit to what they can accomplish. You want them to learn to be Americans, but you are proud of your Hungarian culture and also want them to value that heritage. Your children learn quickly and already speak two languages. You have absolute confidence they will be able to thrive in high school and go on to get good jobs. ✎

Black Activist

You are a black activist in Central City. Over the years you've worked with a number of organizations to promote civil rights. Sometimes you've worked with groups that make alliances with whites; other times you've worked with black-only organizations. You join with whomever you see as capable of fighting racism in Central City and the country as a whole. For years there weren't many black people in Central City. Most blacks came north during World War I. Conditions were horrible in Mississippi. Your family worked as sharecroppers there. It seemed like you were always in debt to the white landlord. Everything you had to buy was expensive; but they paid you next to nothing for the crops you raised. Anyone who protested would be beaten or even killed. Blacks were denied the right to vote and the kids went to crummy schools.

When people heard there were jobs up north, practically your whole county emptied out overnight. But conditions in Central City have become increasingly difficult since the war. Perhaps the biggest problem is job discrimination. Employers hire blacks in only the most dangerous, worst paid and dead-end jobs. The Ku Klux Klan is strong in Central City. They want to make sure that blacks stay poor and powerless instead of demanding good jobs, better housing, and decent schools. You are especially concerned about the education of black children. Although schools are not formally segregated in Central City, you know that black children are discriminated against. One recent study found that 50 percent of black girls in Central City schools were classified as "retarded" and put in "special classes," whereas only 4 percent of native-born whites were classified this way. For this you blame racist administrators and teachers.

Many school officials say that they want to teach children the skills they will need in "real life." They assume blacks will continue to be janitors and maids and so want to teach you to be good—and happy—janitors and maids. But you want your children to get a good academic education so they can become anything they set their minds to.

However, some people complain that this kind of education will make black children resentful. As one judge warned, education should not put "fool ideas of rising and equality into [black] folks' heads, and [make] them discontent and unhappy." In your view, in an unjust society, education *should* make young people discontented. It should fill their heads with dreams of equality and give them the tools—reading, writing, knowledge of their history—that will allow them to make their dreams real. You hope that the more education children have, the unhappier they will be with the racism in Central City and the larger society. A good education should help give children the skills to organize for a better, more just, society. What you want from the superintendent of schools in Central City, and the school system as a whole, is a commitment to fight racism. ❧

IWW Member

You live in Central City, U.S.A., and are a member of the Industrial Workers of the World, the IWW, a radical labor union. You're concerned about school because you care about children, but also because you see schools as a place where people learn about what is expected of them by society. You see changing the schools as part of a larger movement for changing the whole society. Much is now different in America. The society is more and more divided between rich factory owners and workers who own nothing but their own ability to labor. As far as you in the IWW are concerned, the problems of working people will only begin to be solved when workers take over all the workplaces and run them together for the benefit of the whole society—not just for the private profit of the owners. As long as owners run industry for their own profit, there will be continual conflict between them and the workers they control. You believe that workers produce all wealth, so they should control all wealth—what do owners produce?

Thus, the goal of the IWW is not only for higher wages or shorter hours, but to change the whole society. People who produce, who do the work, should run workplaces and all of society. And schools should help people learn the skills to run the whole society. In the IWW you don't believe in the idea of "follow the leader." Your goal is for every worker in the country to be a "leader." Recently, you read a speech by Eugene Debs, an IWW founder. Debs summed up the IWW belief:

> The average working [person] imagines that he must have a leader to look to; a guide to follow, right or wrong....You have depended too much on that leader and not enough on yourself. I don't want you to follow me. I want you to cultivate self-reliance. If I have the slightest capacity for leadership I can only give evidence of it by "leading" you to rely on yourselves.

That's what democracy is all about as far as you're concerned: Everyone is a leader, a thinker, a participant—regardless of race, sex, or class background. And that's what schools should promote for all the students, not just the ones from rich families. Schools should model a truly democratic, classless society. 🖉

HANDOUT ✍

Middle-Class Person

You consider yourself "middle-class"—maybe upper-middle-class. You manage a small variety "five-and-dime" store; your father was a clerk for a large machine shop in town. The changes going on in Central City make you nervous—not so much for yourself, but for your children. When you were young, the common wisdom was that if you went to high school and you graduated, you were guaranteed a good, solid middle-class or business job. You might become a clerk or a factory superintendent, or go on to college to become a lawyer or a doctor. The ticket was high school graduation, and for the most part only the upper and middle classes went to high school.

But now everything is changing. In the last 20 years or so, the population of Central City has tripled. Quite a number of people are coming into town off the farms, but most of the newcomers are immigrants from overseas. These people, many of whom can't even speak English, think that in America the streets are lined with gold. The problem is that the immigrants think that the way to get some of that good American gold is to send their kids to high school. Why is this a problem? Because there aren't enough good jobs to go around. A university did a survey recently, asking high school kids what they wanted to be when they grew up. Just over 90 percent wanted to be some kind of professional person, clerk, or businessperson; only 4 percent wanted to work in a factory. But in the real world, only about 18 percent of the jobs are those kind of decent, middle-class jobs. More than 60 percent are factory jobs or farm work of some kind.

You hate to think of yourself as selfish, but these statistics mean that there are going to be lots of people competing for the jobs that should belong to your children. You know that in a fair competition, your child would succeed. But what is happening now is that all these immigrant kids and farm kids who can barely read or write are crowding into the same classes. Soon, a high school diploma won't be worth anything. You want your child to read classic literature, take mathematics, write essays and research papers, learn the history of this great country, and master the workings of our form of government. But all these slow learners are going to hold everyone back. And they are also disruptive, many of them juvenile delinquents. The world is a different place. Today, good jobs require more education. You might even have to send your children to college. But what if they've had an inferior high school education because of all these rowdy newcomers? ✎

Opting Out and Speaking Up

A national movement grows to opt out of state tests

PEGGY ROBERTSON

Opting out of the state test is not a new idea; for many years parents have been opting children out of state tests, and educators have been sharing the negative effects of excessive standardized testing. However, the stakes have never been so high within our public school system, where the state test is currently tied to students, teachers, schools, and communities in ways that punish our children and drastically affect the future ability of our nation to function as a democracy.

Our movement began as a Facebook site, which I created in August 2011, when it seemed the momentum for national change was finally here. Americans were waking up and the Save Our Schools march helped spark our movement. No Child Left Behind and Race to the Top set in place accountability systems that were failing the 99 percent.

Educators have attempted to reason with politicians, corporate reform educators, administrations, and all involved with the current standardized testing frenzy. We have been silenced at every turn. Many educators go to work in fear of losing their jobs and are forced into silence through what I consider to be abusive working conditions. Many students go to school with high anxiety, fear, and dislike for a school environment that no longer allows their bodies, minds, and spirits to breathe, create, and become individuals in our supposed democratic society. We have hoped that those in charge would listen and focus on strategies to support and improve equity within our public schools as well as create opportunities for children to be innovative through reading, writing, drama, music, art, movement, and more. Instead, our children have been fed tests. And under Race to the Top they will be fed more tests. No matter how much research demonstrating the negative effects of standardized testing we share, the corporate reformers continue to increase the testing mandates.

The Save Our Schools march was the first national protest against the corporate takeover of our public schools. The event attracted thousands of educators and activists and received national coverage, putting in place a new narrative, which I summarize here:

> Our schools are not in crisis. Our public schools should provide a whole and equitable education for all students. The corporate reformers are dicing and splicing our schools using a variety of strategies and resulting in the ever-widening gap between the haves and have-nots. While our schools can always be improved, we are not in crisis. We have a crisis of child poverty, which cannot be

solved by the schools alone. Our test scores are actually quite good when we remove the test scores of children receiving free or reduced lunch. Poverty is the crisis—not bad teachers. We can reclaim our public schools.

> **Many students go to school with high anxiety, fear, and dislike for a school environment that no longer allows their bodies, minds, and spirits to breathe, create, and become individuals in our supposed democratic society.**

I felt we could further the true narrative shared by the Save Our Schools march by creating a national movement to support parents and students in opting out of the state test. Other educators agreed. For example, Tim Slekar, associate professor at Penn State Altoona, had created the Facebook site, "Kids Are More than Test Scores: Boycotting High-Stakes Testing," after he attended the march.

Morna McDermott McNulty, associate professor at Towson University, agreed to help with the Facebook page I had created, which is called "Opt Out of the State Test: the National Movement." Slekar joined us. Within days, other educators joined our efforts: Ceresta Smith, national board certified teacher from Florida and charter Save Our Schools march organizer; Shaun Johnson, assistant professor at Towson University; and finally Laurie Murphy, also a charter Save Our Schools march organizer with resource and program development expertise. The Facebook page grew like wildfire. Within 48 hours, hundreds of members and parents had requested support. Parents wrote, asking how to opt out. They shared their children's stories of abusive situations in schools where the test took precedence over childhood health issues, play, developmentally appropriate curriculum, necessary recess, P.E., music, art, purchase of necessary supplies, and more. The test took precedence over quality teaching and learning. Parents were waking up. The mandates had become so stringent that the children were suffering greatly and parents had had enough.

We could not meet the demands we received nationally and abroad through our Facebook page alone. Now a team of six administrators, we created a website, www.unitedoptout.com, to house all the supports we had available to parents and communities who were attempting to change the narrative about standardized testing and put a halt to the "reform" occurring in their schools. We met weekly through Skype to discuss and strategize. We became a think tank.

> **We will no longer be silenced and fearful of the mandates imposed on the 99 percent by the corporate reformers of the one percent.**

Our movement is not one of simply sharing information. By design, we are intent on creating action—weekly—continual, forceful, and unwavering. We will no longer be silenced and fearful of the mandates imposed on the 99 percent by the corporate reformers of the 1 percent. We live in a democracy that is disappearing quickly, but with movements such as ours, there is hope that our democracy will rise again and public schools will equitably fund education for all of our children once again.

Corporate-owned mainstream media continually spout the following message: Our schools are bad and standardized testing will improve student learning. The research demonstrates that their message is a lie, and many groups, such as FairTest, continue to call them out. Through social media and constant networking, we have begun to organize local and national community protests. We are a community of Opt-Outers, numbering in the hundreds, who share ideas, stories, and strategies for changing the narrative—and we have evidence that the narrative is changing.

As weeks go by, new articles appear chronicling the harmful effects of excessive standardized testing. In addition, parents are writing blogs and articles in which they share their stories of opting their children out of state tests.

United Opt Out National is a movement created to halt corporate education reform by denying reformers the one tool they need to control and topple our public education system—the state test. Without the state test, it becomes impossible to close schools, punish teachers, students, and communities. The test need not be feared. We simply can refuse the test. If **mass** opt out occurs, privatization of our public schools comes to a screeching halt.

The Opt Out movement continues to gain momentum. We are many. They are few. Our voices can be louder and our actions can have impact. We are no longer silent or afraid, and we demand that our public schools be returned to the 99 percent. Why do we support opting out? In the words of Tim Slekar: because we support public schools. ✎

Template for Opting Students Out of State Tests

[Your Name]

Date: [Insert Date]

[Recipient]

[Title]

[Company]

[Address 1]

[Address 2]

[Address 3]

Dear [Recipient]:

I am writing on behalf of my student to opt him or her out of the [test name(s)] test. [He/She] is neither permitted to take the exam during mandated testing days nor during designated make-up sessions. Additionally, I am requesting that the school make accommodations for meaningful alternative activities or assignments that will continue to promote [his or her] academic and intellectual growth. My child will not be in attendance if academically viable alternatives are not available. Furthermore, I must be guaranteed in writing that whatever option is taken, either alternative assignments or absence, my child will not face any negative consequences to, for example, course grades, social or behavioral evaluations, workload, promotion, or future classroom assignments.

Strict adherence to state and federal high-stakes standardized testing, including the extensive classroom preparation that occurs prior to test administration, prevents my student from receiving a well-rounded and engaging educational experience. Until focus on testable skills diminishes to a reasonable extent, I will continue to withhold my child from participation in the testing program, and I ask that you honor that decision to the best of your ability.

I do apologize in advance for the inconvenience or scrutiny that this decision may cause the administration, the school, and staff.

Sincerely,

[Your Name]

[Your Title]

PART 6

Beyond High-Stakes Standardized Testing

RANDALL ENOS

Hallmarks of Good Assessment

THE EDITORS OF *RETHINKING SCHOOLS*

Alternatives to high-stakes standardized tests are being implemented across the country. Although the alternatives vary in focus and scope, they generally share the following principles:

- Support improved learning. The assessment is designed to provide feedback that helps students improve their learning.

- Help teachers teach better. Good assessment provides an array of information that teachers can use to improve their teaching practices and help ensure student learning.

- Are integrated with the curriculum and instruction. Assessment works best when it flows naturally from, and is part of, student work—i.e., a science experiment that becomes part of the student portfolio.

- Are classroom based. Most of the information for the assessment is based on classroom work done by students over a period of time.

- Use a variety of measures. Good assessment does not rely on a single yardstick but compiles data based on individual students' learning as well as schoolwide data such as attendance and graduation rates.

- Involve educators, parents, and the broader community. Improved success for students relies on a positive collaboration among the various forces necessary for school reform to work.

- Don't straitjacket the curriculum. Good assessment procedures provide for flexibility and don't dominate the curriculum. ⊛

Alternatives to Standardized Tests

The only thing worse than requiring students to reduce all learning to a single "correct" answer is reducing assessment and accountability to a single standardized test

BOB PETERSON AND MONTY NEILL

Critics of standardized tests are often asked, "What's your alternative?"
It's a legitimate—and important—question. Parents and community members have the right to know how well their children are learning.

Unfortunately, in part due to rhetoric that equates high standards with standardized tests, many parents believe that standardized tests will give them the answer. At the same time, parents are often the first to understand that a test score cannot capture the complexity of their children.

The issue is how to create alternatives to standardized tests that will inform parents and community members about how well the schools are doing and clue them in to whether their children are learning what they need to know—that is, how to create an alternative approach to accountability. Teachers and parents also need to learn about and promote alternatives to "high-stakes" tests, the term for a single exam that solely or largely determines if a student is promoted, graduates from high school, or gets into college.

Standardized tests are just one type of assessment, although they often get the most publicity. It's also important to recognize that teachers assess students regularly as part of their ongoing teaching. The challenge is to match assessment that is integrated into classroom instruction—which is focused primarily on helping individual children—with assessment that provides school- and districtwide information being demanded by state and federal officials or members of the community.

One of the first steps toward rethinking assessments is to ask, "What is the purpose of the assessment?" and, "Is this purpose worthy or meaningful?" Answering these questions means addressing what is important for students to learn, how we help them learn, and how we know what they have learned.

Too often, the rationale for standardized testing appears overly punitive: "We're going to get these kids and schools to perform better—or else." Such an approach forgets that assessment should serve one primary purpose: to improve student learning. The goal is not to flunk kids, not to wave fingers at lousy teachers, not to make bold pronouncements that will be remembered at election time, not to protect systems from bad publicity by narrowly focusing on boosting test scores, not to give kids more of the same even though it didn't work the first time. The purpose should be to provide information to help the student learn better.

Assessment serves other purposes as well. Community members may want data to see if schools are providing equal opportunity to all students. Policy makers might want to know the effectiveness of various programs. Districts and state legislatures often use tests to hold schools accountable for how well they are spending taxpayers' money. Schools might also use assessment as a way to report to parents, or to summarize and certify a student's achievement. Finally, districts might use changes in assessment policy to help transform the curriculum.

> **One of the first steps toward rethinking assessments is to ask, "What is the purpose of the assessment?" and, "Is this purpose worthy or meaningful?"**

Depending on the purpose, schools might use different forms of assessment. For example, an assessment designed to evaluate how well a school, overall, is teaching its students to read should not be used to decide whether a particular student should or should not be promoted to 4th grade. Furthermore, any assessment should ultimately serve, and not undercut, the primary goal of helping the student.

Alternatives to standardized testing are in use in both the United States and other industrialized countries. Those alternatives include student portfolios, districtwide projects or tasks, and outside review teams that evaluate schools. Evidence is growing to show that these measures do a better job of showing how well students and schools are performing.

The biggest drawback to most of these alternatives is that they challenge this country's predominant approach to thinking and learning—that is, that we can only truly know something if it can be statistically and "objectively" determined and analyzed. History has unfortunately shown that such an approach has been used not just to predict, but also to control the world and those who live in it. For many, the consequences are harmful, not beneficial.

Alternative assessments, on the other hand, require diversity in thinking about the purpose of knowledge and what constitutes knowledge. To challenge statistical ways of knowing is to challenge the status quo and its tendency to marginalize and describe as abnormal those who do not neatly fit into a statistical box. Alternative assessments mean alternative voices, perspectives, and actions. They are the only way for all students to demonstrate a range and depth of important learning, and for many students alternative assessments represent the fairest way to show what they know and can do. For these vitally important reasons, they should be embraced as an important part of accountability.

Other obstacles exist. Alternative assessments are new and, like any innovation, they challenge those who prefer to do things the way they've always done them. It takes time and energy to reeducate teachers, parents, and students in new forms of assessments. Moreover, such assessments cost more because they require more sophisticated teaching, staff development, and scoring. Decent assessment can't be done cheaply, any more than can decent education. That said, a great portion of the time spent on learning and doing alternatives serves as effective staff development.

Nor are alternative assessments a magic bullet. Teachers and parents need to be aware of the strengths and weaknesses of any approach, and how to use it appropriately.

The following is a description of some of the most common forms of alternative assessments.

Portfolio-based Assessment

One of the more promising forms of assessment is what is known as "portfolio-based assessment." The approaches to portfolios vary considerably, but they all rest on records kept by the teacher and on collections of the student's work, called the "student portfolio." During the school year, teachers and students gather work that shows student progress and achievement in various subjects such as English or science. Students are usually encouraged to reflect on the work that has been selected. Such reflection helps students think not only about what they have learned, but also about their own learning processes, all of which contributes to the overall goal of improving student learning.

In some approaches, at the end of a marking period the teacher (or groups of teachers) examines the portfolio and evaluates the work based on a scoring guide. Sometimes students or their peers also score their work. The teacher ultimately records a score on a long-term record, attaching evidence such as a writing sample, or write-up of a science experiment, or a teacher's observation. A particularly strong variant is the "Learning Record," which provides a clear, strong structure to guide how teachers and students gather evidence of and evaluate student learning. This approach is useful for the teacher, student, and parent in determining how well a student is progressing. But, through what is known as "random sampling," it also can be the basis for improved professional development and for school- and districtwide accountability.

Under random sampling, a number of the learning records and student portfolios are selected randomly from each classroom. An independent group—of teachers from other schools, members of the community, or a combination of both—reviews the records and port-folios ("moderation"). If there is a significant difference between the conclusions of the independent readers and the classroom teacher, then a third reader might be called in or a larger sample might be taken from the classroom, in order to determine how well a

> **Performance exams have the advantage over standardized tests in that they drive the curriculum in a relatively progressive way.**

particular teacher consistently applies the agreed-upon assessment guidelines.

Approaches of this sort have been developed in Britain, Australia, and the United States, by organizations such as the New York Performance Standards Consortium (see "Multiple Measures," in this volume), which does this with performance tasks shared across participating schools.

This classroom-based approach has several advantages. For example, the evaluation is based on a wide range of student work done over a long period of time, rather than on a single, paper-and-pencil test taken over a few hours. Further, the approach encourages schools and districts to invest in the professional development of the teachers and outside evaluators (rather than continuing to buy one-shot tests from corporations), and it pushes teachers to reflect more consistently on the quality of student work in their classrooms.

One of the criticisms of this approach is that it works best when there are quality teachers. But such criticism needs to take into account that this classroom approach, over time, can encourage collaboration among teachers and improve their work. If done properly, this approach has teachers regularly talking about students' work and allows more-skilled teachers to help less-experienced teachers. Such portfolio discussions will inevitably include not only how to evaluate student work, but also the nature of the work that is going on in particular classrooms and strategies to get students to do better work. This approach can benefit a weak teacher, certainly more than standardized tests do.

Another criticism of portfolios, especially when teachers have little control over what types of materials are to be included in the portfolio, is that the requirements can "hijack" the curriculum and dominate what is taught. For instance, if a district decides that the English portfolio for 8th graders needs to have an example of a business letter and a five-paragraph essay, the teacher may focus so much on those requirements that little time is left for other important topics such as poetry, creative writing, or literary analysis. One solution is to require a wide range of types of writing in a writing portfolio, as the Learning Record does. Many educators also note that it is better to have a portfolio-driven curriculum, which is based on real student work, than a curriculum shaped by standardized tests and their reliance on random bits of memorized data and procedures.

Another problem with portfolios is logistics. Where does a high school English teacher store more than 100 portfolios? How does an elementary school maintain portfolios as students move up in grades? How does the issue of student mobility influence this kind of record keeping? One creative solution is to videotape portfolios; another is to save the information digitally. Though methods vary, teachers and schools are overcoming these problems. In addition, even young children can learn to maintain their portfolios or Learning Records.

A fourth criticism of the portfolio approach is that it relies too much on the individual judgment of teachers and opens the door to overly subjective evaluation. This concern has been raised most directly where teachers may not be sensitive to the needs and skills of students of color, or non-English speakers, or immigrants. Clearly, this is a serious issue. At the same time, it is a problem that pervades all forms of assessment. Who, for example, chooses the questions on standardized tests? Rarely is it immigrants, or non-English speakers, or educators of color.

If the outside evaluators are sensitive to this potential problem, portfolio-based assessment can be used to identify teachers who are subjectively giving lower evaluations to particular groups of students or teachers whose pedagogical weaknesses lead them to have students focus on mindless worksheets rather than engaging projects. Professional learning can strengthen these teachers. Further, in the culture of shared learning among educators that portfolios can foster, better teachers can counsel out teachers who will not or cannot improve.

Overall, we have found that portfolios are central to high-quality schooling. They can foster collaboration among teachers, focus attention on getting students to do quality work, and provide data to the community on how well a school is performing.

Performance Assessments

Some states and districts have adopted what are called performance examinations. These are tests given to all students, based on students "performing" a certain task, such as writing an essay, conducting a science experiment, or doing an oral presentation, which is videotaped.

For a few years in the 1990s, Milwaukee Public Schools did extensive work developing such performance exams in the areas of writing, science, math, visual arts, and oral communications. For example, 4th or 5th graders had to perform a three- to five-minute oral presentation. In writing, 4th, 5th, 8th, 11th, and 12th graders all had to write and revise essays over a period of two days, based on a districtwide prompt that changed from year to year and covered different genres—from imaginary writing, to narrative essays, to expository essays. Teachers from the district judged the essays—independently and anonymously—using a scale of one to four. Two teachers read each essay, and the final score was based on the sum of the two readers. To reduce subjectivity, if there was a difference of more than one point in the two readers' evaluation, a third reader scored the paper.

Some districts also use these performance exams as a way to check how well classroom teachers are scoring their student portfolios. If large numbers of students are doing well on the performance exams yet score poorly on the student portfolios, or vice versa, it sends a signal that follow-up needs to occur.

Performance exams have the advantage over standardized tests in that they drive the curriculum in a relatively progressive way. In Milwaukee, the assessments encouraged teachers to focus on actual student writing rather than fill-in-the-blank worksheets. They led to more hands-on science experiments where students actually learn the scientific process and how to reflect on and analyze data, rather than merely answer questions at the end of a textbook chapter. The oral presentations were useful way to get students actively involved, rather than merely listening to lectures by the teacher; they

> It's essential that a broad array of parents and staff be involved. Otherwise, both parents and teachers feel that, once again, someone else is telling them how to raise their child or how to teach.

also forced teachers to pay attention to oral communication skills, which cannot be tested with a paper-and-pencil exam. The actual performance assessments, once they were scored, became part of student portfolios. Unfortunately, a combination of factors—mainly costs and the growing national pressures to define achievement as scores on standardized tests—led Milwaukee's school administration to abandon this innovative reform.

Currently, the strongest example in the United States is the New York Performance Standards Consortium. The roughly 30 participating high schools develop and share performance tasks across the schools, and these count as part of a student's overall work.

Teachers who help write the performance assessment tasks (or prompts) learn a lot about how to develop more interesting and academically valuable projects for their students.

Performance exams are performance assessments that most often take the form of projects, from laboratory experiments to group activities to exhibitions (described below), which are done as part of classroom work. (Sometimes the term includes portfolios as well, or these tasks and projects can be important parts within portfolios.) Using performance exams can encourage teachers to use a wider range of activities in the classroom, which can enrich instruction, deepen learning, and provide detailed assessment information.

Performance exams have not been used more widely in part because they take considerable time, both for the classroom teacher and the district. It takes time, expertise—and ultimately, money—to develop the prompts and score the assessments, to say nothing of training teachers in activity-based teaching methods necessary for such performance assessments.

Some very good teachers, particularly those who have spent years developing a cohesive curriculum for their classrooms, may find that the exams disrupt the flow of classroom work, although this shouldn't be the case if the assessments are carefully aligned with good instructional practices.

Finally, another problem is that performance exams, as with any kind of assessment, can tempt teachers to "teach to the test." Even in performance assessment, the emphasis must remain on higher-level thinking skills instead of on recall and memorization. Expecting a wide range of tasks and projects over a year can help prevent over-teaching to one or two tasks.

In a *New York Times* opinion piece in December 2000, Harvard professor Howard Gardner cautioned:

> It might now seem far better to teach students how to write a personal essay than to simply ask them multiple-choice questions about a passage. Yet it is possible even with essay tests to teach students to do well through mimicry rather than through general writing skills.... Educators and parents should value the development of knowledge and skills that go beyond a single test. That is, high performance should be an incidental result of strong general preparation.

Among other problems, reductive scoring guides ("rubrics") can foster "teaching to the writing prompt," thereby also narrowing curriculum and instruction.

As with using random sampling of student portfolios, sampling can also be used with performance exams. The National Assessment of Educational Progress (NAEP), a federal agency that monitors student achievement, uses such a technique. When the NAEP reports, for example, on the progress of U.S. 4th graders, the data is based on a sample of students. NAEP, however, relies primarily on multiple-choice questions with some short-answer written responses.

We believe that performance assessments—including performance exams—can be useful, especially when they are integrated into the ongoing curriculum. They can suffer, however, when they are isolated from daily classroom life and imposed from above.

Proficiency Exit Standards

The assessment known as "proficiency exit standards" combines the approaches of portfolio-based assessment and performance exams; it also sometimes includes standardized tests.

Under this approach, students have to meet certain standards in order to be promoted to the next grade or to graduate from high school. In Milwaukee, for example, the district has developed proficiencies that students need to meet in order to complete 8th grade and graduate from high school. The proficiency standards focus on four broad areas—math, science, communication, and a research project—and are generally considered more rigorous than most standardized exams.

Students are given several ways to show "proficiency" in each of these areas—through portfolios; classroom projects such as science projects, performance exams, standardized test scores; and research papers. The district took this approach because it did not want to rely on any single assessment to determine whether a student could be promoted or graduate.

Exhibitions

Exhibitions of student work are another useful assessment. Perhaps the most common exhibition is also one of the oldest: the science fair. As with any student work, the strength of the approach rests on providing ways for all students to succeed. Many people know stories of parents who do the science fair project for their kid, building elaborate electrical engines or wondrous weather kits. Some schools try to get around this problem by having students work on the projects at school.

> **Rather than just a report card, some schools have begun to develop school-level portfolios.**

In many of the NY Consortium schools, students graduate by exhibition. Students have to demonstrate competencies in core areas of learning. In language arts, math, science, and history they present and defend their portfolio work, which includes extended projects, to a committee of adults, including outside experts. This is somewhat similar to the oral exams common for postgraduate degrees.

At La Escuela Fratney in Milwaukee, at the end of 5th grade (before students leave for middle school), students select some of their work from throughout the year and invite family and community members to an open exhibition. One project that figures prominently is the student-made book, in which students reflected on what they've learned throughout elementary school. The book also includes examples of work from their entire time at Fratney, which teachers have collected as part of their portfolios.

Parent Conferences and Input

One important reason for assessment is to let parents know how well their children are progressing. This purpose cannot be separated from the larger issue of communication between school and home. A number of schools are experimenting with assessment programs that are based on a process of two-way communication.

Some schools, for instance, have lengthy conferences with parents before children even enter kindergarten, to explain the school's programs and get input from the family on the children's strengths and weaknesses. Other schools have adapted their parent-teacher conferences so that they do a better job of letting parents and teachers talk together about the child's progress. The Learning Record builds in teacher interviews with both parents and the student to discuss the child as a learner. In order for such an approach to work, parent-teacher conferences need to go beyond the "five-minutes-per-teacher" syndrome that is particularly common in middle and high schools—where teachers haul out the grade book and talk, and parents listen.

With this approach, schools need to ensure that they give parents a clear idea of the curriculum and a general view of child development. This is particularly important in early elementary grades, where children develop at different rates and ages and children cannot be pigeonholed into a single set of expectations. Likewise, in adolescence, teachers and parents need to communicate about developmental issues and how they may be affecting student performance.

Some schools involve students in the conferences. Students are asked to present work from their portfolios, reflect on what they have learned, and help figure out where they have made good progress and where they still need work. To work best, such an approach needs to be part of a comprehensive effort to ensure that parents know they can raise concerns at any point during the school year, not just at conference time. Soliciting and encouraging such parental input is not easy, but it is essential to developing a true collaboration between home and school.

This issue is, in the final analysis, grounded in difficult questions of the power imbalances in most schools, particularly along lines of race and class. Some schools have taken preliminary steps in trying to address this problem by hiring a parent organizer/liaison, creating a parent center, forming a parent/teacher curriculum committee, or ensuring that principals welcome parental input rather than view it as yet another chore. In some districts, parents are involved in teacher evaluation; how well a teacher communicates with parents is specified as a part of the evaluation.

School Report Cards

Just as parents need to know how well their children are doing, communities have the right to know how well entire schools are performing. Sometimes this happens in a rather distorted way: The local newspaper ranks schools based on a single standardized test or battery of tests. Beyond the cold, hard number, little analysis occurs to explain how or why some schools are performing differently— or even if the test is a valid measure of student achievement. Equally troubling, a school's performance often tells more about the income level of the students' families than the quality of teaching and learning at the school.

A growing number of schools have issued "school report cards"; in fact, many states require such report cards, many of which are posted on websites.

School report cards generally go beyond a listing of test scores, although that data is included. Other information in the report, depending on the state or district, can include attendance; average grade point; the number of Advanced Placement courses; discipline issues such as suspension rates; parental involvement; types of assessment (such as whether performance exams are required in certain subjects) and their results; school mission and governance structure; and so forth. The information is sometimes broken down by race, gender, socioeconomic status, first language, and other important categories, to show how well schools are serving students from diverse backgrounds.

Although such report cards are superior to a simple listing of test scores, there are important cautions: In particular, data can be omitted or manipulated. Some high schools, for example, have a policy of dropping students from a class if they have more than three unexcused absences. As a result, the grade point average in that class can be artificially high because only a select group of students is included. Also, if the primary data on student learning is from standardized test scores, as is often the case, then parents will have far too little information.

Overall, school report cards need to reflect a much richer view of student learning, such as can be found in portfolios and exhibitions. In fact, rather than just a report card, some schools have begun to develop school-level portfolios. Other schools and outside people can evaluate the school by looking at portfolios and by visiting the school.

School Quality Review Teams

Because student success is intimately related to the culture of learning in an entire school, one valuable assessment, known as the "School Quality Review Team," focuses on schoolwide issues. [See the FairTest fact sheet on better school evaluation included in this volume, and Richard Rothstein's book *Grading Education*.]

Students and teachers need time to explore their interests, to pursue matters in depth, and to develop qualities of thinking and working.

Teams of trained educators and community members visit schools, usually for as long as a week. The teams observe classrooms, follow students, examine the curriculum, and interview parents and teachers. Based on their observations, they write up a formal report with specific recommendations for improvement. This approach, modeled on a century-old system in England, has been adopted in a few states and is used in New Zealand and the Netherlands.

To be most effective, the team's recommendations need to be distributed to and acted upon by both teachers and parents, which often requires additional time and resources.

It Won't Be Easy

Adopting these alternatives isn't easy; old ways of doing things are generally more comfortable and familiar. Here are some of the most common pitfalls:

- The primary obstacle is the No Child Left Behind Act (NCLB), the current version of the long-standing Elementary and Secondary Education Act. This law not only effectively mandated standardized testing in reading and math in grades 3-8 and once in high school, plus three grades of science testing, it has also fostered a huge proliferation of "benchmark" and "interim" tests used mainly by districts, and then a growing raft of micro-tests. These are very short multiple-choice testlets, administered usually by computer. (They are falsely labeled "formative" assessments.) In Milwaukee, they have been termed "probes." All this testing has crowded out better forms of assessment and will make it much harder to change course toward high-quality performance and portfolio assessments. It is hard to serve two masters, which is why the NY Consortium won a variance so they only have to administer one of the state's high school exit exams.

- Assuming one can muster the political clout to change the growing emphasis on high-stakes standardized tests, most alternatives take time to develop. Because most are implemented while existing standardized tests continue, teachers are being asked to do more and more assessing—but they are not given any more time to do so. One more task is added to an already filled day, and the performance tests fit badly with standardized test-oriented curriculum and instruction. Sometimes, that causes teacher opposition. It is therefore important to reduce standardized tests as quickly as possible while building the alternatives.

• If such assessments are to provide a true alternative, it's essential that a broad array of parents and staff be involved. Otherwise, both parents and teachers feel that, once again, someone else is telling them how to raise their child or how to teach.

• Many of these alternative assessments are new to just about everyone involved: policymakers, students, teachers, and parents. Everyone needs to have thorough discussions of the pros and cons of various assessments, and clear understanding of the purpose of any particular assessment. Although self-styled "school reformers"—conservatives and liberals alike—often decry the "status quo" mentality of teachers and schools, on the testing issue they are the ones who refuse to "think outside the box" while they rely on traditional, and flawed, methods of standardized testing.

• Such assessments take more work, more time, and more resources. But districts can make great progress with modest resources, as Milwaukee and Nebraska showed when they pursued this path—and as the NY Consortium and other schools continue to show.

• Any assessment is prone to problems of inequity, inadequacy, and subjectivity.

So it is important to recognize and counteract these problems.

We cannot state this too often: The primary purpose of assessment is to improve the quality of teaching and to help students learn better. If the focus is not on student learning, it's misplaced.

District and state officials have the right and responsibility to require schools to provide evidence that all students are learning, but such requirements must not be allowed to control all aspects of schooling—and they should not undermine educational quality. Students and teachers need time to explore their interests, to pursue matters in depth, and to develop qualities of thinking and working. In fact, a really good accountability and assessment system will tell parents and the public that these, too, are part of education. 🖎

A Better System for Evaluating Students and Schools

FAIRTEST: NATIONAL CENTER FOR FAIR & OPEN TESTING

P olls show that most Americans agree we need a better way to assess students and evaluate schools. The question is: What should we do? Any new system must provide reasonable accountability and include assessments that support high-quality learning and school improvement. It must get us out of the downward spiral of producing a nation of children who mostly learn how to fill in bubbles on multiple-choice tests.

FairTest and our allies propose a healthy assessment and evaluation system that would include three key components: limited large-scale standardized testing, extensive school-based evidence of learning, and a school quality review (SQR) process.

Large-scale Tests

Many nations with better and more equal education outcomes test only one, two, or three times before high school graduation and largely avoid multiple-choice questions. Better tests would help, but based on criteria set by the Department of Education, the next batch—to be developed by multistate consortia—aren't likely to be much better. And we'd still waste time and money testing too many grades. Congress should require statewide tests once each in elementary, middle, and high school. States could cut back to what many did before No Child Left Behind (NCLB), when school improvement was faster than it is now.

Local and Classroom Evidence of Learning

If you want to find out what kids know and can do, look at their actual work. That is what many other countries do. By focusing on the classroom, we can assess important learning standardized tests cannot, such as research projects, oral presentations, essays, problem solving, and using computers in real situations. This process enables us to evaluate higher order thinking skills and deeper knowledge than do standardized tests. High-quality assessment improves teaching and learning.

Building the system on local evidence means trusting teachers. Some need to improve how well they assess, so ensuring teachers can work and learn together is important. This is what high-performing nations have done.

> **Congress should require statewide tests once each in elementary, middle, and high school.**

Building the system on local evidence means trusting teachers.

To ensure quality, some other countries have systems where samples of student work from each classroom are re-scored by independent people to verify a teacher's initial score ("moderation"). This has been done well enough to ensure local quality and provide comparability across a state. Schools would explain their results in an annual report.

School quality reviews (SQR)

The SQR is the central tool for school evaluation in places such as England and New Zealand. Instead of test results, their systems focus on a comprehensive school review by a team of qualified professionals every four to five years. This leads to a report describing the school and recommending actions for improvement. Schools that need extra help would be reviewed more frequently.

Countries with a more balanced, comprehensive, improvement-focused assessment and evaluation system produce better educational results with fewer harmful side effects than the system in the United States [See "Multiple Measures," next page.] In FairTest's proposal, the core of the system is local evidence. This is cross-checked and verified by limited statewide testing and periodic school quality reviews. It is a system that trusts but verifies and enables comprehensive reviews. It also combines quantitative and qualitative information, which frees and supports educators to do their jobs well while holding them accountable in a fair way. Our nation would get better assessment, adequate comparability, helpful accountability, and stronger guidance for improvement efforts. These changes will help all schools, especially those serving mainly low-income children, because those schools are more focused on standardized tests.

Real school reform requires a lot more than assessment and accountability. But without healthy assessment and evaluation, the reform enterprise will fail again. ✎

Note

The idea of a three-part evaluation system was developed by the Massachusetts Coalition for Authentic Reform in Education, of which FairTest was a part. See http://www.fairtest.org/call-authentic-state-wide-assessment-system.

See also related FairTest fact sheets on the web at http://www.fairtest.org/fact+sheets.

Multiple Measures

*It's not easy to escape the high-stakes trap,
    but here are some examples of alternatives*

MONTY NEILL

Multiple measures: *the use of multiple indicators and sources of evidence
of student learning, of varying kinds, gathered at multiple points in time,
within and across subject areas. These include but are not limited to: teacher
observations; tests that include multiple-choice, short, and longer constructed
response items; essays; tasks and projects of various sorts done in various modes
including electronic; laboratory work; presentations; and portfolios. They are
used to assess higher-order thinking skills and understanding, including analysis,
synthesis, evaluation, application, problem-solving, and creativity. They are
used for both formative and summative purposes, and many become part of the
learning process itself.*

Examples of Multiple Measures from the United States

The demands of No Child Left Behind (NCLB) have largely stymied the use of
multiple measures in the United States. However, in several parts of the country, teachers and districts are looking beyond bubble sheets to evaluate teaching
and learning.

The Learning Record

The Learning Record (LR) was developed in England as the primary language
record for use with multilingual, multicultural populations in reading, writing,
speaking, and listening. Its structure provides a consistent framework for gathering and evaluating information. It was adapted and expanded in the United States
and was beginning to grow, particularly in many Bureau of Indian Affairs schools,
before being largely swept aside by NCLB requirements.

In the LR, each teacher documents and evaluates student work and progress,
focusing on reading and writing. Thus, a student's LR would include documentation on books the student can read and understand, including evidence showing
his or her understanding of them, as well as samples of writing and teacher observations of the student as a learner. Since the specific books each child reads
vary, the specific evidence varies by student. The LR includes a variety of types of
evidence as well. Each student's progress is documented, summarized in writing,
and placed numerically on a developmental scale.

The LR scales have been validated. Moderation processes (independent review
of records) have established adequate to superior inter-rater agreement between
moderators and the teachers providing the initial scores. This shows that with a
good structure, diverse sources of information can be brought to bear on common

topics, like reading development. The validation process also supports the accuracy of teachers' judgments in placing their students on the developmental scales. Such judgments (numbers) can be aggregated and used to describe overall student attainment and progress. That is, if each originating teacher's judgment is sound (supported by a review of three to five randomly sampled records), then the aggregate information about classrooms and schools can be considered sound.

Learning Record practice and research demonstrate it is a reliable, valid, comparable, and educationally sound method of evaluating individual progress and status using multiple sources of evidence—and of aggregating that information to provide public information about schools.

Work Sampling System

The Work Sampling System (WSS) for children aged 3-8 is similar in some ways to the LR. It was developed by Samuel Meisels, one of the nation's foremost authorities on the assessment of young children. It includes collecting, evaluating, and summarizing observations and examples of student work. It has also been demonstrated to have strong validity and reliability.

The WSS uses three complementary elements to assess student knowledge and development: 1) observations by teachers using developmental guidelines and checklists, 2) collection of children's work in portfolios, and 3) summary reports. The developmental guidelines used in teacher observations are based on national content standards and current knowledge of child development. The guidelines give all observations the same basis of description and evaluation. Observations and the collection of materials for portfolios continue throughout the school year. Schools distribute summary reports to parents and students three times a year: in fall, winter, and spring.

Pearson now owns the WSS; information on it is available at www.pearsonassessments.com. See also, www.fairtest.org/work-sampling-system and www.fairtest.org/trusting-teacher-judgment.

New York Performance Standards Consortium

The Consortium includes 28 public high schools, most in New York City. They have received a variance from the state that allows their schools to use only one of five mandated Regents exams (language arts) and instead use their combination of consortium- and school-based performance assessments to meet NCLB's Adequate Yearly Progress (AYP) and for graduation requirements. The Consortium's website reports:

> Consortium schools have devised a system of assessment that consists of eight components including alignment with state standards, professional development, external review, and formative and summative data.

Consortium schools have documented how their work meets and exceeds New York State Regents standards through a system of rigorous commencement-level performance-based assessment tasks. Performance on these tasks is reflected on student transcripts and results are used for college admission:

> The tasks require students to demonstrate accomplishment in analytic thinking,
> reading comprehension, research writing skills, the application of mathematical
> computation and problem-solving skills, computer technology, the utilization
> of the scientific method in undertaking science research, appreciation of and
> performance skills in the arts, service learning, and school to career skills. Experts
> external to the schools, from universities and the business world, participate in
> reviews of student work.

The Performance Assessment Review Board, Inc.—an external body of educators, test experts, researchers and members of the legal and business world—monitors the performance-based assessment system and systematically samples student work.

Consortium members use performance assessments instead of Regents tests in a series of graduation-level tasks: analytical comparative essays in literature, social studies research papers, original science experiments, and applications of higher-level mathematics, as well as proficiencies in oral defenses and exhibitions of their work.

Although the Consortium relies on performance assessments, these include a variety of kinds of tasks and projects over the various subjects, providing multiple opportunities for students to demonstrate their learning in different ways over time. It is therefore a multiple measures system.

Common rubrics are used to help ensure consistency in scoring. The Consortium validated the use of the rubrics in four subjects through shared rescoring of sample work.

For more information, see http://performanceassessment.org/consortium/index.html.

Nebraska STARS

Prior to NCLB, Nebraska developed its Statewide Teacher-led Assessment and Reporting System (STARS), composed of local assessments that met statewide standards, including that they be based on the state's academic content standards (or state-approved equivalent local standards), ensure consistent scoring, be unbiased and developmentally appropriate with mastery levels set appropriately, and that students must have an opportunity to learn the content. In most districts, local educators helped develop the assessments. Independent experts reviewed each local system. If it was not approved, it was revised until it met the criteria. The state then audited the district assessment system periodically and if a district proposed major changes.

The nature of the assessments varied. Districts often used criterion-referenced tests standardized within the district. Most incorporated more extended, classroom-based work, including tasks and projects. These elements had a positive impact on teaching and learning. The state system included a statewide writing examination, and it administered a norm-referenced test at three grades.

Although these were not used for accountability, they served as a check on the validity of the local assessments. Independent reviews, such as by the Buros Institute for Mental Measurements, found the districts generally produced strong assessments and were willing to improve.

Though then-U.S. Education Secretary Rod Paige expressed support for Nebraska's system, his successor, Margaret Spellings, opposed the state's efforts. Approval for the system was blocked , and legislators in the state voted to switch to a single-test model.

Wyoming's "Body of Evidence"

Wyoming has implemented a "Body of Evidence" approach as part of its high school graduation requirements. These are locally developed assessments designed to indicate students have met state graduation standards. The state's website says, "The philosophy at the heart of the Wyoming Body of Evidence system is to provide multiple measures to assess student mastery of the content standards; in this way, no single assessment can disqualify a student from graduation."

The Body of Evidence is a collection of a student's work that proves understanding of concepts and the ability to perform certain required skills. In keeping with the emphasis on locally designed approaches, Wyoming allows four different ways for a district to design a Body of Evidence, and districts can choose the way or combination of ways that best suits their needs. As in Nebraska, a district's assessment must meet specified criteria. Districts must:

- Provide evidence of student achievement directly related to the Wyoming state standards.
- Give students multiple opportunities and multiple ways (i.e., not just more chances to take the same tests) to demonstrate their knowledge and skills relating to the standards.
- Be fair to all students, including those with disabilities or who are learning English, and provide accommodations.
- Allow education professionals to decide what's "good enough" in a fair and reasonable way.
- Create assessments that are similar across schools and classrooms within the same school district both within a given year and across years.
- Answer these two questions: Does the student know enough to graduate? And does the evidence support the answer?

The state website says, "Each district's Body of Evidence system is reviewed through a peer review process facilitated by the Wyoming Department of Education."✎

This article was excerpted from a more comprehensive look at multiple measures, which is available at www.fairtest.org/sites/default/files/MultipleMeasures.pdf. For more information, see www.k12.wy.us/SA/BOE.asp and www.fairtest.org/wyoming-steers-clear-exit-exams.

Their Report Card—and Ours

How do we know if schools are doing a good job?
And how can we make them better?

PORTLAND AREA RETHINKING SCHOOLS

According to Oregon's Department of Education, state-mandated standardization of curriculum and increased testing will inspire—or frighten—educators and students to perform at higher levels. This strategy emphasizes measurable objectives and scores that can be compared from student to student, school to school, community to community. It emphasizes the necessity of holding all students to "high standards." In practice, this strategy increasingly turns schools into test-prep academies. Test-led reform sucks joy out of learning and discourages teacher and student creativity. What is not measured on the tests—for example, critical thinking, discussion skills, the arts—becomes more and more neglected. Of course, equating student achievement with higher test scores may, in fact, raise test scores. But it will not help nurture more knowledgeable, motivated, or caring students.

The Department of Education's school "report cards" exemplify the hollowness of this reform strategy. The state judged student performance strictly in terms of standardized test results; "school characteristics" were assessed based on one criterion: the percentage of a school's students taking state tests. We're reminded of the saying, "Not everything that matters can be measured and not everything that can be measured matters." If one aim of school reform is to make schools more accountable, then surely we need to capture a fuller portrait of school life.

Portland Area Rethinking Schools proposes an alternative school reform strategy. Unlike state testing that is premised on a belief that learning can and should be quantified—and assessment results used to compare, reward, and punish—we believe that assessments should be collaborative endeavors, grounded in school communities. We believe that school life and student achievement can only be assessed—and improved—with participatory inquiries that offer rich descriptions of a school's educational practice.

Below is a draft of our alternative report card. In important respects, the process of collecting data for the report card is itself an essential part of the product. Real school reform must be democratic, drawing on the collective efforts of teachers, students, administrators, parents, and the broader community. We encourage school communities to use the questions below as the basis of discussions to assess and improve school life.

> **We believe that school life and student achievement can only be assessed—and improved—with participatory inquiries that offer rich descriptions of a school's educational practice.**

Curriculum

1. How is the content of the curriculum meaningful, interdisciplinary, multicultural, and academically rigorous for all students?

   a. How are high academic expectations communicated to and maintained for all students?

   b. How are reading, writing, math, discussion skills, and the arts taught across the curriculum?

   c. How are historic, artistic, and scientific contributions of diverse cultures, families, social classes, and genders represented in each content area?

   d. How does the curriculum encourage all students to see themselves as social and environmental problem-solvers capable of making the world a better place? Does the curriculum have real-life links?

   e. How are students encouraged to take initiative in choosing directions in their learning? How are the needs, dreams, and interests of individual students incorporated into the curriculum?

2. Are sufficient resources available to meet the curricular mission of the school?

   a. Are sufficient high-quality materials available to meet the needs of all students?

   b. What is the range of actual class sizes?

   c. Do students have access to mentors and tutors?

   d. Is the library welcoming and accessible to all students and staff?

   e. Are reading, writing, math, and/or other specialists available for students and staff?

   f. What elective opportunities are available to students?

   g. What technology resources are available to all students? With what frequency are they available? Are students penalized for not having access to technology at home?

   h. What school time is scheduled for teachers to plan, develop, and discuss curriculum?

   i. How does professional development support the curriculum and instruction outlined above?

   j. Do new and struggling teachers have access to mentors?

   k. What is the number of courses taught by teachers not teaching in their certificated area?

Student Assessment

1. How is assessment used to promote student learning?

   a. How do assessment results influence subsequent instruction in the classroom and program modification in the school?

b. What actions are taken to avoid misapplication of assessment results through tracking or stigmatization?

c. How is it ensured that the frequent use of feedback from assessments offers students the opportunity to grow?

2. How is it ensured that assessment complements the curriculum and desired outcomes?

a. How is it ensured that assessment allows students multiple ways to demonstrate their learning?

b. How is it ensured that self-reflection and self-evaluation are part of the assessment system?

c. How is it ensured that students are aware of the learning goals on which they will be assessed and the assessment process that will be used?

d. How are accommodations made for ESL and other students with special needs?

Equity for All Students

1. Historically, so-called ability grouping has discriminated against poor, working class, and students of color by offering educational programs of unequal quality to different students. How does the school group its students (e.g., honors, advanced, remedial, scholars, International Baccalaureate)? How does the school know that these grouping practices do not result in unequal educational experiences?

a. Describe the rationale and practice for your grouping.

b. How are students placed in these classes?

c. What impact does grouping have on equity for students of color and students with learning or physical disabilities, as well as on gender equity?

d. If inequity in placement exists, what procedures are in place to review curriculum and placement practices?

e. If students are grouped for short-term educational purposes, what records are available to demonstrate individual progress and movement from group to group? How often are students reassessed? How many students move? How often?

2. What accommodations are made for the needs of students with attendance and tardy problems: students who work to support their families, travel to home countries, take care of younger or older family members?

3. Is evidence of historical, literary, artistic, and scientific contributions of diverse cultures represented in each content area? In teachers' lesson plans? In the book room? On bulletin boards? During assemblies?

4. Who is represented and honored in the school? Consider the hallways, library, and overall school environment. Does the racial, ethnic, linguistic, and class composition of extracurricular leadership and special academic programs reflect the student body?

How are low-income, minority, or second-language students encouraged to participate?

5. What measures does the school take to ensure that students with physical disabilities are fully integrated into school life?

6. How does the school equalize opportunities for success by ensuring that all students have access to computers, field trips, materials for projects, supplies, and electronic equipment?

7. Describe how each class demonstrates high expectations for all students. How does the school present academic, professional, and trade options to students?

8. Does the staff reflect a range of cultures? What recruitment strategies are in place to hire teachers of color and second-language speakers?

Health and Safety

1. Describe your discipline policies and programs that promote respect and conflict intervention and resolution. Specifically, how are students involved in these programs?

2. How does the school promote the physical safety and the emotional well being of students? Are programs built into the curriculum to address such needs as violence and sexual harassment prevention, suicide intervention, sex education, and prevention of drug and alcohol abuse?

3. How are marginalized students identified and protected at your school? What policies and strategies are used to counter racist, sexist, or homophobic language and put-downs? How is respect taught in the school curriculum?

4. How accessible are mental health and crisis services at the school? Is nursing staff provided? Describe safe places students can go during personal distress. Describe any formal or informal mental health services available to students.

5. What is the selection and quality of cafeteria food? Are restricted or organic diets available? What are the school policies about serving milk and meat products from hormone-injected animals or other genetically modified foods? How often and under what criteria is the water tested in the school? Do students have access to pure water?

6. How is the student environment protected from other chemical ingredients of unknown or potentially harmful effects, like ingredients in cleaning solutions, herbicides, pesticides, or airborne contaminants?

Parents and Community in the Life of the School

1. How does the school include parents, students, and community in decision-making?

   a. What adaptation and/or encouragement is made for working, non-English-speaking, reluctant, marginalized, and/or parents of color?

b. What power does the community have in decision making?

c. Does the site council accurately reflect the social class, racial, ethnic, and linguistic diversity of the community?

2. When and how are parents informed and included regarding student progress (e.g., academic assessments, absences, tardiness, and misconduct)?

a. How does the school ensure that parents understand their students' progress?

3. How do school and community interact for mutual benefit?

a. Is there broad representation of community organizations in the life of the school: unions, women's organizations, religious institutions, senior centers, environmental and social justice organizations, businesses, etc.?

b. What community service projects are in place?

c. How is school networked to other community services? How does the school facilitate connecting students and families to community and governmental resources?

d. How are community members invited to contribute?

e. How does the school include and coordinate volunteers?

f. How are families/community members who cannot volunteer during the school day included in direct support of the school?

g. How are the school facilities and people utilized as a resource of the community?

4. How do the school and community help students make the transition between schools?

a. How does the school reach out to the community during transition points—i.e., from preschool into kindergarten or 1st grade? From elementary to middle school? From middle school to high school? From high school to college?

b. How effective are these efforts?

5. What audiences beyond the classroom do students have for their work and ideas?

a. In the school, how are parents and/or community members invited to give feedback on student work or portfolios? Are there student author presentations, science fairs, gallery displays, etc.?

b. Outside the school, are there readings in the community, projects that connect the generations, student research and input to community boards or committees, etc.?

6. What informational events does the school hold?

a. Describe the events (open houses, parent conferences, etc.), who attends, and the percentage of the various groups attending.

b. What adaptation and/or encouragement is made for working, non-English speaking, reluctant, marginalized parents, and/or parents of color?

c. How does the school accommodate parents' special needs—for example, daycare?

District and State Support

1. In what ways do the school district and state support the school community in achieving the above aims?

2. In what ways do the school district and state hinder the school community in achieving the above aims?

3. What strategies are being pursued by the school community to challenge any policies or practices that hinder efforts to provide all students with quality education?

Basketball and Portfolios

LINDA CHRISTENSEN

It was 5:30 on finals day. Most students left the building at noon, giving teachers a chance to work on their grades before the weekend or prepare for the new classes starting on Monday. They had three hours; the possible uses for their time were endless. I was in the library's prehistoric computer lab with a roomful of students who were still writing, revising, and polishing work for their portfolios.

Lloyd had walked out of the lab and into the adjoining library. At 5:30, college basketball comes on cable. Lloyd slid onto the library table, obviously through with portfolios for the day. "Hey, Ms. Christensen, why do we have to write these evaluations anyway? You've got all my work in there. You're the teacher. Just read my work and give it a grade. Why do *I* have to evaluate it?"

His eyes moved back to the TV where Arizona was playing UCLA. I looked over at him. Somehow this year he'd moved from his one- or two-line papers without punctuation to essays, scrappy and sometimes not quite full enough to be called "done," but a big improvement over last year's meager output. He wasn't ready for college writing yet, and our class was ending.

"Do you watch videos after your basketball games?" I asked, knowing that the coach always scheduled mandatory postgame reviews.

"Yeah, every day after our game we got to go watch those videos," he answered without taking his eyes off Damon Stoudamire.

"Why do you think Coach Harris makes you watch your game after you already played it? Couldn't he just tell you what you did?"

"Because then we can see our mistakes—and what plays we're running that work. We look at videos of teams we're going to play, too, so we can see what kind of offense and defense they've got. We can see who to match our players up with. We learn their plays so we can outwit them at the basket." He shifted on the table, still not seeing how his writing portfolio had anything to do with post-game videos. I turned off the TV and we sat and made comparisons between basketball videos and writing portfolios. With Lloyd it was basketball, with Harold it was wrestling; with Tawni and Aaron it was dance. The connection between teaching, practicing, performing, reviewing, and critiquing is a common thread between disciplines. It also gives me a way to connect the students' passion with learning to evaluate their own writing.

Portfolios: Grading, Evaluation, Assessment?

I've had students make portfolios for years. When I first started keeping

> **When the teacher evaluates a piece, it takes an essential part of the learning experience away from the student and gives the act of judgment and power to the teacher.**

writing folders, I called them portfolios, but they were really glorified work folders where students stored everything from false starts and ugly "I didn't want to write that poem anyway" fragments along with polished pieces. Now I've come to see portfolios as places where students keep the journey of their writing, but also as a place where they analyze their work, their process, and their progress, so they can take what they know and apply it to the next piece that comes along—just as my basketball players view their videos to improve their next game.

While most students enjoy rummaging through their folders and don't mind tossing their work from one folder to another, they are resistant to reflection. Lloyd's comment that I'm the teacher therefore I should just do the evaluation is common. Most students aren't accustomed to standing back from their work and assessing it. The routine has been write it, turn it in, the teacher grades it, get it back. End of cycle. When the teacher evaluates a piece, it takes an essential part of the learning experience away from the student and gives the act of judgment and power to the teacher. Ultimately, students learn a great deal more about their writing if they learn to "watch the postgame video" and critique their "play." But it's hard to get them to that point.

As a classroom teacher and director of the Portland Writing Project, I'm skeptical of legislators and school bureaucrats mandating portfolios. The ones I've seen designed for English classrooms too often dictate types of writing students must include and then provide ways to score them so that, once again, student achievement can be reduced to a single digit number—easily compared across cities, states, and the nation. (Although these days, I'd take any portfolio assessment over the rash of multiple-choice tests that drag our students through weeks of testing.)

I'm not interested in reducing my students to a single digit. I am concerned about their growth in writing and thinking. Frankly, I've never found district or state reading and writing scores to be reliable or useful in my classroom practice. I use portfolios to shape my instruction for individual students, but I also see portfolios as a tool to move students from object to subject in their education. For a critical teacher, portfolios are an evaluation method that pushes students to participate with their teacher in their assessment rather than being *judged* by teacher-as-outside-authority.

But let me be clear: I'm not a hands-off kind of teacher. Some of my colleagues believe the portfolio belongs to the student; therefore, the student should be allowed complete freedom to select and control the content. I disagree. There are places and times when students have control; for example, at the end of my class, students make a book of their writing where they choose all of the pieces. Jessica, a terrific poet, put poetry and pictures in her book; Aaron made his a collection of fiction writing. With portfolios, I try to establish and negotiate higher expectations. I'm setting the standards. Each grading period in each class, I determine the kinds of writing that students must include in their portfolios.

One term in Literature and U.S. History, the students needed a literary analysis, a historical fiction piece, and a research paper on either a resistance movement or a person who worked for change. Students *also* included poetry, interior monologues, and film critiques, but unless they completed satisfactory drafts of the requirements, they didn't pass. I provided lots of work time, models, and demonstrations. These tasks were not *assigned*; they were *taught*. I spent two to three afternoons a week in the computer lab after school, working with students who either needed extra help or who wanted more work time.

> Tyrone, a thoughtful rapper, would like to write every assignment—from museum critique to historical fiction—as a rap; but if I allowed that, I wouldn't be providing him a rigorous education.

Partly, my insistence on variety and standards comes from real world concerns: I'm at the high-stakes end of education; I work with mostly with juniors and seniors. Tyrone, a thoughtful rapper, would like to write every assignment—from museum critique to historical fiction—as a rap; but if I allowed that, I wouldn't be providing him a rigorous education. He already knows how to write raps. He doesn't know how to write essays. As more colleges move toward portfolios as entrance criteria rather than or in addition to SATs, I want my students, who tend to score poorly on these tests, to be able to demonstrate their range.

Beyond the college connection, I want to push students to think more deeply about the world, to make connections in their essays between literature and life in their neighborhood. I don't just want pretty words and adept dialogue; I want searing analysis. My students walk out the school door into a social emergency. They are in the center of it. I believe writing is a basic skill that will help them understand that emergency and work to change it.

The portfolio in my classroom fulfills several duties: It showcases students' work in a variety of genres; it demonstrates their journeys as writers—from early to polished drafts as well as stumbling first attempts at poetry, fiction, and essay to later, more accomplished pieces. But it also provides a space for student and teacher to reflect on the change and growth in writing and thinking as well as pointing out a trajectory for future work.

Over the years, I've made some discoveries and fine-tuned my approach to portfolios. Some terms I'd end up with amazing evaluations, where students had obviously internalized discussions on craft and content; other terms, the analysis was thin—even when I could see remarkable changes in students' writing. Sometimes I knew I'd crammed too much work in at the end of the term; other times, it was obvious that the portfolio prompts were too meticulous or too broad. And still other times, it was clear that my teaching was off target. Although I'm still struggling with the evaluation process—as well as the teaching process that precedes it—I've learned some lessons along the way.

Time Is Important

Students need enough time between their entry into the class and the analysis of their writing to see change or growth. Often the portfolio evaluation written after the first nine weeks of class is weak. Students are just finding the "basket," learning to dribble. I'm still working at moving them from perfunctory "for-the-teacher writing" to committed writing, from all-rhyming poetry to free verse, from aimless diatribes to essays with support. After nine weeks, they haven't traveled the pathway often enough to see it clearly. But it's important to begin the process, so they are critiquing their own work. They also need to begin noting how they work, what they do to move out of a writer's block, how to get a first draft finished, what to do when they start a paper, or how to embed quotes. In short, they need to become critics of their own learning.

I used to jump into the writing evaluation at the end of the quarter without giving students time to reread their pieces. Now I devote a 90-minute class period for students to transfer papers from their work folders to their writing portfolios. Before they begin, I bring in one of my portfolios and talk about pieces I chose to put in and why. Some are samples of my best writing; others are pieces I want to work on, and some show how much my writing has improved. I show them all the drafts of my pieces—including the false starts and comments from my writing friends. I want them to see that most people do not create a perfect draft the first time. This is a noisy 90 minutes as students read and talk about their writing (mostly, but not always, on task). It's when I hear students say, "I didn't realize how much work I completed." Or "Look, I didn't even know how to line my poetry out." And sometimes, "I wrote better pieces last year."

I learned that if I expect a thorough analysis of their writing, then I need to give that signal by weighting the evaluation as heavily as I do a major writing assignment. I need to give models, criteria, set standards, and give them adequate time to complete the task. I also need to practice patience. It takes as much time to teach students how to think about and write a reflection on their writing as it takes to teach them how to write a literary or historical analysis. Older students with more experience tend to write better analyses than younger, less-experienced writers. I have to praise the effort and push them to the next level.

Models and Prompts for Portfolio Reflection

When I first started asking students to critique or examine their own writing, I underestimated their need for models of self-reflection. I expected them to "do it" without knowing what they were doing. Bobby Harris, Jefferson's basketball coach, wouldn't spend two hours watching a game video without telling his players what to look for—or developing the criteria together.

"What is self-reflection?" Johnny asked, "What do you mean, 'What did I learn from my writing?'" Amber didn't understand how to use examples from her work for support. Students need to see what I want. They need models of past portfolio evaluations so they can gain a sense of how to look at their writing— just as they needed examples of former students' essays or historical critiques so they could see what embedded and block quotes look like in a text. Now, I guide them through the process by asking them to read over their papers, making a list of what they know about writing and where that knowledge shows up in their papers. They use this as an outline to write their reflections, pulling examples from their essays, poems, and narratives as proof of their growth.

I discovered that students took their own writing more seriously after they listened to conversations by writers about writing. For this reason, I read selections from William Stafford, Tess Gallagher, Donald Murray, and Toni Morrison writing about their writing. Students are fascinated, for example, to discover that the idea for Toni Morrison's novel *Beloved* came from an old news article explaining how a woman killed her children because she didn't want them to grow up in slavery.

> My students walk out the school door into a social emergency. They are in the center of it. I believe that writing is a basic skill that will help them both understand that emergency as well as work to change it.

I also save samples of students' written reflections from previous years. I provide guidelines to get students started, but leave them loose enough so that students have room to follow their passions. Sometimes inexperienced writers take the model and copy it exactly, substituting examples from their writing, but using the knowledge of the model. They are not really thinking deeply—they are mimicking. I've come to see this as a stage in their evolution. Some students like more specific prompts, while others find them stifling, so I vary the prompts and allow them choice. When a student says he or she can't get excited about this (or any) assignment, I say, "Find your passion." They know they have to write an evaluation of their work. Renesa, for example, couldn't put pen to paper until I showed her an article by a local columnist on writing. She wrote her evaluation as an advice column for writers, and typed it in newspaper format—including her picture and examples from her writing to prove her point. Frank wrote his as a letter to my future students telling them what they could expect to learn about writing, giving examples from his own writing.

Some terms I ask my class to focus their evaluations on one genre—essay or fiction, perhaps. Using colored pencils or highlighters on their essays, they have to identify types of evidence, introduction styles, and block and embedded quotes, and they must analyze their content and conclusions. In fiction, they have to point out dialogue, blocking, imagery, flashback, and interior monologues. Aaron discovered that he rarely used dialogue. Shameica realized that she didn't use blocking and wondered if that was why people got confused about who was speaking in her story. Tony saw that he didn't use evidence from Andrew Jackson's speech on the Cherokee removal; in his critique, he had no quotes to support his position that Jackson was a "racist pig." The act of coloring their draft made the holes concrete.

Sometimes I ask students to draw a picture or write a poem that describes themselves as writers and then write a paragraph explaining the image to me. Gabriella drew a sculptor with a block of clay. She wrote: "I am the potter with clay, molding, shaping, by taking off pieces and discarding pieces until I have a piece

I discovered that students took their own writing more seriously after they listened to conversations by writers about writing.

of art." Jim wrote that he was a chef and his writing is dough that he pinches and pulls into just the right shape. Licy drew a jar full of candy to describe herself as a contributor to the class: "My writings and contributions are like the taste of candy itself—some sweet, some sour. Like melting bits of chocolate, I melt cultural information to teach the class something about Mexicans. Like the wrinkled wrapper, I make a sound so everyone knows I am aware. I am here."

One obvious lesson I learned was that students should share their insights with the class. At the beginning of the new term, students showed their metaphors and drawings. These become conversation starters about the craft of writing. As students talked about their drawings or poems, they also shared their roadblocks and their detours. Johanna was a planner who ran into difficulty because her drafts never went as she predicted. The information didn't present itself as neatly as she initially hoped it would. Lisa needed to doodle to get started. Anthony said that seeing all of my drafts freed him to get started because he knew he didn't have to get it right the first time. Peter taught some classmates his method of outlining that was flexible enough to allow for surprises, but gave his piece "river banks" to contain the flow. The point of our class discussion isn't to make students all work the same way through a piece of writing; it is meant to encourage them to find alternative strategies, so if they aren't successful they can try someone else's for a spell to see if it helps.

Portfolios are one small part of the total classroom, but an important part because it's where I measure not only the students' success and growth, but my own as well. I can lay the foundation of expectations at the beginning of the grading period and help students meet those criteria. The compiled work and the evaluation of it allow both student and teacher to reflect on what worked, on our mistakes, what can we do better next time. Perhaps because evaluations give us time to pause and look back, they also rehearse us for our next performance—whether it's writing an essay or making a three-point outside shot in the state tournament. ☙

WRITING PORTFOLIO 🖎

Criteria

At least three pages handwritten, two pages typed (size 12 font).
This must be thorough and use examples from your work.

Writing can be a process of discovery. When asked about all of his failed experiments, Einstein responded, "Those weren't failures. I learned what didn't work each time." Sometimes our writing "works," other times it doesn't. One of the purposes of a portfolio is to give you time to reflect on what you've learned about writing—either through your mistakes or your successes. When you figure out what makes you a successful writer and articulate that on paper or in dialogue, you are more likely to transfer that knowledge to your next writing project. Find your passion in this assignment. Find a way to make it meaningful to you.

Procedure

1. Look back through your work folder. I want you to begin this portfolio by just reading through your papers. As you read, look at the kind of growth you've made over the year. Take some notes on the changes you've witnessed in your writing.

2. Find pieces that you want to put in your portfolio. Remember to find examples for each genre: narrative, expository, persuasive, and poetry. Think about what these pieces will show an audience about your writing talent.

3. Choose either the Pulitzer (See "Portfolio Evaluation—Pulitzer") or the Profile style of portfolio (See Jim Jackson's Portfolio). Please note that both of these will use essay criteria—whether you write them as a letter or as a speech:

Introduction

Question

Anecdote

Quote

Wake Up Call

Evidence:
Specific evidence/quotes/citations from your work.
(*This section will vary depending on your topic choice.*)

- Explanations of how to write a specific genre

- Discussion about revision or getting started

- Discussion of your writing strategy

Conclusion

Another Path Is Possible

Despite the pressures of high-stakes testing,
  two Chicago principals keep an eye on what matters

GREG MICHIE

It's mid-March—testing week in Chicago—and for many administrators in the city's schools, that means a laser-like, 24/7 focus on one thing: the Illinois Standards Achievement Test (ISAT). But Amy Rome, the principal at National Teachers Academy (NTA), an elementary school on the near South Side, has spent the past 15 minutes in a hallway brainstorming session with a representative from a neighborhood social service agency. The mother of several NTA students has been evicted from her apartment in a nearby public housing development, and the social service worker has come seeking Amy's help in finding temporary housing for the woman and her children.

As Amy sees it, this is an integral part of her job. Ask her about her school's vision—even during ISAT week—and you won't hear references to test scores or mantra-like chants of the latest educational jargon. "At NTA we're about knowing our kids and our families," she says. "We're about relationship building, student support, and collaborative problem-solving with the community. We believe the community's challenges are the school's challenges."

Although she laments the obsession with high-stakes accountability that has beset the city's schools over the past decade or so, she also believes that her students' scores matter. "Using a single test score as the basis for assessing our kids is unfair," she tells me later. "It puts them at a disadvantage, and we don't like that. But at the same time, it's the reality of how students are being evaluated right now, so we have to be responsive to it. We absolutely don't teach to the tests, but it's cheating a child to dismiss the idea that they need to do well on them. We try to view testing as a way to navigate better opportunities for our students. It matters to us because it impacts their future."

But rather than allowing the crush of federal demands to dictate their direction, Amy and her staff have worked hard to see through the thicket and clear a different path. They've focused not only on a more rigorous curriculum that encourages critical thinking, but also on broad-based supports for students and families and on making NTA "a place where kids want to be."

Early Struggles

The school's full name is rarely heard these days, but when NTA opened to much fanfare in 2002, it was known as the National Teachers Academy. Nearly all of its students were African American and came from two nearby public housing developments. At the time, the central office's plan was to create a national model of professional development: a neighborhood school where a staff of "master teachers" guided a corps of student interns. NTA's striking $47 million structure included a four-story classroom building and a connected community center with a swimming pool and gymnasium.

But from the beginning, NTA struggled. When Amy arrived in 2004 to serve as a liaison for the University of Illinois at Chicago (UIC), which had been asked by the district to help jump-start the school, NTA was already on its second principal. Tardiness was high and attendance was spotty. Teachers were reluctantly implementing a scripted reading program. Few extracurricular opportunities were available for students. Parent involvement was minimal. Test scores were among the worst in the city. And morale, in general, was sinking.

> "The most important thing was building a team. The quality of a teacher in the classroom is what makes it or breaks it for kids. And we have some amazing teachers."

As UIC's liaison, Amy worked with the school's new administration and university faculty to target specific challenges. Her first project was to tackle the school's excessive tardiness problem. After a semester of talking with parents, distributing alarm clocks to families who needed them, and pairing younger children with older ones who could help them cross busy streets on their way to school, tardiness shrank from 10 to 15 percent each day to less than 3 percent.

But numerous challenges lingered, and the environment among staff at the school remained tense. Before the end of the year, the new principal left, and her replacement didn't last much longer. In 2006, Amy was chosen as the school's fourth principal in five years.

Connecting with Parents

As a classroom teacher in Chicago for nearly a decade, Amy had long believed that building strong relationships with parents and community members was crucial. As principal, one of her first priorities was to make parents feel welcome at NTA and to provide them with opportunities for meaningful involvement. She reinvigorated a "parent room" that had gone largely unutilized, equipping it with a computer, phone, photocopier, and information on job training and GED classes. She met with parents every Friday morning to discuss their concerns and solicit their counsel. And she encouraged teachers to do all they could to communicate their desire to have parents and caregivers visit their classrooms.

"The building started to feel more like a community school," Amy says. "It gave us more opportunities to better understand the community, and it gave parents more opportunities to understand what we were trying to do with the kids. They really got in the mix of how the school works and started advising us. So now they call to let me know when something important is happening in the community, or come by to give feedback on what we're doing in the school, or just to help us keep an eye on safety."

Other initiatives built on these connections. The entire staff went on neighborhood walks before school began in the fall to connect with residents and reinforce the importance of students being present on the first day. A full-fledged in-school health clinic, initiated through the UIC partnership, opened to address the many unmet medical needs in the community. Teachers voted to scrap the canned reading program in favor of a balanced literacy approach that they developed themselves. And Amy used new hires and new partnerships to bring additional programming and resources: an art therapy program, an adolescent nurse psychologist, a drumming group, and a hip-hop yoga class.

"The most important thing was building a team," she says. "The quality of a teacher in the classroom is what makes it or breaks it for kids. And we have some amazing teachers."

A Climate Where Learning Becomes Possible

Walk around NTA these days, and you're struck by all the good things that are happening. Outside a pre-kindergarten classroom, photographs of "guest readers" include several moms, a dad, an auntie, and an older sister. Inside, kids brainstorm ideas for how to pick up and move a heavy dresser:

"Pour some of the stuff out," says Marcus.
"Use a string," says Omani.
"I'd get my big brother to help," adds someone else.
"Excuse me," a little boy with tight braids says. "We could all carry it together!"

"Yeah!" several voices call in unison, agreeing that it's a brilliant idea. The teacher, Connie, calls four students to the front of the class and, in what seems like an act of magic, they lift the dresser that none of them alone could budge. The rest of the class applauds and then settles down to listen to a read-aloud of *Carrying*, a book about how people in various places around the world transport different things.

Upstairs in the music room, 4th graders beat out call-and-response drum rhythms. It's a wonderful, open space—"The energy is good," says Holly, the teacher—with oversized windows lining the entire north side and the words "dream," "believe," "explore," and "unite" splashed on other walls. There's a circle of 22 painted drums, four congas, and, on a raised platform, xylophones, metallophones, and a glockenspiel.

"Oh, that's so gorgeous," Holly says to the kids as they beat out a pattern in unison.

Since the students have spent most of the morning glued to their desks filling in test bubbles, Holly knows that music class may be a time for them to release frustrations. "I understand you had a really tough, stressful morning," she tells them. With every beat on the drums and every mallet strike on the xylophones, I can almost see the tension being lifted from the kids' shoulders. One student, Raymond, goes a little overboard with his drumming technique and is asked to sit out for a while, but for the most part, the next 45 minutes are full of movement, singing, and syncopated rhythms—kids being given the time and space to connect with their creative spirits. It shouldn't feel like such a novelty, but on the South Side of Chicago, in the middle of a school day, it does.

> With every beat on the drums and every mallet strike on the xylophones, I can almost see the tension being lifted from the kids' shoulders.

Later, in a physical education class, the teacher, Aaron, begins by having his 8th graders put on pedometers. They discuss whether the gadgets measure the volume or intensity of exercise, and then huddle up to play a team-building game. At the end of the period, Aaron has all the students check their pedometers to see how many steps they took during the 50-minute class. The kids then sit in a circle and Aaron asks them to hold up between one and five fingers, giving themselves two grades: one for effort and one for attitude. He asks if anybody wants to nominate a classmate for a sportsmanship award, and hands shoot up. "I nominate Kiara," one boy says, "because she got frustrated but she didn't quit." Several other kids follow by nominating another of their peers.

When I ask Aaron how he developed such a supportive atmosphere among these teenagers, he says it's mostly due to the trusting relationships he's built with them—not just in the classroom, but also coaching and working with them after school. "Sometimes kids need to be helped to find the language to say nice things to each other," he says. "I want them to feel safe here, and I want them to feel cared for. That's when learning can happen. We're trying to create a climate here where learning becomes possible."

It's a philosophy Amy has actively promoted and the entire school has embraced: creating a climate where real learning becomes possible. And it's not a coincidence that when you ask Amy to let you visit a few classrooms, she includes the music and PE classes. At some schools, these have become afterthoughts, little more than once-weekly diversions in the quest for higher test scores. But Amy believes that the drumming and the team-building exercises and the parent center and the yoga classes have done just as much to create a climate for learning as the balanced literacy program and the renewed focus on academic rigor have.

"It's so great to see the kids learning," she says. "To see them motivated, to see them feeling good about themselves, to see them believing that it's cool to be academically smart."

Telpochcalli: Culture at the Center

A few miles away, on the city's Southwest Side, Telpochcalli, a small public elementary school that serves 260 mostly Mexican immigrant students, has been doing things differently for 15 years. Telpochcalli, which means "house of youth" in Nahuatl, a language spoken by indigenous groups in central Mexico, was founded in 1994 by a group of teachers, including current principal Tamara Witzl.

"We made a commitment to do things differently here from the beginning," Tamara says. "And we hold each other to that commitment." The school's approach is constructed on four pillars: building a strong professional learning community, working in genuine partnership with the surrounding community, educating students to be fully bilingual and biliterate, and infusing Mexican art and culture into all subject areas. All of these come together, Tamara says, to create an environment that keeps social justice at the center of the school's mission.

Educating Against the Grain

Telpochcalli's approach goes against the grain of current educational policy in almost every way. The past decade has seen relentless attacks against bilingual education nationally, and in Chicago the push has been toward moving students out of bilingual classrooms and into English-only classes as quickly as possible. Tamara sees a strong correlation between these developments and the increased focus on standardized test scores. But despite these realities, she says Telpochcalli is committed to bilingualism for the long term. "We believe it's a good thing for all students. We want our kids to value and hold on to their home language and to learn English as well, to be truly bilingual and biliterate."

One of the most tragic casualties of the preoccupation with testing in many urban schools has been the arts. At Telpochcalli, Tamara not only seeks out grants to fund artists-in-residence and after-school programs in guitar, video production, and folkloric dancing, but she also actively promotes the infusion of the arts in every subject area during the school day. The hallways and classrooms are alive with creativity—colorful student paintings and pottery, vibrant floor-to-ceiling murals, marimbas, video cameras, the sounds of Mexican *corridos* or *rancheras* spilling out of an open classroom door.

Like Amy, Tamara keeps an eye on test scores, but she refuses to let such concerns overwhelm the broader vision of Telpochcalli. "We believe in the popular education model," she says. "Building capacity and using education as a means of doing that." It makes sense, then, that the school is a true community center, offering ELL (English language learner) classes for adults, aerobics and sewing courses, men's basketball nights, domestic violence workshops, and a lot more. In a given week, more than 400 people use the building outside of school hours.

"We want to be open and available to kids and families," Tamara explains. "We're continually stretching ourselves, and we're committed to meeting people's needs when they come to us and how they come to us. You have to make very overt, constant efforts to keep the doors open and keep working with people."

That work doesn't end at the schoolhouse door. In 1998, Tamara joined a group of neighborhood parents, educators, and activists in founding a nonprofit organization, the Telpochcalli Community Education Project, which operates both inside and outside schools in efforts "to bring about a more united, better educated, safer, and socially prepared community."

> "We believe it's a good thing for all students. We want our kids to value and hold on to their home language and to learn English as well, to be truly bilingual and biliterate."

It isn't just the work Tamara and her staff do that is nontraditional. The way they work together is unconventional as well. Rather than the top-down administrative model—resurgent, perhaps, because of so many federal and district mandates—Telpochcalli is about shared leadership and consensus building. To help make that possible, the school's teachers decided early on that they needed more opportunities to come together to share ideas, develop curriculum, and grow professionally. So they agreed to restructure the day—scheduling longer teaching days Monday through Thursday—so that every Friday afternoon would be dedicated to whole-staff gatherings and professional development.

Visionary Leadership

As principal, Tamara sees her role largely as helping to facilitate the shared vision. Although her days are partly filled with the kinds of tasks one might expect of a school administrator—answering calls and emails, helping to monitor hallways and lunchrooms, completing district-required paperwork—she believes her most valuable contribution lies in supporting others in their work. "I try to help people solve problems and stay connected with one another," she says. "I help seek out resources and supports. And a major part of what I do is remaining firmly committed to our work and our way of working—so that we don't roll back into the same old, same old."

Tamara acknowledges that being part of a small school has made it easier in some respects to resist the "same old, same old" and navigate the pressures of federal policy. She calls herself a "hard-core small schools person," and believes that the nature of larger buildings with hundreds more students can lead principals to fall back, sometimes unintentionally, on traditional forms of leadership. She also thinks the "enormous fear factor" of not raising test scores may inhibit some administrators from thinking more creatively. "But our approach is, if it's an idea that is supportive of what we're trying to do, then we try to find a way to make it work."

It's hard to blame principals for being fearful. The entire framework of federal education policy relies on threats and punishment for schools that don't "perform." Superintendents or district CEOs pass that fear on to their subordinates, who pass it on to principals, who pass it on to teachers, who pass it on to students. But Tamara and the teachers at Telpochcalli serve as a reminder that it doesn't have to be that way—that it's possible, even under the cloud of high-stakes testing,

It's hard to blame principals for being fearful. The entire framework of federal education policy relies on threats and punishment for schools that don't "perform."

to hold on to a vision of schools as they could be.

Yet the cloud still hovers overhead. Although NTA's reading and math scores have risen dramatically in the past three years, the school still doesn't meet federal expectations. And though Telpochcalli has raised test scores in all other categories, it continues to miss the mark in reading.

For Tamara, this says far less about what's happening at the schools than it does about the inherent limits of No Child Left Behind's measures—as well as the law's disregard for the influence of outside-school factors such as poverty and substandard health care on students' school performance. "There are some really good reasons the data looks the way it does," she says. "If we're serious about leveling the opportunities, we need to get serious at the policy level about having wraparound support systems for kids and families."

In the meantime, mandates and dictums rain down on principals on a seemingly daily basis, and how they respond—determining which require serious attention, which should be sent straight to the recycle bin, and which fall somewhere in between—can make a huge difference in what sort of learning environment is promoted and nurtured at a school. It's a team effort, of course, and Amy and Tamara are quick to acknowledge the crucial roles played by their teachers, staff, parent volunteers, and other partners. When discussing their schools' approaches, they both talk about "we" far more than "I." Still, it's hard to overstate the importance of courageous, visionary, imaginative leadership—especially in times like these.

Amy and Tamara agree that it's difficult work, but also deeply satisfying. "What we do at Telpochcalli requires flexibility and stability and a commitment to doing it day after day after day," Tamara says. "It's not easy to sustain. But I wouldn't want to do it any other way."

Amy adds: "When you think about the scope of the job, there are so many things you have to do that it can be pretty overwhelming. It can be hard to focus on the things that really matter. But despite the craziness, we're inspired by the commitment everybody in the school makes—especially the kids. The hope and the possibility you see in the kids keep you coming back every day." ✎

Steady Work

Finland builds a strong teaching and learning system

LINDA DARLING-HAMMOND

One wonders what we might accomplish as a nation if we could finally set aside what appears to be our de facto commitment to inequality, so profoundly at odds with our rhetoric of equity, and put the millions of dollars spent continually arguing and litigating into building a high-quality education system for all children. To imagine how that might be done, one can look at nations that started with very little and purposefully built highly productive and equitable systems, sometimes almost from scratch, in the space of only two to three decades.

As an example, I am going to briefly describe how Finland built a strong educational system, nearly from the ground up. Finland was not succeeding educationally in the 1970s, when the United States was the unquestioned education leader in the world. Yet that country created a productive teaching and learning system by expanding access while investing purposefully in ambitious educational goals using strategic approaches to build teaching capacity.

I use the term "teaching and learning system" advisedly to describe a set of elements that, when well designed and connected, reliably support all students in their learning. These elements ensure that students routinely encounter well-prepared teachers who are working in concert around a thoughtful, high-quality curriculum, supported by appropriate materials and assessments—and that these elements of the system help students, teachers, leaders, and the system as a whole continue to learn and improve. Although no system from afar can be transported wholesale into another context, there is much to learn from the experiences of those who have addressed problems we also encounter.

The Finnish Success Story

Finland has been a poster child for school improvement since it rapidly climbed to the top of the international rankings after it emerged from the Soviet Union's shadow. Once poorly ranked educationally, with a turgid bureaucratic system that produced low-quality education and large inequalities, it now ranks first among all the OECD nations (Organisation for Economic Co-operation and Development—roughly, the so-called "developed" nations) on the PISA (Program for International Student Assessments), an international test for 15-year-olds in language, math, and science literacy. The country also boasts a highly equitable distribution of achievement, even for its growing share of immigrant students.

> **These new immigrants speak more than 60 languages. Yet achievement has been climbing in Finland *and* growing more equitable.**

Inquiry is a major focus of learning in Finland, and assessment is used to cultivate students' active learning skills by asking open-ended questions and helping students address them.

In a recent analysis of educational reform policies, Finnish policy analyst Pasi Sahlberg describes how, since the 1970s, Finland has changed its traditional education system "into a model of a modern, publicly financed education system with widespread equity, good quality, large participation—all of this at reasonable cost." More than 99 percent of students now successfully complete compulsory basic education, and about 90 percent complete upper secondary school. Two-thirds of these graduates enroll in universities or professionally oriented polytechnic schools. More than 50 percent of the Finnish adult population participates in adult education programs, and 98 percent of the cost of education at all levels is covered by government rather than by private sources.

Although there was a sizable achievement gap among students in the 1970s, strongly correlated to socioeconomic status, this gap has been progressively reduced as a result of curriculum reforms started in the 1980s. By 2006, Finland's between-school variance on the PISA science scale was only 5 percent, whereas the average between-school variance in other OECD nations was about 33 percent. (Large between-school variation is generally related to social inequality.)

The overall variation in achievement among Finnish students is also smaller than that of nearly all the other OECD countries. This is true despite the fact that immigration from nations with lower levels of education has increased sharply in recent years, and there is more linguistic and cultural diversity for schools to contend with. One recent analysis notes that in some urban schools the number of immigrant children or those whose mother tongue is not Finnish approaches 50 percent.

Although most immigrants are still from places like Sweden, the most rapidly growing newcomer groups since 1990 have been from Afghanistan, Bosnia, India, Iran, Iraq, Serbia, Somalia, Turkey, Thailand, and Vietnam. These new immigrants speak more than 60 languages. Yet achievement has been climbing in Finland *and* growing more equitable.

Strategies for Reform

Because of these trends, many people have turned to Finland for clues to educational transformation. As one analyst notes:

> Most visitors to Finland discover elegant school buildings filled with calm children and highly educated teachers. They also recognize the large autonomy that schools enjoy, little interference by the central education administration in schools' everyday lives, systematic methods to address problems in the lives of students, and targeted professional help for those in need.

Leaders in Finland attribute the gains to their intensive investments in teacher education—all teachers receive three years of high-quality graduate level preparation completely at state expense—plus a major overhaul of the curriculum and assessment system designed to ensure access to a "thinking curriculum" for all students. A recent analysis of the Finnish system summarized its core principles as follows:

- Resources for those who need them most.

- High standards and supports for special needs.

- Qualified teachers.

- Evaluation of education.

- Balancing decentralization and centralization.

The process of change has been almost the reverse of policies in the United States. Over the past 40 years, Finland has shifted from a highly centralized system emphasizing external testing to a more localized system in which highly trained teachers design curriculum around the very lean national standards. This new system is implemented through equitable funding and extensive preparation for all teachers. The logic of the system is that investments in the capacity of local teachers and schools to meet the needs of all students, coupled with thoughtful guidance about goals, can unleash the benefits of local creativity in the cause of common, equitable outcomes.

Meanwhile the United States has been imposing more external testing—often exacerbating differential access to curriculum—while creating more inequitable conditions in local schools. Resources for children and schools—in the form of both overall funding and the presence of trained, experienced teachers—have become more disparate in many states, thus undermining the capacity of schools to meet the outcomes that are ostensibly sought. Sahlberg notes that Finland has taken a very different path. He observes:

> The Finns have worked systematically over 35 years to make sure that competent professionals who can craft the best learning conditions for all students are in all schools, rather than thinking that standardized instruction and related testing can be brought in at the last minute to improve student learning and turn around failing schools.

Sahlberg identifies a set of global reforms, undertaken especially in the Anglo-Saxon countries, that Finland has *not* adopted, including standardization of curriculum enforced by frequent external tests; narrowing of the curriculum to basic skills in reading and mathematics; reduced use of innovative teaching strategies; adoption of educational ideas from external sources, rather than development of local internal capacity for innovation and problem-solving; and adoption of high-stakes accountability policies, featuring rewards and sanctions for students, teachers, and schools. By contrast, he suggests:

> Finnish education policies are a result of four decades of systematic, mostly intentional, development that has created a culture of diversity, trust, and respect within Finnish society in general, and within its education system in particular.... Education sector development has been grounded on equal opportunities for all, equitable distribution of resources rather than competition, intensive early interventions for prevention, and building gradual trust among education practitioners, especially teachers. Equity in opportunity to learn is supported in many ways in addition to basic funding.

Finnish schools are generally small (fewer than 300 pupils) with relatively small class sizes (in the 20s), and are uniformly well equipped. The notion of caring for students educationally and personally is a central principle in the schools. All students receive a free meal daily, as well as free health care, transportation, learning materials, and counseling in their schools, so that the foundations for learning are in place. Beyond that, access to quality curriculum and teachers has become a central aspect of Finnish educational policy.

Improving Curriculum Content and Access

Beginning in the 1970s, Finland launched reforms to equalize educational opportunity by first eliminating the practice of separating students into very different tracks based on their test scores, and then by eliminating the examinations themselves. This occurred in two stages between 1972 and 1982, and a common curriculum, through the end of high school, was developed throughout the entire system. These changes were intended to equalize educational outcomes and provide more open access to higher education. During this time, social supports for children and families were also enacted, including health and dental care, special education services, and transportation to schools.

By the late 1970s, investment in teachers was an additional focus. Teacher education was improved and extended. Policy makers decided that if they invested in very skillful teachers, they could allow local schools more autonomy to make decisions about what and how to teach—a reaction against the oppressive, centralized system they sought to overhaul.

This bet seems to have paid off. By the mid-1990s, the country had ended the highly regulated system of curriculum management (reflected in older curriculum guides that had exceeded 700 pages of prescriptions). The current national core curriculum is a much leaner document—featuring fewer than 10 pages of guidance for all of mathematics, for example—that guides teachers in collectively developing local curriculum and assessments. The focus of 1990s curricular reform was on science, technology, and innovation, leading to an emphasis on teaching students how to think creatively and manage their own learning.

There are no external standardized tests used to rank students or schools in Finland, and most teacher feedback to students is in narrative form, emphasizing descriptions of their learning progress and areas for growth. As in the National Assessment of Educational Progress (NAEP) exams in the United States, samples of students are evaluated on open-ended assessments at the end of the 2nd and 9th grades to inform curriculum and school investments. The focus is on using information to drive learning and problem solving, rather than punishment.

Prospective teachers are competitively selected from the pool of college graduates— only 15 percent of those who apply are admitted—and receive a three-year graduate-level teacher preparation program, entirely free of charge and with a living stipend.

Finland maintains one exam prior to attending university: the matriculation exam, organized and evaluated by a matriculation exam board appointed by the Finnish Ministry of Education. Although not required for graduation or entry into a university, it is common practice for students to take this set of four open-ended exams that emphasize problem-solving, analysis, and writing. Teachers use official guidelines to grade the matriculation exams locally, and samples of the grades are re-examined by professional raters hired by the matriculation exam board. Although it is counterintuitive to those accustomed to external testing as a means of accountability, Finland's use of school-based, student-centered, open-ended tasks embedded in the curriculum is often touted as an important reason for the nation's success on the international exams.

The national core curriculum provides teachers with recommended assessment criteria for specific grades in each subject and in the overall final assessment of student progress each year. Local schools and teachers then use those guidelines to craft a more detailed curriculum and set of learning outcomes at each school, as well as approaches to assessing benchmarks in the curriculum. According to the Finnish National Board of Education, the main purpose of assessing students is to guide and encourage students' own reflection and self-assessment. Consequently, ongoing feedback from the teacher is very important. Teachers give students formative and summative reports both through verbal and narrative feedback. Inquiry is a major focus of learning in Finland, and assessment is used to cultivate students' active learning skills by asking open-ended questions and helping students address them.

In a Finnish classroom, it is rare to see a teacher standing at the front of a classroom lecturing students for 50 minutes. Instead, students are likely to determine their own weekly targets with their teachers in specific subject areas and choose the tasks they will work on at their own pace. In a typical classroom, students are likely to be walking around, rotating through workshops or gathering information, asking questions of their teacher, and working with other students in small groups. They may be completing independent or group projects or writing articles for their own magazines. The cultivation of independence and active learning allows students to develop metacognitive skills that help them to frame, tackle, and solve problems; evaluate and improve their own work; and guide their learning processes in productive ways.

Improving Teaching

Greater investments in teacher education began in the 1970s with the expectation that teachers would move from three-year normal school programs to four- to five-year programs of study. During the 1990s, the country overhauled preparation once again to focus more on teaching diverse learners higher-order skills like problem-solving and critical thinking in research-based master's degree programs. Preparing teachers for a research-based profession has been the central idea of teacher education developments in Finland.

Prospective teachers are competitively selected from the pool of college graduates—only 15 percent of those who apply are admitted—and receive a three-year graduate-level teacher preparation program, entirely free of charge and with a living stipend. Unlike the United States, where teachers either go into debt to prepare for a profession that will pay them poorly or enter with little or no training, Finland made the decision to invest in a uniformly well-prepared teaching force by recruiting top candidates and paying them to go to school. Slots in teacher training programs are highly coveted, and shortages of applicants are virtually unheard of.

Teachers' preparation includes both extensive coursework on how to teach—with a strong emphasis on using research based on state-of-the-art practice—and at least a full year of clinical experience in a school associated with the university. These model schools are intended to develop and model innovative practices, as well as to foster research on learning and teaching. Teachers are trained in research methods so that they can "contribute to an increase of the problem-solving capacity of the education system."

Within these model schools, student teachers participate in problem-solving groups, a common feature in Finnish schools. The problem-solving groups engage in a cycle of planning, action, and reflection/evaluation that is reinforced throughout the teacher education program and is, in fact, a model for what teachers will plan for their own students, who are expected to incorporate similar kinds of research and inquiry in their own studies. Indeed, the entire system is intended to improve through continual reflection, evaluation, and problem-solving at the level of the classroom, school, municipality, and nation.

Teachers learn how to create challenging curriculum and how to develop and evaluate local performance assessments that engage students in research and inquiry on a regular basis. Teacher training emphasizes learning how to teach students who learn in different ways, including those with special needs. It includes a strong emphasis on "multiculturality" and the "prevention of learning difficulties and exclusion," as well as on the understanding of learning, thoughtful assessment, and curriculum development. The egalitarian Finns reasoned that if teachers learn to help students who struggle, then they will be able to teach all students more effectively and, indeed, leave no child behind.

Most teachers now hold master's degrees in both their content area and in education, and they are well prepared to teach diverse learners—including special-needs students—for deep understanding, and to use formative performance assessments on a regular basis to inform their teaching so it meets students' needs. Teachers are well trained both in research methods and in pedagogical practice. Consequently, they are sophisticated diagnosticians, and they work together collegially to design instruction that meets the demands of the subject matter as well as the needs of their students.

"Teachers should not be seen as technicians whose work is to implement strictly dictated syllabi, but rather as professionals who know how to improve learning for all."

In Finland, like other high-achieving nations, schools provide time for regular collaboration among teachers on issues of instruction. Teachers in Finnish schools meet at least one afternoon each week to jointly plan and develop curriculum, and schools in the same municipality are encouraged to work together to share materials. Time is also provided for professional development within the teachers' workweek. As is true in many other European and Asian nations, nearly half of teachers' school time is used to hone practice through school-based curriculum work, collective planning, and cooperation with parents, which allows schools and families to work more closely together on behalf of students. The result is that:

> Finnish teachers are conscious, critical consumers of professional development and inservice training services. Just as the professional level of the teaching cadre has increased over the past two decades, so has the quality of teacher professional development support. Most compulsory, traditional inservice training has disappeared. In its place are school- or municipality-based longer-term programs and professional development opportunities. Continuous upgrading of teachers' pedagogical professionalism has become a right rather than an obligation. This shift in teachers' learning conditions and styles often reflects ways that classroom learning is arranged for pupils. As a consequence of strengthened professionalism in schools, it has become understood that teachers and schools are responsible for their own work and also solve most problems rather than shift them elsewhere. Today the Finnish teaching profession is on a par with other professional workers; teachers can diagnose problems in their classrooms and schools, apply evidence-based and often alternative solutions to them, and evaluate and analyze the impact of implemented procedures.

The focus on instruction and the development of professional practice in Finland's approach to organizing the education system has led, according to all reports, to an increased prevalence of effective teaching methods in schools. Furthermore, efforts to enable schools to learn from each other have led to "lateral capacity building": the widespread adoption of effective practices and experimentation with innovative approaches across the system, "encouraging teachers and schools to continue to expand their repertoires of teaching methods and individualizing teaching to meet the needs of all students."

A Finnish official noted this key lesson learned from the reforms that allowed Finland to climb from an inequitable, mediocre education system to the very top of the international rankings:

> Empowerment of the teaching profession produces good results. Professional teachers should have space for innovation, because they should try to find new ways to improve learning. Teachers should not be seen as technicians whose work is to implement strictly dictated syllabi, but rather as professionals who know how to improve learning for all. All this creates a big challenge...that certainly calls for changes in teacher education programs. Teachers are ranked highest in importance, because educational systems work through them.

Finland has undertaken these elements in a systemic fashion, rather than pouring energy into a potpourri of innovations and then changing course every few years, as has often been the case in many communities in the United States, especially in large cities. And while this small nation—about the size of a mid-sized U.S. state—has conducted this work on a national level, similar strategies have been employed at the state or provincial level in high-scoring Australia, New Zealand, and Canada, and provinces like Hong Kong and Macao in China, also with positive outcomes.

They demonstrate how it is possible to build a system in which students are routinely taught by well-prepared teachers who work together to create a thoughtful, high-quality curriculum, supported by appropriate materials and assessments that enable ongoing learning for students, teachers, and schools alike. ✎

Teaching in Dangerous Times

*In this era of demands for teacher quality, it is crucial
to develop culturally relevant ways to assess teachers*

GLORIA LADSON-BILLINGS

In the popular book, *Dangerous Minds*, the former-Marine-turned-teacher LouAnne Johnson is credited with turning around the "class from hell"—a group of urban African American and Latino students on the road to failure in school and life. This book and the subsequent motion picture were more of the "teacher-as-savior" genre that constructs an image of teachers, particularly white teachers, as "rescuing" urban students of color from themselves, their families, and their communities.

Unfortunately, most of the teachers in this genre pay little or no attention to the academic achievement of their students. Thus, while many audiences applaud the Hollywood teacher-images' amazing social work, interpersonal, and cross-cultural communications skills, few real-life educators would point to any of these histrionic teachers as exemplary classroom instructors.

Given the changing demographics of the student body in the United States and the bifurcation of public school student populations into groups of haves and have-nots, it is important to understand that, rather than confront dangerous minds, teachers of urban students of color are teaching in dangerous times. One of the most urgent issues facing this perilous era and the cadre of teachers who serve in it is that of being able to more accurately measure what students know and are able to do.

Communities of color, which historically have raised questions about the potential biases built into traditional test measures, have challenged the purpose and design of many of the new assessments. This scrutiny has been accompanied by a focus in the educational community at large on teacher assessment.

Rather than rely on the old "input" model, in which teacher-worthiness is judged by the kinds of courses teachers have completed, there have been increasing calls for more authentic forms of assessment for teachers. These new assessments target "outputs"—what teachers know and are able to do.

Educational researchers and scholars of color have long suspected that traditional teaching assessment techniques systematically screen out teachers of color from the teaching field. For example, in 1997, I was personally told that during a recent round of testing for the National Board for Professional Teaching Standards, *no* candidates of color passed the Early Adolescence/English Language Arts Assessment.

Rather than confront dangerous minds, teachers of urban students of color are teaching in dangerous times.

Do proposed new "authentic" teacher assessment techniques continue in this vein? And, if so, do alternative assessments need to be formulated, and what proficiency or skill areas must these assessments address?

In this article, I would like to look briefly at problems in some of the most popular teacher assessment techniques and then propose other possible measures that can be used to assess teachers.

Teacher Testing

Since the mid-1980s, the nation has seemed fixated with testing its teachers. Predictably, these testing measures have had an adverse impact on the already shrinking pool of African American teachers. Though few would argue that school districts certify incompetent teachers, those states calling for teachers to be tested typically fail to engage in a process that holds schools and colleges of teacher education responsible for ensuring that their graduates meet minimum standards.

The problem of teachers not passing competency tests seems inconsequential when compared to the larger issue of what these tests reveal about teachers' ability to teach. For example, all California teachers who have received regular teaching certificates within the past 10 years have passed that state's teacher competency test. Yet, would one argue that all of California's teachers are good teachers? Creating tests as screens or barriers to admission seems to appease the public outcry for higher standards, even when those standards have no relationship to performance.

The more relevant question might be: How equitable and reliable are teacher assessment measures for ensuring that teachers will be effective in classrooms of urban children of color?

Teaching Contexts

Many new teacher assessments fail to consider the very different contexts in which teachers find themselves. More pointedly, teachers of color are more likely to find themselves in poor, urban school communities than are white teachers.

The example of one assessment center activity that I personally critiqued describes a case in point. In this instance, the videotape prepared and presented to the assessors by an African American teacher who taught in an overcrowded, underfunded urban public school yielded assessor discussion only about how stark and bare her classroom seemed compared to those of other examinees. This teacher did not have an intricate, handmade spider's web draped across her classroom as a visible reminder of a reading unit's insect theme, as did the suburban teacher who submitted a video. Nor did the African American teacher have a big comfortable sofa, beanbag chairs, pillows, and a carpeted floor, as did the teacher from a school in a college-town district.

In my later conversation with the African American teacher, I learned that because of overcrowding she did not have a real room for her classes and instead taught out of a makeshift closet. Additionally, the school was on a year-round schedule. This meant that every nine weeks she was required to take down everything in her "room" and reassemble it after the break. Nothing in the teacher assessment process was designed to take into consideration teaching under these circumstances. Further, if new assessments continue to discount the inequities already built into schools by virtue of unequal funding and other material resources, then they will continue to discount the creative ways some teachers deal with scarcity and push students to higher intellectual heights.

> **Teachers cannot yell "cut" and re-teach a "scene" each time a student is confused or behaving inappropriately. Teaching is more episodic, random, and unpredictable than movies.**

Videotaping and Portfolios

I'd like to briefly touch on two popular innovations in teacher assessment: videotapes and portfolios.

Because videotaping gives us the luxury of "seeing" teaching, it has gained increased credibility. However, videotaping a classroom also reveals how cameras do, indeed, lie.

At best, a video is an artificial representation of teaching. Even unedited, a video reveals but a partial view of the classroom setting and what transpires there. It can capture only selected slices of classroom life.

Teachers cannot yell "cut" and re-teach a "scene" each time a student is confused or behaving inappropriately. Teaching is more episodic, random, and unpredictable than movies. The dynamic of the classroom creates ups and downs, zigs and zags, that may come across as confused and unfocused through the flat, unforgiving lens of a video camera.

Further, when a videotape is used for assessment and evaluation, teachers, as vested participants, often choose to "create" a tape that features the best of their teaching. Schools and districts with resources and personnel equipped to produce high-quality videotapes can make mediocre teaching appear much better than it really is. Conversely, excellent teachers with limited access to good equipment and videographic skills may be left with poor-quality tapes that fail to illuminate any of the magic that transpires in the classroom.

Similar problems can emerge with portfolio assessment.

On the surface, this seems a fair and equitable way to assess teaching: Allow teachers to show what they believe is their best work, and/or the products of that work, and judge it.

However, this also has its equity pitfalls. Imagine, for example, a teacher who was prepared at one of the nation's research institutions. She probably heard about teaching portfolios; perhaps she was both taught and required to construct a portfolio during her student teacher semester. By contrast, a colleague who was prepared at a small, historically black college did not have the same access to portfolio preparation training. Both are good teachers, but one is more capable of using a portfolio to document abilities and skills.

A Culturally Relevant Approach

If the most common teacher assessment techniques fall short, especially for students and teachers in urban areas, what proficiency or skills areas must the assessments address?

My previous work with teachers who are successful with African American students suggests that some ways to rethink teacher performance include looking at teachers' abilities to engender success among their students in three key areas academic achievement, cultural competence, and sociopolitical consciousness.

Additionally, assessments that consider aspects of teachers' culture might prove more equitable for teachers of color.

Academic Achievement

Regardless of the elegance of one's teaching performances, the bottom line is always how much learning takes place. Do students demonstrate competence in academic areas? Are they able to formulate questions, propose solutions, apply knowledge to new and different situations?

Most portfolio assessments require teachers to supply examples of individual students' work. Rarely do they set performance criteria for a teacher's entire class. However, a central focus on helping as many children as possible achieve academically is one of the hallmarks of culturally relevant teaching. Consequently, assessment of culturally relevant teaching practice would require teachers to show evidence of academic achievement for all their students or to provide educationally defensible explanations of why any students do not meet this criteria (e.g., consistently poor attendance, identified special needs, and so forth).

One way to determine teachers' ability to enhance students' academic achievement is to collect baseline data at the beginning of the school year and compare those findings to end-of-year data. Often, students from upper-income, dominant-culture communities come into a classroom knowing much of what their teachers purport to teach them. Thus, their typically superior performance on standardized measures is actually an indication of what they already know.

Unless a teacher's students are demonstrating academic progress, one cannot contend, with good conscience, that the teacher is exemplary. Indeed, it is not the teacher's method or strategy that should be the criteria for good teaching, but rather the academic accomplishments of students. Do students who were previously unable to read demonstrate an ability to read after spending a year in a teacher's classroom? Can students who were not able to compute and solve problems at the beginning of the school term provide evidence that they can do so by the end? These students' performances should be the benchmarks upon which we put our confidence in teacher effectiveness, and they do not have to be demonstrated solely on standardized tests. However, effective teachers must be prepared to provide powerful examples of what their students know and can do.

Cultural Competence

This second area does not lend itself to conventional forms of measurement. Its goal is to ensure that teachers support the home and community cultures of students, while helping students become proficient in the cultures of schooling and education.

What makes this difficult is the finding that far too many teachers in U.S. schools possess only a surface understanding of culture—their own or anyone else's. As noted in another of my earlier studies, many middle-class, white, American teachers fail to associate the notion of culture with themselves. Instead, they believe that they are "just regular Americans," while people of color are the ones "with culture." This notion of regularity serves a normalizing function that positions those who are "not regular" as "others." Not recognizing that they, too, are cultural beings prevents these teachers from ever questioning taken-for-granted assumptions about the nature of human thought, activity, and existence.

> Do students who were previously unable to read demonstrate an ability to read after spending a year in a teacher's classroom? Can students who were not able to compute and solve problems at the beginning of the school term provide evidence that they can do so by the end?

Culturally relevant teachers know when to introduce relevant examples from their students' backgrounds and experiences to make learning more meaningful. For example, when the African American students of a teacher I will call Ms. Deberaux indicated that the only females who could be princesses were white, blond-haired, and blue-eyed, she quickly brought out a copy of John Steptoe's *Mufaro's Beautiful Daughters* for them to read. This lavishly illustrated children's book, with its richly detailed story of African royalty and traditions, provided her students with the necessary counter-knowledge to challenge their misguided notions about nobility and people of African descent.

The goal of fostering cultural competence requires teachers to help raise students' awareness of prejudice and discrimination as well as their ability to react to and constructively cope with these negative social realities. For example, before a teacher I will identify as Ms. Lewis took her inner-city African American students on a camping trip, she talked candidly with them about the fact that they would be coming in contact with white students and counselors. She encouraged them to think proactively about what they might do if any white person exhibited insensitive or racist attitudes toward them.

Fostering cultural competence also requires teachers to support students' home language/dialect while simultaneously teaching them Standard English. That is, rather than chastise students for using the language/dialect they use when speaking with family and friends and in their communities, effective teachers help students understand when and where code-switching, or the alternate use of Standard English and home language/dialect in formal and informal settings, is preferable or necessary.

Unfortunately, nothing in the current teacher assessment battery addresses how well teachers foster cultural competence within their students. Perhaps this is because few test constructors have ever considered the importance of cultural competence for students, nor would they even recognize it when teachers demonstrate it.

One example that came to my attention involved an art teacher in a predominantly African American high school. The classroom video submitted by this teacher depicted a demonstration lecture by a cosmetologist the teacher had invited to her class to discuss the intricate hair braiding done by black African women as an art form. The assessors rated this teacher's submission poorly, claiming that cosmetology belongs in vocational education, not art. Their lack of understanding of the relationship between hair and art in African societies kept them from accepting a broader notion of the relevance of this demonstration.

Sociopolitical Consciousness

In addition to ensuring that students achieve academically and are culturally competent, culturally relevant teachers develop a sociopolitical consciousness in their students. The use of the term "sociopolitical consciousness" is important, lest readers equate it with the more simplistic, almost vacuous term "critical thinking."

Whereas there certainly is nothing wrong with critical thinking per se, what often masquerades as critical thinking in most classrooms is a set of prescriptive steps and practices that may reflect important processes but that are attached to relatively inane content. For instance, students might be asked to imagine that they are legislators who must decide whether or not to provide aid to a country that is deforesting its rain forest. Although this is a serious ecological issue, how can students come to think critically about it given only vicarious knowledge?

A different kind of critical thinking—what I term sociopolitical consciousness or an activist civic and social awareness—is demonstrated by Bill Tate in his focus on a teacher he calls Sandra Mason. According to Tate, Ms. Mason's middle school mathematics students came to class upset each morning because their route to school was impeded by indigent panhandlers who aggressively approached them for money to purchase cheap liquor from one of the many liquor stores near the school. Instead of ignoring the students' concerns, Ms. Mason decided to incorporate the problem of negotiating around these alcohol-dependent throngs into a classroom lesson. Her students examined city zoning ordinances and learned that their city was divided into "wet" and "dry" zones that determined where alcoholic beverages could be sold. The schools that served poor communities of color were located in wet zones. The students calculated the amount of money that was being generated by the liquor stores in the school neighborhood (and lost to the community since most of the store owners lived elsewhere), and they developed an action plan for rethinking zoning in the city. This involvement with real problems raised the students' sociopolitical consciousness and made mathematics a more meaningful activity for the students. It also made teaching more challenging for Ms. Mason, but it enabled her to help her students understand that what happened in school had relevance for their everyday lives.

How should teachers' abilities to develop students' sociopolitical consciousness be assessed? Certainly, this is a more complex skill than can be exhibited on a pencil-and-paper test. Yet, if we say that students must exhibit this trait, then teachers have to demonstrate their ability to teach in ways that support that kind of learning.

> The goal of fostering cultural competence requires teachers to help raise students' awareness of prejudice and discrimination as well as their ability to react to and constructively cope with these negative social realities.

Concluding Thoughts

In the longer essay upon which this article is based, I outline some possible ways one might promote assessments for teachers that value and reward culturally relevant teaching. Here, I want to underscore a question that looms over any assessment practice: Who gets to handle whose business?

If assessment practices both powerful and subtle enough to evaluate academic achievement, cultural competence, and sociopolitical consciousness could somehow be devised, who would carry them out?

The complexities of the new types of assessments required will demand assessors who are capable of cultural translations of pedagogical expertise. These assessors would have to be able to answer several questions, such as the following:

• When is direct instruction the right methodology to use?

• How does one determine the difference between a teacher who is unduly harsh or one who is warmly demanding?

• What difference does it make if teachers slip in and out of a students' home language to make a point to their students?

• Can all assessors determine the pedagogical significance of teachers' culturally specific behaviors?

• How is it that African American teachers so regularly and predictably fail current assessments, yet the presence of white teachers is no assurance that African American or other students of color will achieve?

• What is the nature of the technical problems related to designing culturally relevant teacher assessments?

• Can teacher assessments be considered without a concomitant look at student assessment? In other words, can failing students have successful teachers?

These questions are important because more states and local districts are looking at new ways to assess both preservice and inservice teachers. What these assessments will look like, what opportunities teachers will have for demon-

If we understand teaching as a highly complex endeavor undertaken by professionals, then we are compelled to develop assessments that are highly sophisticated and nuanced.

strating teaching competence, and how these assessments will include or exclude potential teacher candidates need careful and critical examination.

The work of teaching is both complicated and complex. How we educators come to understand it has implications for how we assess it. If we construct teaching as a set of technical tasks, then we will devise assessments designed to score these tasks. However, if we understand teaching as a highly complex endeavor undertaken by professionals, then we are compelled to develop assessments that are highly sophisticated and nuanced. Regardless of how we construct teaching as a profession, the challenge of ensuring high-quality performance from teachers and students remains. Without improvement in both, we will continue to live in dangerous times. ✏

This article is condensed from Gloria Ladson-Billings (1998),"Teaching in Dangerous Times: Culturally Relevant Approaches to Teacher Assessment." The Journal of Negro Education, *67, 255-267. Reprinted with permission from* The Journal of Negro Education, © *1998 Howard University. www.journalnegroed.org.*

Teachers Teaching Teachers

*In Portland, teachers work together to create
teacher-centered professional development*

LINDA CHRISTENSEN

"Teachers teaching teachers is like the blind leading the blind," a literacy "expert" told senior Portland Public Schools (PPS) administrators in the fall of 2005, while discussing my three-year writing proposal, which included classroom teachers sharing strategies and lessons to improve writing in Portland Oregon's elementary schools. Instead, elementary teachers will get yet another outside expert with a program and a large price tag.

During my seven years as a curriculum specialist designing professional development in Portland Public Schools, I wanted teachers to see themselves as curriculum producers, as creative intellectuals rather than technicians serving out daily portions of someone else's packaged or downloaded materials. I attempted to create spaces where teachers could work together to develop their own curriculum and discuss education issues.

School districts write mission statements about creating citizens of the world, but more and more, they want teachers to become robotic hands who deliver education programs designed and shipped from sites outside of our classrooms.

If we want an educated citizenry, we need teachers who know how to think about their students' needs and write their own curriculum in community with others.

In recent years, federal education policy has pushed administrators to grab quick solutions to get a fast "bump" in their test scores. Instead of taking the time to build teacher capacity by improving instruction or creating schools as learning communities where teachers have opportunities to have honest discussions about classroom practice, share successful lessons and strategies, or examine student work together, more and more administrators opt for what I call "boxed" professional development—from fill-in-the-blank writing curricula to "stick-the-kid-on-the-computer" reading and math programs.

When high school language arts teachers in Portland were asked by the Professional Development Committee—a group founded by the school district and the Portland Association of Teachers—which professional development programs had the greatest impact on their students' learning, they overwhelmingly named the Portland Writing Project, the Summer Literacy

> **I wanted teachers to see themselves as curriculum producers, as creative intellectuals rather than technicians serving out daily portions of someone else's packaged or downloaded materials.**

Curriculum Camp, and the Professional Development Days—which were all led by classroom teachers.

Teachers stated that these three programs were practical and related specifically to their content. The programs gave them models of new strategies and curricula, hands-on practice, and time for collaboration and implementation. Teachers also said they appreciated the support of ongoing professional development, instead of the one-shot variety. What struck me in reading the surveys and talking with teachers was that the top-down approach of telling teachers what to do without engaging them in active learning is as ineffective in professional development as it is in the classroom.

In the same way that some teachers insult students by assuming that they have no knowledge, history, culture, or language, some schools and school districts insult teachers by assuming that they come to professional development without any prior knowledge or expertise. For example, last year a literacy "expert" came to town with her bag of tricks. She landed at a school that had a literacy team representing teachers across the disciplines. Instead of finding out what they knew, she proceeded to teach them about "think-alouds," graphic organizers, textbook previewing, and reading strategies they'd already been implementing in their classrooms.

Another common professional development pitfall is the series of overheads, which is currently being replaced by the dancing PowerPoint presentation, with too-simple bulleted points about complex issues like inclusion of special education students or English Language Learners in mainstream classrooms, as if naming a problem constitutes addressing it. Without any modeling, discussion, or time to plan for implementation, the leaders of these inoculation sessions expect teachers to take the theory back and apply it in their classrooms. This is like taking students to the Louvre, showing them great art, and expecting them to reproduce it without giving them any lessons on drawing and painting.

Portland Writing Project

The Portland Writing Project (PWP), a collaboration between Portland Public Schools and the Oregon Writing Project at Lewis & Clark College, is one of the 189 sites of the National Writing Project (NWP). The Portland Writing Project models the pedagogy it hopes teachers will take back to their classrooms, but it also encourages teachers to constantly reflect on their classroom practice and revise their teaching based on their observations. Like the NWP, the PWP doesn't preach one way to teach writing; it teaches the writing process. But in Portland, we also help teachers learn to develop their own curriculum.

Every summer for most of the past 20 years, 25 K-12 Portland Public Schools teachers have gathered to share writing strategies and lessons with each other during an intensive (9 a.m. to 4 p.m.) four-week class; they receive 10.5 university credits for participating. At our site, my co-director and I choose a multicultural novel that situates our teaching in a period of U.S. history, so teachers can learn to integrate history, reading, novel study, writing, and students' lives into their lessons.

For a number of years we read *Nisei Daughter*, Monica Sone's autobiography, which takes place during the Japanese-American internment. The participants, co-directors, and I developed role plays and writing assignments using the book, primary source documents, children's books, or other parallel texts on the topic. While the co-directors and I provide the framework for the summer institute, each teacher develops and teaches a writing lesson

> **The top-down approach of telling teachers what to do without engaging them in active learning is as ineffective in professional development as it is in the classroom.**

that contributes to the unit. For example, Alexis Aquino-Mackles, a 1st-grade teacher, read a section of *Nisei Daughter* that described how Sone's family burned "everything Japanese: Japanese dolls, music, swords, Japanese poetry." Then she read a section from *Farewell to Manzanar* where a Japanese-American mother breaks her family's heirloom dishes one at a time rather than sell them to the vultures who lurked in Japanese-American neighborhoods during the evictions and bought families' valuables at ridiculously low prices prior to the internment. She gave each member of our class a broken piece of pottery and had us write an interior monologue from the character's point of view about that moment.

Tanya McCoy, a high school science teacher, asked each of us to bring a baggie full of soil from our garden. After conducting experiments on the soil and discussing how different the soil would be in the mostly desert-like settings of the internment camps, we wrote about our experiments.

Our intention is not for teachers to grab this particular unit and slavishly follow the lessons; instead we aim to equip teachers to think in interdisciplinary terms and see themselves as curriculum developers, not consumers of other people's curriculum. The work around *Nisei Daughter* is an important example, but only because it provides a model for how teachers of any grade level or content area might approach developing units of study. I intentionally model curriculum that struggles with racism and inequality of all kinds, that encourages teachers to think about engaging students in why there is inequality and oppression, and that looks for places of solidarity, hope, and alternatives.

All the teachers in the PWP also participate in reading groups, writing response groups, role plays, and simulations. They write every assignment. They learn the strategies by *doing* the strategies, not by having someone *talk about* "participatory, engaging, hands-on curriculum." They know revision strategies because they use them as they write and revise their own narratives, essays, and poetry. They can teach students methods for opening narratives or strategies for knocking their classmates' socks off with their dialogue because they learn how to write like writers during the institute. Teachers also reflect after each activity on how they will use or adapt the strategies in their classrooms. They meet in grade-level groups throughout the four weeks to plan for the following year. Their activity, their plans, and their growth provide the content and the goal of this kind of professional development.

The intent of the PWP is not to "fix" broken teachers; rather, it provides a rich environment for teachers to practice literacy, and to have hard conversations about thorny issues that surface in their classroom practice. This is the kind of dialogue that simply can't happen in top-down trainings or when teachers are handed a packaged curriculum created at Princeton.

Of course, not all teachers who attend the summer institute bring stellar practice. Some are victims of bad writing instruction themselves; others have internalized the need to look outside of their classroom for answers, to find an expert or guru to follow instead of becoming their own experts. During the four weeks, the co-directors and I work with participants to tease out what they do know and what they can share. We try to validate and expand their knowledge—in the same way we respond to students in our classrooms.

PWP teachers continue to meet monthly during the year following the summer institute. (Some teachers have continued to come to these meetings for a number of years, and almost 100 teachers gather for our yearly writing retreat in February.) They discuss the implementation of strategies in their classroom. They bring in student work to examine, successful lessons to share, and problems to ponder and solve.

Because many teachers have not *experienced* a classroom that engages their hearts and minds while also teaching them to read and write critically, it is essential that professional development do more than *describe* good classroom practice. We can't just hand teachers a program to implement. Teachers need to participate in this kind of pedagogy as a student experiences it in order to understand why this kind of instruction is necessary. For example, Ellie Hakala, a second-year language arts teacher, said at our October PWP meeting, "I never realized how important students' sharing their work was until I went through the Writing Project. When I wrote a great piece, I wanted everyone to hear it, not just my small group. I wanted to hear what others had written. Now my students want to share all the time as well."

Summer Curriculum Camps

In collaboration with a group of language arts teachers representing each of our high schools, I designed the Curriculum Camp specifically to give teachers time to create curriculum and to bring a more diverse, multicultural, contemporary reading list into our high school language arts classrooms. Instead of just buying the books and putting them in book rooms across the city, I wrote a grant to pay teachers to come together and write curriculum guides to help teach the novels. Of course, it would have been cheaper and faster to buy prepackaged curriculum for teachers to open each fall and follow the directions. But our group wanted to hone teachers' capacities to create curriculum from the ground up, so we chose to take the time and spend the money to share and build teacher knowledge. Because the novels, like the ones we chose for the Portland Writing Project, included sensitive cultural, racial, and gender issues as well as historic events that not all teachers were familiar with, we knew it was important to spend time researching background knowledge and talking about how to teach the novels. We wanted to expand the repertoire of instructional strategies that teachers use, but we also wanted to link those strategies to deeper, more challenging content.

Our intent was to integrate the canon, but also to share the expertise of our skilled teachers as we wove reading and writing strategies into these study guides. (Many of these teachers had participated in the Portland Writing Project sometime during the past 20 years.) Many of us needed to learn how to teach reading and writing skills more effectively. Using the PWP model of teachers teaching teachers, we took turns teaching workshops that shared effective strategies while we built our units.

> **The intent of the Portland Writing Project is not to "fix" broken teachers; rather it provides a rich environment for teachers to practice literacy, and to have hard conversations about thorny issues that surface in their classroom practice.**

We received a grant from the privately funded Portland Public School Foundation for $40,000—enough to purchase sets of books for every high school and to pay two teachers from each school their hourly wage for 30 hours of work. Other teachers volunteered to come for credit. They were hungry for a community where they could learn and share with each other. At the end of the first summer one teacher wrote, "I have learned that we are our best resources."

Six years later, we continue to meet for a week each summer, scrounging money from various grants or the district's coffers. In fact, more than 90 percent of PPS high school language arts teachers, as well as a number of ESL, special education, and social studies teachers, have attended at least one summer camp.

We spend part of each morning discussing provocative readings and topics or attending reading or writing workshops that participants asked us to provide. We talk about the tough issues: how to differentiate our curriculum with an increasingly diverse student body, how to work with students who don't speak or write Standard English, how to teach students to design their own essay topics, etc. Then teachers move into work groups to develop curriculum on new novels, nonfiction texts, or hot topics. For example, teachers have created curriculum on *Persepolis*, *Kite Runner*, *Fences*, *Thousand Pieces of Gold*, as well as *Fast Food Nation*, *Nickel and Dimed*, and *Smoke Signals*.

The Curriculum Camp provides another lesson for professional development: New teachers need time to grow their practice with skilled professionals. During the Summer Curriculum Camp, first-year teachers and veteran teachers a year or two from retirement work side-by-side developing curriculum and learning new skills. As one first-year teacher wrote, "Being new to teaching, the greatest thing about the Literacy Project has been…learning tons about everything, soaking up as much as I can. Up to this point, I really had a limited collection of strategies to use."

During the first summer of the literacy camp, I told my colleagues that I was less interested in the curriculum guides we produced than in the process of teachers working together and learning from each other. Mistake. The guides are also important. They are the written legacy of our summer work. But the guides also indicate our curricular weaknesses and blind spots. Some are brilliant. Others limp along with too many internet downloads and not enough inspired teaching. Some miss the point.

After each summer, I review the guides to see what lessons we learned and what we missed as we create our work for the following summer.

If we purchased guides for the books or distributed anthologies with questions and writings mapped out for the teachers, we would miss these opportunities to learn together to build curriculum for the students who populate *our* schools. Although published guides may be slicker in presentation than ours, they lack the creative struggle of teachers making decisions about the *best* way to introduce the book, the *best* way to teach *how* to read this particular text.

Professional Development Days

How do teachers get better at their craft? How do we create "lifelong learners" in the teaching profession? If we don't reach beyond our classrooms to learn new strategies or engage in debates with our colleagues, we can grow rigid and narrow. No matter how long we've been teaching or how good we are, we can always benefit from gathering with colleagues and sharing new curriculum ideas and strategies, talking about new issues that have surfaced, or discussing old issues that we still need to tackle.

As teachers, professional development needs to provide us with time-outs from our work, so we can step back and ask the questions about our daily practice that needle us. We need time to think, discuss, debate, find new strategies and resources for our classrooms and ourselves. Too often professional development is provided in tiny morsels from 3:30 to 5:30 p.m. after we have taught all day—or squeezed into an hour one morning a month. Fortunately, the Portland Association of Teachers and Portland Public Schools hammered out an agreement to provide five paid professional development days for teachers each year. Originally, the days were set aside to give teachers time to become familiar with the state standards, work samples, and scoring rubrics. Typically, these days have been divided between school-based professional development and district professional development.

During the seven years I worked as the high school language arts curriculum specialist, I met regularly with the high school literacy leaders, a group composed of one language arts liaison from every comprehensive and alternative high school. Together, we decided to commit our professional development days to disseminating the curriculum guides developed during the summer, sharing strategies, discussing the impact of district or state initiatives on our classrooms (like high school reform), or bringing in occasional speakers to address hot issues, like untracking.

A few years ago we started developing interdisciplinary workshops with social studies, ESL, and special education teachers. These days broke us out of our classrooms and content areas to share our practice, but also helped us disseminate the curriculum we developed each summer. We engaged as intellectuals with other teachers in meaningful discussions about our content—and the world. Instead of sitting in rows, listening to some "expert" tell us about effective classroom practice, we experience it.

> **Instead of sitting in rows, listening to some "expert" tell us about effective classroom practice, we experience it with our colleagues.**

For example, on a recent professional development day, Carmel Ross and Lisa Walker, two of the teachers who developed curriculum for *Bronx Masquerade*, shared one of the strategies from their summer work. They led participants on a treasure hunt, a prereading activity that develops background knowledge prior to entering a unit of study. Their interactive workshop taught about the main characters of the Harlem Renaissance and demonstrated how to get "TAG, ELL, SPED, and Johnny out of their seats and into your curriculum."

In another workshop, Hyung Nam, a social studies teacher, led language arts, social studies, and ESL colleagues in a lesson on "Institutional Racism and Segregation in the Post-Civil Rights Era and in Portland." His lesson asked: How do segregation and racial disparities persist after the Civil Rights Era? How does Portland's history of segregation and environmental racism compare to the national history? Hyung's lessons explored the multiple causes of racial segregation and environmental racism while helping students understand how institutional racism is perpetuated today. His workshop included a mock tribunal and examination of local history with ongoing segregation and racism.

Teachers not only learned new pedagogy, but they also walked away with information, including handouts and historical documents on the structural features of racism to use with their students. They experienced learning by participating in the trial, not by reading about it. They engaged in conversations about racism in their city and learned how to teach about it at the same time.

Teachers who present—and over the years we have worked to enlist as many teachers as presenters as possible—learn twice as much. They not only engage as participants in the workshops throughout the day, but they also gain clarity about their own practice by sharing it with other teachers. In presenting to their colleagues, they teach their lessons, but they also teach the underlying assumptions about good pedagogy and content knowledge that animate their work.

Teacher-centered professional development doesn't happen unless districts—and school administrators and curriculum leaders—have intimate knowledge of teachers' practice. Just putting teacher X in front of the faculty will not lead to the kind of professional development I am advocating. Curriculum leaders must make the effort to listen to teachers' conversations when they talk about their classrooms and their students; they must observe teachers at work with students and colleagues; and they must look for exemplary practice and curricular expertise. Ultimately, they must have a vision of professional development that puts classroom teachers at the center. 🖋

Taking Teacher Quality Seriously

A collaborative approach to teacher evaluation

STAN KARP

So what's the alternative? If narrow, test-based evaluation of teachers is unfair, unreliable, and has negative effects on kids, classrooms, and curricula, what's a better approach?

By demonizing teachers and unions, and sharply polarizing the education debate, the corporate reform movement has actually undermined serious efforts to improve teacher quality and evaluation. For example, there is a lot of common ground among educators, parents, and administrators on the need for:

- better support and evaluation before new teachers get tenure (or leave the profession, as nearly 50 percent do within five years).
- reasonable, timely procedures for resolving tenure hearings when they are initiated.
- a credible intervention process to remediate and if necessary remove ineffective teachers, tenured or non-tenured.

Good models for each of these ideas exist, many with strong teacher union support. But overreaching by corporate reformers has detached the issue of teacher quality from the conditions that produce it. Class sizes are growing and professional development budgets are shrinking. Federal and state plans are pouring hundreds of millions of dollars into data systems and tests designed to replace collaborative professional culture and experienced instructional leadership with a kind of "psychometric astrology." These data-driven formulas lack both statistical credibility and a basic understanding of the human motivations and relationships that make good schooling possible. Instead of "elevating the profession," corporate reform is eroding it.

But better alternatives do exist. One promising model is the Professional Growth System (PGS), from Montgomery County, Maryland, which has taken a collaborative approach to improving teacher quality for more than a decade. Several defining features make the Montgomery model very different than the test-based "value-added" or "student growth" approaches. The Montgomery County professional growth system:

- was negotiated through collective bargaining rather than imposed by state or federal mandate.
- is based on a clear, common vision of high quality professional teaching practice.
- includes test scores as one of many indicators of student progress and teacher

performance, without rigidly weighted formulas.

> **Overreaching by corporate reformers has detached the issue of teacher quality from the conditions that produce it.**

- includes a strong PAR (peer assistance and review) component for all novice and underperforming teachers, including those with tenure.
- takes a broad, *qualitative* approach to promoting individual and systemwide teacher quality and continuous professional growth.

Developing and sustaining good teachers, rather than "getting rid of bad ones" has always been the main goal of the Montgomery system. But real consequences for persistently poor performance are part of the process. *New York Times* education reporter Michael Winerip wrote that the program "has worked beautifully for 11 years," providing teachers with "extra support if they are performing poorly and getting rid of those who do not improve."[1] In 11 years, the PAR process has led to some 500 teachers being removed from the classroom in a countywide system of about 150,000 students with approximately 10,000 teachers and 200 schools. Over the same period, nearly 5,000 teachers have successfully completed the PAR process.[2]

But PAR is only part of a professional growth system designed to improve teacher capacity throughout the system, not just identify and remove ineffective teachers. It's a qualitative approach growing out of a shared vision of high-quality professional practice. The PGS begins with "six clear standards for teacher performance, based on the National Board for Professional Teaching Standards" and includes "performance criteria for how the standards are to be met and descriptive examples of observable teaching behaviors."

The six standards are[3]:

- Standard 1: Teachers are committed to students and their learning.
- Standard 2: Teachers know the subjects they teach and how to teach those subjects to students.
- Standard 3: Teachers are responsible for establishing and managing student learning in a positive learning environment.
- Standard 4: Teachers continually assess student progress, analyze the results, and

adapt instruction to improve student achievement.

• Standard 5: Teachers are committed to continuous improvement and professional development.
• Standard 6: Teachers exhibit a high degree of professionalism.

An extensive system of supports and professional development activities, including detailed protocols for assessing progress towards these goals, is outlined in various handbooks, evaluation rubrics, and contractual agreements. The system also provides resources necessary to turn these ambitions into real commitments.

For example, the PAR system relies on 24 "consulting teachers" who are recruited from master teachers with five years of experience in Montgomery County Public Schools (MCPS). The consulting teachers (CTs) make a commitment to work for three years as CTs and then return for at least two years to a school in a teaching or other non-administrative position. CTs receive special training to work intensively with an average of 16-18 "clients" who include new teachers and experienced teachers referred to PAR by their principals. The supports provided by CTs include:[4]

• Informal and formal observations
• Written and verbal standards based feedback
• Equitable Classroom Practice ("Look-fors")
• Coaching sessions
• Lesson planning
• Model lessons
• Co-teaching modeling
• Peer observations
• Classroom management
• Time management
• Alignment of school supports

Consulting teachers document their work, but do not conduct formal evaluations. Their reports go to the PAR panel, which is made up of eight teachers appointed by the Montgomery County Education Association (MCEA) and eight principals appointed by the administrators' association. The panel reviews the documentation and makes a recommendation for non-renewal/dismissal, an additional year of PAR, or "release" to the "regular" PGS evaluation process that covers all staff. If either the client or the principal disagrees with the panel's recommendation, then he or she can initiate an appeals process that allows all parties to present additional information and speak to the panel, which ultimately reaffirms or alters its original decision. A tenured teacher dismissed through PAR does retain tenure rights and can appeal a dismissal decision. But in practice, the PAR process generally documents fully the basis for such decisions and formal challenges to PAR decisions are rare.

Although the system is spelled out in detail, what really makes it possible is the level of trust and cooperation that grew out of years of developing a collaborative approach to issues of teacher quality. The commitment to collaboration between the MCEA and the district is summarized in unusual contract language:

> **"Good teaching is nurtured in a school and in a school system culture that values constant feedback, analysis, and refinement of the quality of teaching."**

> We define collaboration as a process in which partners work together in a meaningful way and within a time frame that provides a real opportunity to shape results. The purpose of the process is to work together respectfully to resolve problems, address common issues, and identify opportunities for improvement. To be successful, the collaborative process must be taken seriously and be valued by both parties. The process must be given the time, personal involvement and commitment, hard work, and dedication that are required to be successful. The partners will identify and define issues of common concern, propose and evaluate solutions, and agree on recommendations.[5]

"It wouldn't work without the level of trust we have here," MCEA president Doug Prouty told *The New York Times*. Jerry D. Weast, former superintendent of the Montgomery County system, added, "It took three to five years to build the trust to get PAR in place. Teachers had to see we weren't playing gotcha."[6]

Beyond PAR, the larger PGS system is based on a belief that "good teaching is nurtured in a school and in a school system culture that values constant feedback, analysis, and refinement of the quality of teaching." Formal performance evaluations are part of "a multiyear process of professional growth, continual reflection on goals and progress meeting those goals, and collegial interaction." The aim is to support "a collaborative learning culture among teachers in each school, integrating individual growth plans into school plans, and utilizing student achievement and other data about student results."[7]

Besides teachers, there are separately articulated PGS standards and evaluation protocols for administrators, non-classroom professionals, and support staff. Ideally, this contributes to a schoolwide sense of accountability and collective purpose that helps sustain healthy school communities, and there is significant evidence that it works.

Peer Review Success Story

Over the past decade, student achievement as measured by Maryland's state assessments has increased across the board in every student subgroup—by race, ethnicity, and income level. Achievement gaps have narrowed at all grade levels and in both math and reading. In grades 3 and 5 math, and grade 7 reading, the gap narrowed by 16 points; in grades 3 and 5 reading, it narrowed by more than 20 points.[8]

Beyond the test scores, 84 percent of Montgomery County's students go on to college and 63 percent earn degrees.[9] The collaborative approach has also extended beyond teacher evaluation issues. For example, Broad Acres elementary school serves a population almost completely composed of students of color and free/reduced lunch students. In 2000, it was on the verge of state takeover and a "reconstitution" that would have included wholesale replacement of school staff and leadership. But a collaborative approach, initiated by MCEA and embraced by the school leadership, led to a sustained process of renewal and reform that has dramatically improved student performance and school culture. According to the school's principal, "The reason Broad Acres succeeded was teacher leadership; and everyone holding themselves accountable for every student."[10]

These successes and the national debate about teacher quality have brought new attention to the Montgomery County PGS/PAR model. Secretary of Education Arne Duncan told MCPS Superintendent Weast, "You're going where the country needs to go."[11] Yet the PGS approach is exactly the opposite direction from federal policies.

Under the Obama administration's Race to the Top competition, states were pressured to tie teacher evaluation to student test scores. Maryland won a $250 million grant by promising to base teacher ratings on state test results. Implementing the grant in MCPS would have meant dismantling a successful system developed by collective bargaining that works to improve results for teachers and students. After failing to get a waiver from the U.S. Department of Education to continue using the PGS system, the Montgomery County school board withdrew from the state's Race-to-the-Top plans and had to forfeit its $12 million share of the grant funds.

If federal policy were serious about improving teacher quality it would be investing precisely in programs like peer assistance and review, which have significant costs. One Harvard study estimates the cost at $4,000-$7,000 per participant.[12] Instead the federal government has poured hundreds of millions into the development of more test-based data systems and pressed states to use them to rate both teachers and the college certification programs they came from. It's wasted money chasing bad policy.

Montgomery County is not the only district that has implemented collaborative, peer approaches based on collective bargaining. Long-standing peer review programs in Toledo and Cincinnati, Ohio; Rochester, New York; and elsewhere have shown various degrees of success. A recent in-depth study of two California districts using PAR programs reached some striking conclusions about the current push for new and better teacher evaluation models.[13]

The study compared the types and quality of support provided by CTs in two districts using PAR, one near San Diego, the other near Sacramento. It also compared the work of the CTs with the more traditional performance reviews done by principals. Finally, it observed and analyzed the work of the joint labor-management PAR panels that reviewed the evaluations and recommendations of both the principals and the CTs.

"What we found," wrote the study's authors, "belies conventional wisdom.... integrating support and evaluation can be a more effective approach to improving instructional practice than isolating one from the other. The programs...clearly show that PAR is a rigorous alternative to traditional forms of teacher evaluation and development."

"In an era when policy makers are calling for better teacher evaluation, our research shows that peer review is far superior to principals' evaluations in terms of rigor and comprehensiveness. Equally important, peer review offers a possible solution to the lack of capacity of the current system to both provide adequate teacher support and conduct thorough performance evaluations."

The study confirmed another benefit that Montgomery teacher union leaders and administrators had previously demonstrated. Collaboration about core issues like teacher quality and evaluation has ancillary benefits. The PAR panels "turned out to be problem-solving arenas where district officials and union leaders collaboratively addressed operational and policy problems that might otherwise have ended up as grievances or gone unresolved.... We were struck by the collaborative labor-management interactions that form the foundation of PAR. Though both [districts] have in the past experienced rocky union-district relations, PAR has served as a springboard for building strong connections. More than simple collaborative efforts, through PAR, management and unions are doing the hard work of confronting tough, high-stakes issues and reaching accord on how to proceed when decisions carry real and human consequences."

Just as with student assessment, evaluation can be a tool for improving teaching and learning or an instrument of bad policy and external control. The key in both cases is to make sure that people, not tests, are the point of departure and that real collaboration among all parties shapes the process. ⟡

Endnotes

1. Michael Winerip, "Helping Teachers Help Themselves," *The New York Times*, June 5, 2011.

2. MCPS Schools at a Glance, 2010–2011, Office of Shared Accountability Montgomery County Public Schools. Webinar presentation by MCPS Consulting Teacher Team, Office of Human Resources and Development, July 25, 2011.

3. MCPS Teacher Professional Growth System Handbook, 3.

4. MCPS webinar presentation, July 25, 2011.

5. Bonnie Cullison, former MCEA president, U*nion Leadership: How Teacher Professional Growth Systems Can Help Transform Schools, The Union Role in Systemic Change*, Coalition for Educational Justice presentation, Sept. 24, 2011.

6. Winerip, *The New York Times*, June 5, 2011.

7. MCPS Teacher Professional Growth System Handbook, 1.

8. Cullison.

9. Winerip.

10. Kevin Hart, "Collaboration Results in Transformation at Maryland School," March 11, 2010.

11. Winerip.

12. "A User's Guide to Peer Assistance and Review: Costs and Benefits of PAR," Harvard Graduate School of Education, available at http://www.gse.harvard.edu/-ngt/par/costs/.

13. Julia E. Koppich and Daniel C. Humphrey, "Getting Serious About Teacher Evaluation," Education Week, October 12, 2011.

Pencils **Down**

Author Biographies

Wayne Au, a former public high school social studies and language arts teacher, is an editor at *Rethinking Schools* and is an assistant professor in the education program at the University of Washington, Bothell Campus. He contributes regularly to *Rethinking Schools* and, among his many publications, is author of *Unequal By Design: High-Stakes Testing and the Standardization of Inequality*.

Ann Berlak has taught social foundations of schooling for more than 40 years. She is the author, with Sekani Moyenda, of *Taking It Personally: Racism in Classrooms from Kindergarten to College*.

Bill Bigelow is the curriculum editor of *Rethinking Schools*. He taught high school social studies in Portland, Oregon, for many years, and is the author and editor of numerous books, including *Rethinking Globalization* and *A People's History for the Classroom*.

Melissa Bollow Tempel is licensed in bilingual and elementary education and has a master's degree in cultural foundations of education with an emphasis on race relations in education. She has been teaching since 2000 and currently teaches 1st grade at La Escuela Fratney, a dual-language public school in Milwaukee. She is on the steering committee for the teacher activist group Educators' Network for Social Justice.

Peter Campbell is a parent, educator, and activist who served in a volunteer role for four years as the Missouri state coordinator for FairTest before moving to Portland, Oregon. He taught multiple subjects and grade levels for more than 20 years. His daughter's name has been changed in his article for this book.

Linda Christensen is the director of the Oregon Writing Project, located in the graduate school of education at Lewis & Clark College. She is the author of *Reading, Writing, and Rising Up: Teaching about Social Justice and the Power of the Written Word* and *Teaching for Joy and Justice: Re-Imagining the Language Arts Classroom*. She taught high school language arts for 30 years and worked as language arts curriculum specialist in Portland, Oregon.

Andie Cunningham teaches at Lewis & Clark College in Portland, Oregon.

Ruth Ann Dandrea is a public school educator who has spent the last 35 years happily teaching high school English. She spends her summers paddling a yellow kayak on Adirondack waterways.

Linda Darling-Hammond is the Charles E. Ducommun Professor of Education at Stanford University where she has launched the Stanford Educational Leadership Institute and the School Redesign Network. She has also served as faculty sponsor for the Stanford Teacher Education Program. She is a former president of the American Educational Research Association and member of the National Academy of Education. Her research, teaching, and policy work focus on issues of school restructuring, teacher quality, and educational equity.

Kelley Dawson Salas teaches 5th grade at a Milwaukee Spanish immersion school. She is an editor of *Rethinking Schools*.

Dan DiMaggio scored standardized tests for three years in the Twin Cities, Minnesota, until he was blacklisted for writing the article reprinted in this book. He is now a graduate student in the department of sociology at New York University.

Elaine Engel Keswick currently teaches 1st grade part time in Carlsbad, California. She lives in Oceanside, where she manages Lights On Tutoring, a math tutoring company that provides tutoring to students from economically disadvantaged homes.

Todd Farley is the author of *Making the Grades: My Misadventures in the Standardized Testing Industry*. He has written about standardized testing in *The New York Times*, *Christian Science Monitor*, *Washington Post*, *Detroit Free Press*, *The Huffington Post*, *Education Week*, *Edutopia*, and *Rethinking Schools*.

Tiny (a.k.a. Lisa) Gray–Garcia is a poverty scholar, revolutionary journalist, lecturer, Indigenous Taino, Roma mama of Tiburcio, daughter of Dee, and the cofounder of *POOR Magazine* and author of *Criminal of Poverty: Growing Up Homeless in America*. Her newest book, to be released in 2012, is entitled *Poverty Scholarship: a PeopleSteXt— the Population Brings the Popular Education*.

Amy Gutowski has worked in the Milwaukee Public Schools for 10 years. She currently teaches 3rd grade and is hoping common sense and compassion will return to education.

Asa Hilliard, now deceased, was a professor of educational psychology who worked on indigenous ancient African history (ancient Egyptian), culture, education, and society. He was the Fuller E. Callaway Professor of Urban Education at Georgia State University, and he was the author of numerous books and articles on education, particularly the education of African American children.

Meredith Jacks lives in Brooklyn and teaches 8th-grade writing at a public school in Chinatown.

Sarah Knopp has been teaching public school in Los Angeles Unified School District since 2000, is a teacher union activist, and the coeditor of *Education and Capitalism* (Haymarket Books 2012).

Gloria Ladson-Billings is the Kellner Family Professor in Urban Education at the University of Wisconsin in Madison, and she is an H. I. Romnes Fellow. She is the author of *Crossing Over to Canaan: The Journey of New Teachers in Diverse Classrooms* and *The Dreamkeepers: Successful Teachers of African American Children*, among many publications.

Tom McKenna teaches writing and humanities at the Portland YouthBuilders (PYB) school in Portland, Oregon. After retiring from Portland Public Schools in 2005, Tom has continued to teach at PYB and Portland State University, while conducting workshops with the REACH Center located in Bellingham, Washington. Tom is active in the Portland Rethinking Schools group and writes about teaching, education policy, and the lives of students—the reason why we teach.

Kelly McMahon taught kindergarten for Milwaukee Public Schools for eight years. She is currently teaching at the early childhood level in Iowa.

Greg Michie teaches at Concordia University in Chicago. His latest book, *We Don't Need Another Hero: Essays and Stories from Chicago Schools*, will be published in 2012 by Teachers College Press.

Barbara Miner is a Milwaukee-based journalist specializing in education and social issues. She is a former managing editor of *Rethinking Schools*, where she co-edited several books including *Keeping the Promise? The Debate Over Charter Schools*, *Rethinking Columbus*, and *Failing Our Kids: Why the Testing Craze Won't Fix Our Schools*. Her articles have appeared in a range of publications, from *The New York Times*, to the *Milwaukee Journal Sentinel*, *The Nation*, and *The Progressive*.

Monty Neill is the executive director of the National Center for Fair & Open Testing (FairTest, www.fairtest.org), and he chairs the national Forum on Educational Accountability, an alliance working to overhaul the No Child Left Behind/Elementary and Secondary Education Act. Among many publications, he is co-author of *Failing Our Children*, a report analyzing NCLB and providing guidance toward new, helpful accountability systems. He also authored *Implementing Performance Assessments: A Guide to Classroom School and System Reform*, and *Testing Our Children: A Report Card on State Assessment Systems*, the first comprehensive evaluation of all 50 state testing programs.

Sharna Olfman is a clinical psychologist and editor of the *Childhood in America* book series. Her books include *All Work and No Play: How Educational Reforms are Harming Our Preschoolers* (2003), *Childhood Lost* (2005), *The Sexualization of Childhood* (2008), and *Drugging Our Children* (2012).

Amalia Oulahan is a copy editor who received her bachelor's degree in journalism from Northwestern University in 2010. Before that, she attended Milwaukee Public Schools for her entire K-12 career.

Bob Peterson is the president of the Milwaukee Teachers' Education Association (MTEA). He taught 5th grade at La Escuela Fratney, a two-way bilingual school in Milwaukee, and is the founding editor of *Rethinking Schools*. He co-edited (with Bill Bigelow) *Rethinking Columbus: The Next 500 Years* and (with Michael Charney) *Transforming Teacher Unions: Fighting for Better Schools and Social Justice*.

Peggy Robertson is a former public school teacher and current administrator for United Opt Out National. She is the mother of two boys and maintains a blog focused on education at pegwithpen.blogspot.com.

Jay Rosner, a test fairness advocate and the executive director of the Princeton Review Foundation, has been providing admission test preparation information and resources to underrepresented high school and college students since 1995. He is the proud father of two daughters.

Melissa Schieble is assistant professor of English education at Hunter College of the City University of New York. She taught high school English in Wisconsin and England, and she researches the application of critical theories of language and literacy in English teaching and teacher education.

Ruth Shagoury teaches at Lewis & Clark College in Portland, Oregon.

Alan Stoskopf is a senior teaching and research fellow in the Ed.D. program at Northeastern University. Currently, he is co-writing a book with James Fraser from New York University on progressive education in urban public schools in the early 20th century.

Kathy Williams is a former editor of *Rethinking Schools* whose career in the Milwaukee Public Schools spanned 34 years. She taught for 20 years and has retired as director of the district's Division of Research and Evaluation.

Maja Wilson taught in Michigan's public schools for 10 years. She is pursuing her doctorate in composition studies at the University of Hampshire, and she teaches literacy methods courses at the University of Maine. She is the author of *Rethinking Rubrics in Writing Assessment* (Heinemann, 2006).

Sören Wuerth is a writer, activist, and educator. He currently teaches English and social studies at Robert Service High School in Anchorage, Alaska.

Maika Yeigh teaches at Willamette University in Salem, Oregon.

Pencils Down

Index

A

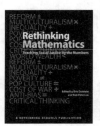

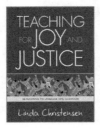

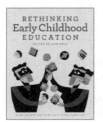